Breaking into the Monopoly

Library of Economic History

General Editors

Peer Vries, University of Vienna
Regina Grafe, Northwestern University, Evanston

VOLUME 4

The titles published in this series are listed at brill.com/lehi

Breaking into the Monopoly

Provincial Merchants and Manufacturers' Campaigns for Access to the Asian Market, 1790-1833

By

Yukihisa Kumagai

BRILL

LEIDEN · BOSTON
2013

Library of Congress Cataloging-in-Publication Data

Kumagai, Yukihisa.
Breaking into the monopoly : provincial merchants and manufacturers' campaigns for access to the Asian market, 1790-1833 / by Yukihisa Kumagai.
p. cm. -- (Library of economic history ; v. 4)
Includes bibliographical references and index.
ISBN 978-90-04-24172-5 (hbk. : alk. paper)
1. East India Company--History. 2. Great Britain--Commerce--Asia. 3. Asia--Commerce--Great Britain. 4. Monopolies--Great Britain--History--19th century. 5. Trade associations--Great Britain--History--19th century. I. Title.

HF486.E6K86 2012
382.095'041--dc23

2012036031

This publication has been typeset in the multilingual "Brill" typeface. With over 5,100 characters covering Latin, IPA, Greek, and Cyrillic, this typeface is especially suitable for use in the humanities. For more information, please see www.brill.com/brill-typeface.

ISSN 1877-3206
ISBN 978-90-04-24172-5 (hardback)
ISBN 978-90-04-24177-0 (e-book)

This book is printed on acid-free paper.

CONTENTS

LIST OF TABLES AND FIGURES

Tables

Figures

ABBREVIATIONS

ACC	American Chamber of Commerce
EIA	East India Association
EIC	East India Company
MCCM	Manchester Chamber of Commerce and Manufacturers
WIA	West India Association

ACKNOWLEDGEMENTS

Without support from a number of people, I could not have completed my research and published this book. After I started my research at the University of Glasgow in 2001, I received invaluable guidance and advice from Dr. Duncan Ross, Professor Michael French, Professor Tony Slaven, Professor Catherine Schenk, and Professor Ray Stokes.

My research also was supported by academic scholars outside my university. In particular, I would like to express special thanks to Professor Tom Tomlinson, who introduced me the records of the Glasgow East India Association, and Dr. Anthony Webster, who was willing to give me precious advice for my research.

I also received assistance from friends with whom I shared the same time and space in Glasgow, especially Dr. Duncan Connors, Dr. Niall Mackenzie, Per Eide Anders, and Dr. Stephen Sambrook.

To improve and reshape the original manuscript into the current form, I owe a particular debt to Professor Regine Grafe and the anonymous reader, who gave me very helpful feedback and comments.

I would like to thank my parents, Ryoichi and Shizuko, who believed in my academic success and supported me financially for many years until I could finally stand on my own two feet as an academic scholar. Finally, my heartfelt thanks go to Ying Zhan, who is always beside me sharing all the happiness and sadness in my life.

INTRODUCTION

In many countries, the gap in political influence and economic power between the capital and the provinces creates tension; this rivalry is a very common phenomenon. In the history of the United Kingdom, beginning in the medieval era, London held a disproportionately significant position in the political and economic spheres, mainly because of its geographical proximity to the centre of national politics. This advantage brought large wealth to London's commercial and financial interests, especially through overseas commercial and trading activities. Meanwhile, their provincial rivals always sought opportunities to snatch the lion's share from them.

During the second half of the eighteenth and early nineteenth centuries, as the Industrial Revolution proceeded, the manufacturing interests of newly growing provincial cities increased their influence on national politics. The classic view emphasised the significance of the Industrial Revolution, commonly explaining that Britain's adoption of a free trade policy after the 1820s largely bowed to demands from provincial manufacturing interests. These interests had gained both economic and political power through industrial growth. In fact, until the first half of the twentieth century, Britain was regarded as an industrial society. Nevertheless, after the 1960s, a number of historians and economists began to revise this old view. For instance, Tom Nairn and Frank Longstreth focused their attention on the peculiarity of the British economy.[1] In their theoretical arguments, these two scholars put the City of London or the financial capitalists in a polarising position against the industrial capitalists. As a political entity, London held a large advantage and victimised the industrial capitalists in the formation of British economic policy. For instance, Longstreth regarded Joseph Chamberlain's Tariff Reform campaign for the manufacturing interests at the turn of the nineteenth century as the first significant attempt of industrialists to challenge the dominance of the City (or financial capitalists) on British economic policy.[2] According to his argument, the campaign was eventually unsuccessful mainly because the campaigners could not

[1] T. Nairn, "The Twilight of the British State", in *New Left Review*, Jan.–April, 1977, pp. 3–61; F. Longstreth, "The City, Industry and the State", in C. Crouch (ed.) *State and Economy in Contemporary Capitalism*, 1979, pp. 157–90.

[2] Ibid., pp. 162–3.

overcome internal divisions within the industrial sectors. In the following decade, statistical studies on the geographical and occupational distributions of wealth in the United Kingdom as well as extensive studies on the commercial and financial activities of the City of London supported their argument.[3] These studies focused attention on the economic supremacy of London and Southeast England.

These new views on the British economy culminated in the introduction of the 'gentlemanly capitalist' thesis. During the 1980s, Peter Cain and Anthony Hopkins defined British capitalism as 'gentlemanly capitalism', a form of capitalism in which aristocratic landed interests and financial and service sectors, particularly those of the City, played the primary role in forming Britain's economic and foreign policy after the Glorious Revolution.[4] According to their argument, the industrial sector located in the north played a less important role in Britain's imperial expansion than historians had traditionally assumed. This point became one of the main controversies in British economic and imperial history. In Cain and Hopkins' model, the gentlemanly capitalists and British policy-makers always reached a consensus with political and economic views based on sharing an aristocratic sense of values. Therefore, it was always difficult for outsiders such as provincial industrialists to break into this interlocked and closed society, and the City's interests always reflected the governmental policies.

The introduction of the 'gentlemanly capitalist thesis' by Cain and Hopkins led to great historical debates during the 1990s. At the same time, this controversy made historians recognise the necessity of more elaborate studies on the lobbying activities of provincial commercial and manufacturing pressure groups as well as their relationship with London.[5] Regarding this point, the accumulation of studies on the activities of provincial

---

[3] W.D. Rubinstein, "Wealth, Elites and the Class Structure of Modern Britain", in *Past and Present*, No. LXXVI, 1977, pp. 91–112 and "The Victorian Middle Classes: Wealth, Occupation and Geography", in *The Economic History Review*, New Series, Vol. XXX, No. 4, 1977; C.H. Lee, "Regional Growth and Structural Change in Victorian Britain", in *The Economic History Review*, New Series, Vol. XXXIV, No. 3, 1981, pp. 438–552; S.D. Chapman, *The Rise of Merchant Banking*, 1984.

[4] P.J. Cain and A.G. Hopkins, "Gentlemanly Capitalism and British Expansion Overseas I. The Old Colonial System, 1688", in *The Economic History Review*, New Series, Vol. XXXIX, No. 4, 1986, pp. 501–25, and "Gentlemanly Capitalism and British Expansion Overseas II, New Imperialism, 1850–1945", in *The Economic History Review*, New Series, Vol. XL, 1, 1987, pp. 1–26.

[5] R.E. Dumett (ed.), *Gentlemanly Capitalism and British Imperialism: The New Debate on Empire*, 1999, p. 39.

pressure groups in national politics during the first few decades of the nineteenth century is relatively shallow, despite the fact that this period was a significant turning point in Britain's economic policy, from traditional mercantilism to free trade. Case studies on this topic could reassess the connection between the merchants and manufacturers from the provinces, particularly from Lancashire and western Scotland, and Britain's economic and imperial policies. To seek answers, this book will explore the efforts of provincial lobbyists to access East Indian markets during the first half of the nineteenth century.

There is no doubt that in British Imperial history India was the single most significant colony for Britain's world power before the end of the Second World War. However, until the upheaval of 1857–58, the British government did not control the country directly. Instead, the central institution of British dominance over India was the East India Company (EIC), whose features changed significantly from a commercial company to a governmental organisation after the acquisition of Bengal in 1756. As one of the major instruments of British Imperialism, the EIC and its affairs have attracted historians' interest. Many historians regarded the abolition of the EIC's monopoly in the first half of the nineteenth century as a result of the increase in the economic and political influence of provincial manufacturing towns and outports in the course of the Industrial Revolution. The rise of British manufacturing industries increased the demand for new markets for manufactured products and for the importation of raw materials and food. In his study on the development of local commercial policy, Arthur Redford described how Manchester's manufacturers organised their pressure group and advocated for the expansion of their access to world markets, including those of India and the Far East, during the first half of the nineteenth century.[6] D.J. Moss analysed Birmingham's campaigns against the Orders in Council and the renewal of the EIC's Charter during the period from 1812 to 1813.[7] He argued that the case of Birmingham indicated the rise of provincial towns and the growth of "the power of organised public opinion." More than three decades later, it appears that the traditional view regarding the increase in provincial manufacturers' influence on nineteenth-century British economic and imperial policies

6 A. Redford, *Manchester Merchants and Foreign Trade, 1794–1858*, 1934.

7 D.J. Moss, "Birmingham and the Campaigns against the Orders in Council and East India Company Charter 1812–1813", in *Canadian Journal of History*, Vol. XI, Issue 1, 1976, pp. 173–88.

is still attracting support. Nick Robins, for example, has described the events leading to the opening of the East India trade from a similar viewpoint.[8] In contrast, Anthony Webster's 1990 study examined the government's motives in the case of the renewal of the Charter of 1813 and briefly explained that provincial manufacturing towns and outports had different interests during the movement.[9] He argued that both London and provincial lobbyists failed to exercise their decisive influence on the state. Instead of these economic interest groups, he stressed the government's role in the making of wartime economic policy, although he has revaluated the impact of provincial pressure groups more positively in his most recent work.[10]

Apart from these studies, other works have explored the efforts of provincial lobbyists for access to the East Indian markets during this period. Sydney Checkland illustrated Liverpool's campaign of 1812–13 as a part of John Gladstone's biography.[11] He described Gladstone's role in the free trade campaign as well as his views on the East India trade. His 1958 article and the work of Brian Tolley also referred briefly to Liverpool's free trade movement in the context of the debates over the Orders in Council.[12] Meanwhile, regarding the free trade movement of the 1820s and early 1830s, Douglas Eyles examined the economic interests of Manchester, Liverpool, Birmingham, Exeter, and Sheffield along with their lobbying activities in favour of a total abolition of the EIC's Charter.[13] Kenneth Charlton studied the campaign of Liverpool merchants against the EIC's monopoly in the 1820s and the early 1830s.[14] In his article, Charlton focused on the significant roles of these merchants' anti-slavery sentiment and the shift in their

---

[8] N. Robins, *The Corporation that Changed the World: How the East India Company Shaped the Modern Multinational*, 2006, pp. 146–9.

[9] A. Webster, "The Political Economy of Trade Liberalization: The East India Company Charter Act of 1813", in *The Economic History Review*, New Series, Vol. XLIII, No. 3, 1990, pp. 404–19.

[10] A. Webster, *The Twilight of the East India Company: The Evolution of Anglo-Asian Commerce and Politics 1790–1860*, 2009, p. 58.

[11] S.G. Checkland, *The Gladstones: A Family Biography 1764–1851*, 1975, pp. 59–62 and pp. 71–2.

[12] S.G. Checkland, "American versus West Indian Traders", in *The Journal of Economic History*, Vol. XVII, No. 2, 1958, pp. 141–60; B.H. Tolley, "The Liverpool Campaign against the Orders in Council and the War of 1812", in J.R. Harris (ed.), *Liverpool and Merseyside*, 1969, Chapter 5.

[13] D. Eyles, "The Abolition of the East India Company's Monopoly 1833", unpublished PhD thesis, University of Edinburgh, 1955, pp. 184–98.

[14] K. Charlton, "Liverpool and the East India Trade", in *Northern History*, Vol. VII, 1972, pp. 55–72.

economic interests from the West Indies to the East Indies during their campaign.

Although these two free trade campaigns against the EIC's commercial monopoly were significant events for provincial merchants and manufacturers' efforts to expand their markets around the world, the studies mentioned above and other previous studies have failed to conduct detailed research to reconstruct a complete picture of their lobbying activities. Therefore, this book will comprehensively examine how those individuals with provincial mercantile and manufacturing interests organised their campaigns to gain free access to Asian markets from 1812–13 and 1829–33. The analysis will include various aspects of their motives, strategies, methods, and networks. It will also assess the influence of the provincial interests over national politics and the relationship between provincial mercantile and manufacturing interests and gentlemanly capitalists in nineteenth-century Britain.

This book will investigate the two campaigns organised by merchants and manufacturers in Glasgow, Liverpool, and Manchester against the renewal of the EIC's Charter between 1812 and 1813 and between 1829 and 1833. Manchester's case, however, will be confined to the later period due to the lack of historical sources. As a result of the renewal of the Charter of 1813, the India trade was opened to all British subjects, and then, after the next renewal of the Charter of 1833, the Company's monopoly of the China trade was abolished. As mentioned previously, in the traditional view, historians have regarded these events as resulting from an increase in the political influence of provincial manufacturing towns and outports in the course of the Industrial Revolution. The three cities formed a core part of the lobbying activities of several provincial manufacturing towns and outports. During that period, Glasgow, Liverpool, and Manchester had different local economies; Liverpool was largely dependent on commercial activities based on its port; Manchester was the centre of the cotton manufacturing industry in Lancashire; and Glasgow played roles as both a trading port and a manufacturing centre in western Scotland. This book will explore how these three provincial cities, with their distinct economic interests, organised and developed their free trade campaigns in competition and collaboration with the London mercantile interests and their nexus. To examine the strategies, methods, and networks of provincial lobbyists and the degree of their influence in forming Britain's imperial policy, the author has analysed numerous primary sources on the provincial campaigns against the EIC's monopoly, especially the records of the Glasgow East India Association (EIA) stored at Glasgow's Mitchell Library, which have rarely attracted historians' attention until Webster's recent work.[15]

This work will also provide answers to the question of how the Scots contributed to the formation of the British Empire by focusing on the lobbying activities organised by Glasgow's merchants and manufacturers in particular. Regarding this question, Thomas Devine and Michael Fry illustrated their positive participation in socio-economic and political activities of the empire.[16] Nevertheless, previous studies on the debates surrounding the Charter renewal tend to emphasise the political influence of manufacturing interests in Lancashire. Similarly, although Cain and Hopkins had opposing stances on the degree of political influence of provincial manufacturers on British imperial policies, the Anglo-centred view of their 'gentlemanly capitalist thesis' also failed to pay attention to the role of Scotland in British imperialism. This monograph will reveal that, in the campaigns for free access to the East, Glasgow played a very significant role, along with Liverpool.

To establish the scene, the next chapter will describe a narrative account of the EIC and the development of the East India trade between the 1790s and the 1830s. This chapter will also examine the internal and external debates regarding the future of the Company's monopoly between 1793 and 1813. Then, the later chapters will examine the campaigns of the provincial lobbying groups in Glasgow, Liverpool, and Manchester between 1812 and 1813 and between 1829 and 1833, respectively. These chapters will include an analysis of the compositions of economic interests for those who joined the campaigns to identify their motives for attempting to open the East India trade. They will also focus on the strategies, methods, and networks of their lobbying while evaluating their impacts on the negotiations regarding the renewal of the EIC's Charter during these two periods.

---

[15] A. Webster, "The Strategies and Limits of Gentlemanly Capitalism: The London East India Agency Houses, Provincial Commercial Interests, and the Evolution of British Economic Policy in South and South East Asia 1800–1850", in *The Economic History Review*, Vol. LIX, No. 4, 2006, pp. 743–64.

[16] T.M. Devine, *Scotland's Empire*, 2003; M. Fry, *The Scottish Empire*, 2001.

CHAPTER ONE

DEFENDING THE MONOPOLY: THE EAST INDIA COMPANY, 1790S–1830S

Introduction

The history of the EIC can be divided into two different phases. In the first 150 years, the Company was a monopolistic trading organisation for the East India trade, with limited political and military functions. In the rest of the period, the Company developed its roles as an administrative institution for India and, at the same time, gradually ceased its commercial functions. The Company's effective acquisition of Bengal after the battle of Plassey brought about changes within the organisation. With the expectation of huge revenues from the land, India was no longer only the Company's private interest but became the national interest of Britain. Nevertheless, as the Company struggled to manage its commercial activities in the traditional framework of the East India trade, it gradually lost its monopolistic trading activities and, eventually, its political operations as well. To provide the background of the provincial lobbyists' two campaigns against the renewal of the Company's Charter, this chapter will focus on the experience that the Company had in its internal and external politics and commercial activities in Asia and at home from the 1790s to the 1830s. It will also provide an overview of the relationship between the state, non-Company private traders and provincial manufacturers, and their debates over the future of the monopolistic trade during this period.

The Company in a New Phase and the Growth of Private Traders

The grant of *diwani* of Bengal, Bihar, and Orissa by the Mughal Emperor in 1765 added a new role to the Company's activities. They were to collect the landed revenues, expected to generate between £2 million and £4 million annually to the Company.[1] In the eighteenth century, the EIC was one of the state's main sources of financing; thus, it recognised that the military and

[1] H.V. Bowen, "Investment and Empire in the Late Eighteenth Century: East India Stockholding, 1756–1791", in *The Economic History Review*, New Series, Vol. XLII, No. 2, 1989, p. 187.

political events in Bengal were significant for the Treasury.[2] However, it was soon proved that the traditional and successful framework in which the EIC had been operating its trading activities for many years was no longer expedient in the new phase and required reforms since it was facing several crises in India and at home.

In the following decades, the EIC suffered severely from the consequences of Clive's conquest of Bengal. The Company showed its inability to cope with the new political and economic situations, both in India and at home. The Court of Directors failed to control the rapid expansion of the Company's territories in India against their wishes or to regulate the misconduct of Company servants, which became a target of criticism in Britain. Since few Directors understood India's local matters, there was a gap between the perceptions of the Directors in London and the reality in India.[3]

Moreover, the will of the Company was not unified in the administrators' struggle for power.[4] The Directors had several different occupational backgrounds and commercial interests. John Bourne's work identified the Directors' seven main backgrounds: bankers, ship-owners, so-called 'free merchants', City merchants, retired servants of the EIC, maritime service with the EIC, and the Indian bar.[5] Their occupations were strongly related to the Company's commercial activities. The merchants of the City were involved in the sales of East Indian products in Britain and in other European countries and in the supply of merchandise for export to India. The 'free merchants' (or free traders), who secured the EIC's permission to engage in the intra-Asia trade, were an indispensable element of the Company's operation in the East Indies. The financiers provided capital and insurance to the Company's trading businesses. Those who were related to the shipping businesses also supplied the Company with the ships and personnel necessary for voyages. Furthermore, in the second half of the eighteenth century, the shares of those who had worked as

---

[2] H.V. Bowen, "No Longer Mere Traders: Continuities and Changes in the Metropolitan Development of the East India Company, 1600–1834", in H.V. Bowen, M. Lincoln, and N. Rigby (eds.), *The World of the East India Company*, 2002, p. 26; J. Keay, *The Honourable Company: A History of the English East India Company*, 1993, p. 379. For example, William Pitt (the Elder), who formed a cabinet in June 1766, regarded the revenues as "a kind of gift from heaven" for the repayment of debts amassed during the Seven Years' War.

[3] P. Lawson, *The East India Company: A History*, 1993, pp. 104–16.

[4] P.J. Marshall, *Problems of Empire; Britain and India 1757–1813*, 1968, Introduction 1.

[5] J.M. Bourne, "The Civil and Military Patronage of the East India Company", unpublished PhD thesis, Leicester University, 1977, pp. 38–49. He defines 'free merchants' as "merchants who had secured the EIC's permission to proceed to India (necessary before 1833), but who did not belong to the Company's service".

Indian civil or military servants gradually increased in the Court. As the investment in the Company's stocks and its dividends became more promising than ever, after the acquisition of *diwani*, these men of different backgrounds strove to seize the initiative in the management of the Company for their own interests in the Courts of Directors and Proprietors. Consequently, the Company's internal politics were in turmoil. Orders from Leadenhall Street were often inadequate and too late, and men in India had to take action in response to local crises.[6] The Directors tried to prevent further territorial conquests, but the local commanders often exploited the fear of external intervention, especially from the French, and magnified the severity of local crises as an excuse for a series of wars and conquests.[7] Once the Company achieved its territorial possessions, it had to defend them and needed to ally with Indian neighbours. This did not allow the EIC to choose isolationism and resulted in its further involvement in complicated local politics and wars.[8] Accordingly, the British territories under the Company grew at a rapidly accelerating rate. Due to this 'principal-agent problem', the Company also failed to prevent its servants from accumulating private fortunes in a corrupt manner. As a result, the increase in war and administrative expenses greatly affected the Company's trading activities. That is to say, it prevented the Company from diverting the land revenues to their import trade.

A shortage of capital for purchasing goods for return cargoes was usually offset by borrowing in India. This borrowing often took the form of issuing bills of exchange on London to those who wanted to send their private fortunes from India to Europe. For the Company, issuing bills was one of the important means of financing its commercial and other activities in India because bullion exports to India, which had been a main export from Britain since the beginning of the East India trade, were virtually stopped after Clive's conquest.[9] However, since issuing the bills on London meant that the debts of the Company in India were effectively converted into those of the head office in London, the total amount of bills that the Company could issue in India depended on its ability at home to clear these bills. If the supply of bills of exchange in Bengal exceeded the

---

6 Principal-agent problems were always concerned in the activities of early chartered companies. See Ann Carlos, "Principal-Agent Problems in Early Trading Companies: A Tale of Two Firms", in *The American Economic Review*, Vol. 82, No. 2, 1992, pp. 140–5.

7 D.M. Peers, "Between Mars and Mammon: The East India Company and Efforts to Reform its Army, 1796–1832", in *The Historical Journal*, Vol. 33, No. 2, 1990, p. 388.

8 D.K. Fieldhouse, *The Colonial Empires: A Comparative Survey from the Eighteenth Century*, 1982, pp. 167–8.

9 Marshall, *Problems of Empire*, p. 85.

Company's solvency at home, the Company would experience financial difficulties at home.[10] Therefore, the maintenance and further development of the channel of Indian remittances through commodity exports from the East Indies to Europe were of primary concern in the formation of Britain's imperial policy for India after the second half of the eighteenth century.

The EIC's territorial expansion over India not only needed more human resources to maintain its administrative and military operations but also attracted private traders and adventurers who looked for new opportunities for economic success. Consequently, the rise in the number of British subjects in India increased demand for remittances to their home. According to Peter Marshall, before the 1790s, if individuals wanted to transfer their savings to Britain, their remittance at the hands of the EIC took a variety of forms: (1) the purchase of privileged cargo space from Company servants; (2) investment in precious stones, mainly diamonds; (3) the purchase of bills of exchange from the Company; and (4) some exceptions applied to such people as the captains of the Company's vessels for carrying cargoes on their own account.[11] Among these forms, the use of bills of exchange was most important. Although the Company's bills offered British settlers more opportunities to send their fortunes to their home country than the use of its commodity trade, the amount of bills was limited and the Company could not supply enough bills to such individuals. Making remittances from India to Britain under the monopolistic trading pattern ultimately depended on the Company's ability to increase the volume of trade and to realise commercial profits at home.

However, even when the facilities of the Company were not available, its servants or private merchants still had a couple of alternative means of remittance. The first choice was sending East Indian goods to European ports using a false flag. Of course, during this period, this kind of conduct violated the Navigation Acts. The second choice was extending foreign traders credit—in other words, the purchasing of bills of exchange from non-British European or American merchants and clearing the bills through their agents in Europe. For instance, between 1785 and 1790, the London agents of the so-called 'new' French EIC received bills of exchange amounting to £757,177 from India rising to just under £1 million by 1793.[12] In the

---

[10] Ibid., p. 84.

[11] P.J. Marshall, *East India Fortunes: The British in Bengal in the Eighteenth Century*, 1976, pp. 220–4.

[12] H. Furber, *John Company at Work: A Study of European Expansion in India in the Late Eighteenth Century*, 1948, p. 50. The 'new' French East India Company was founded in 1785.

Danish case, there is evidence that, from 1783 to 1793, £858,216 was remitted to England in the Danish EIC's bills of exchange and approximately £2 million through Danish private merchants in the same period.[13]

The structural defects of remittance under the monopolistic Company were significantly related to the growth of private merchants in the East Indies during this period. As Marshall described, the private British merchants existed in Asia long before 1756.[14] This private intra-Asian trade was called a 'country trade', in which the Company had less interest and, thus, allowed them to operate with few restrictions. Because Clive's conquest of Bengal provided firmer foundations for the British private traders' commercial activities in Asia, India experienced rapid development of its trade in the second half of the eighteenth century. As trade expanded, the organisational structure of private trade developed. In the seventeenth and early eighteenth centuries, private trading organisations usually took the form of joint-stock or small partnerships with senior Company servants.[15] For example, during this period, the governors of Madras, who were not only in charge of the Company's official trade but also operated the intra-Asian trade on their own accounts, took the initiative to organise a large group of investors to purchase shares in one or more vessels.[16] By the late eighteenth century, such organisations became far more solid and permanent and were called agency houses.

In the late 1780s, Charles Cornwallis, the Governor-General of India, carried out several institutional reforms to improve the administrative activities and sweep away the corruption of Company servants. One of his most important reforms was the prohibition of private trade conducted by the Company's civil servants. Before the reform, Company servants were granted contracts to secure Indian products for export by the Board of Trade under the contract system, which was a hotbed of corruption.[17] Nevertheless, it is also true that this system effectively checked any challenges against the Company's monopoly.[18] After the reform, this contract system was abolished and Company servants could work for either the

---

13 Ibid., pp. 123 and 135.

14 P.J. Marshall, "Private British Trade in the Indian Ocean before 1800", in P.J. Marshall, *Trade and Conquest*, 1993, Chap. XIII, originally published in A.D. Gupta and M.N. Person (eds.), *India and the Indian Ocean 1500–1800*, 1987.

15 Ibid., p. 295.

16 Ibid., p. 287.

17 K.N. Chaudhuri, "Foreign Trade and Balance of Payments (1757–1947)", in D. Kumar (ed.), *The Cambridge Economic History of India, Vol.2: c.1757–c.1970*, 1983, Chap. X, p. 816.

18 A. Webster, *The Twilight of the East India Company: The Evolution of Anglo-Asian Commerce and Politics 1790–1860*, 2008, p. 25.

commercial or administrative branch of the Company's institutions in India. Its servants of the commercial branch were still allowed to operate trade on their own accounts. Meanwhile, in return for earning higher salaries, those who worked for the administrative division were prohibited from conducting their own trade. As a result, in British trading activities in India, private merchants who were developing as agency houses replaced Company servants and increased their influence.

The activities of private merchants extended over several types of financial and trading businesses.[19] After the ban on their private trade, Company servants who usually earned high salaries and held savings in India needed an alternative means of remittance. They utilised the agency houses as well as the Company's bills of exchange as a medium of remittance. They lent the agency houses money out of their savings and later received money from their agents in Britain. The agency houses used this capital for their business. They established their own networks of local trade by accommodating local European planters with loans and directly trading with native merchants. Such Indian merchandise was not only used for their intra-Asian trade but it was also an important source of the Company's trading activities. The networks of the agency houses provided the EIC with Indian products, such as cotton textiles and opium, which were exported to China in exchange for tea, and they diversified the range of products sold in Europe. Moreover, the EIC depended on them for their acceptance of its bonds issued in India. Therefore, after the Cornwallis reform of 1780s, the agency houses established themselves as an indispensable element in the Company's operation in the East India trade, and the relationship between the Company and the agency houses was not competitive but mutually supportive. The position of the houses was crucial to Britain's trade with the East Indies.

Critics and the Charter Act of 1793

By the fourth quarter of the eighteenth century, as the East India trade grew, it was gradually recognised that the monopoly of the EIC was an

---

[19] Regarding the activities of the agency houses, see A. Webster, "An Early Global Business in a Colonial Context: The Strategies, Management, and Failure of John Palmer and Company of Calcutta, 1780–1830", in *Enterprise & Society*, Vol. 6, Issue 1, 2005, pp. 98–133; S. Chapman, *Merchant Enterprise in Britain: From the Industrial Revolution to World War I*, 1992, Chapter 4; Marshall, "Private British Trade in the Indian Ocean before 1800"; A. Tripathi, *Trade and Finance in the Bengal Presidency 1793–1833*, 1979.

obstacle to the development of the trade and a bottleneck in the flow of remittances, so anti-monopolistic campaigns were gradually developed. Contemporary British intellectuals, often representing the ideas of Adam Smith, reinforced the theoretical arguments of these campaigns. In his famous work *The Wealth of Nations*, Smith pointed out the negative consequences of the East India monopoly from two angles. First, he used the example of the Dutch EIC, which could be applied to the British case, too, and argued that the monopoly prevented capital from being distributed adequately among the nation's economic activities.[20] In his view, by limiting the capital available for the East India trade, the monopoly deprived the British of the substantial benefits raised from a further increase in British manufacturing exports to India and the general development of trade that could be achieved under the condition of free trade. The second point was the incompatibility of the Company's commercial and administrative functions. Smith expressed the opinion that "the government of an exclusive Company of merchants is, perhaps, the worst of all governments for any country whatever".[21] Although the EIC, as the sovereign of India, should have acted for the welfare of the Indian nation, its commercial function prevented it from doing so. In his view, not only could neither Britain nor India benefit from the East India monopoly but also it actually damaged the economic interests of both countries. In Glasgow's case, Smith's free trade philosophy was widely accepted even before the publication of his famous book in 1776, and its merchants and manufacturers who adapted his views, notably Kirkman Finlay, led the city's campaigns against the Company's monopoly.[22]

While the theoretical arguments surrounding the East India monopoly became more sophisticated, the actual campaigns against the Company were organised by two main groups in the 1790s. One of these groups was private traders, including the agency houses in Asia and those in London, which were closely linked with each other. The other was provincial manufacturing interests. This was the first serious challenge to the Company's privileges since the merger of the 'original' and 'new' East India Companies in 1708. Among them, the group that initially demanded free access to Asian markets was British private merchants residing in India. Their main

---

20 A. Smith, M. Cannan (ed.), *An Inquiry into the Nature and Causes of the Wealth of Nations*, 1904, p. 131.

21 Ibid., p. 72.

22 J.A. Gherity, "Adam Smith and the Glasgow Merchants", in *History of Political Economy*, Vol. 24, No. 2, 1992, pp. 358–9.

concern was that the Company failed to provide them with adequate shipping services for their exports to Britain.[23] The private traders regarded the shipping service provided by the Company as too expensive and too inflexible and the quota of space on its ships as too small to compete efficiently with their competitors in the British and European markets.

Historians have advanced several reasons for the Company's high shipping costs. Because the ships that the Company employed for the trade were designed for possible war use, they were too large and over-equipped for simply carrying out trade.[24] In addition, far more ships were engaged in trade than were actually needed. For instance, one report to a parliamentary committee in 1773 stated that, although only 55 ships were actually necessary for the trade, the EIC possessed 87 ships, and the Company actually sent 30 ships to the East Indies in spite of the fact that 24 ships were enough to carry all cargo.[25] Ralph Davis also pointed out that the monopoly discouraged the EIC from adopting new technologies that would allow the Company to reduce its freight rate.[26] Without competition, the Company did not need to improve its shipping efficiency. Those who were exclusively engaged in the businesses related to the Company's shipping, such as shipowners, shipbuilders, and captains, largely exploited it. They organised themselves as the 'Old Shipping Interest', and their representatives in the Court of Directors could exercise significant influence on the formation of the Company's policy.[27] As they largely benefited from the trading structure, which kept the Company's shipping costs high, they always resisted changes that would lead to the reduction of the Company's shipping cost.

These characteristics of the Company's shipping became the target of criticism. One contemporary argued that:

> It is the complicated abuses arising from patronage, from the collusion and confederacy of the builders, owners, and husbands of the Indiamen, that made me think it necessary to hinder, if possible, their mutual influence…[28]

Moreover, by the time of the beginning of the negotiations on the renewal of the EIC's Charter, private traders had established themselves as one of

---

[23] S. Imada, *Pakusu Buritanika to shokuminchi Indo* [*Pax Britannica and the Colonial India*], 2000, chap. 1, especially section 1–4.

[24] Marshall, *Problems of Empire*, p. 81.

[25] Ibid.

[26] R. Davis, *The Rise of the English Shipping Industry in the Seventeenth and Eighteenth Centuries*, 1962, p. 265.

[27] Marshall, *Problems of Empire*, p. 81.

[28] A. Brough, *Consideration on the Necessity of Lowering the Exorbitant Freight of Ships Employed in the Service of the East-India-Company*, 1786, p. 35.

the significant interest groups within the Company. The most notable figure who represented them in the Court of Directors at the time was David Scott. In his previous career, he had been the senior figure of Scott, Tate & Adamson, one of Bombay's agency houses, before he left the firm and returned to the United Kingdom.[29] Then, he established David Scott & Co., a London-based agency house. Later, with support from Henry Dundas, the President of the Board of Control, Scott obtained a seat in the Directorship of the EIC. As his career shows, although he was one of the Directors, he had a close connection to agency houses both in India and in London and held critical views regarding the Company's privileges that the 'Old Shipping Interest' had enjoyed for many years.

As the expiration of the Charter was approaching, on 14 January 1793, Dundas sent his notice to the Company to start negotiations on the renewal of its privileges.[30] By that time, the Ministry had shaped its ideas of moderate reforms in the traditional framework of the East India trade. In his early communication, Dundas had suggested to the Company an idea he called a 'regulated monopoly'. This meant that the monopoly must be regulated to ensure for the merchants and manufacturers certain and ample means of exporting to India to satisfy the demand for British products and of importing raw materials at a reasonable rate.[31] The long-established structure of the East India trade encountered several problems during the second half of the eighteenth century. Nevertheless, Dundas still regarded the Company as the best vehicle for remittance from India, although trade with India needed to be extended further by all possible means, including the creation of greater opportunities for non-Company mercantile interests.[32]

As Amales Tripathi and Webster argued, the group that could exercise significant influence on the negotiations of the renewal of the Charter was private traders, i.e., the agency houses, in Asia and London, which were represented by Scott in the Court of Directors.[33] Given Scott's status as one of the Directors, it is understandable that he preferred to seek ways to extend facilities for non-Company private trade with Asia by modifying the

---

[29] Webster, *The Twilight of the East India Company*, p. 26–7.

[30] *Papers Respecting the Negotiation for a Renewal of the East-India Company's Exclusive Trade*, No. I, Article No. I, Letter from Dundas to the Chairman of the EIC, dated 14 January 1793.

[31] *Papers Respecting the Negotiation*, No. I, Article No. IV, Letter from Dundas to the Chairman, dated 16 February 1793.

[32] Webster, *The Twilight of the East India Company*, p. 31.

[33] A. Tripathi, *Trade and Finance in the Bengal Presidency 1793–1833*, 1979, pp. 28–35; Webster, *Twilight of the East India Company*, pp. 36–8.

Company's traditional monopolistic trade. He held a too-large stake as well as a high social position in the Company to try to abolish its privileges immediately and to create a new trading system. Furthermore, because the relationship between the Company and the agency houses in India and London was of mutual dependence, their arguments on the opening of the East India trade were also relatively moderate. One private trader, who is assumed to be John Cochrane, a private trader in India, argued in his memorial to Dundas that, while the Company should retain its privilege of import trade in articles such as saltpetre and certain types of piece goods, it should make a concession to the private traders for all other items.[34]

In the debates on the renewal of the Charter in 1793, one of the most significant questions related to the Company's commercial branch was how the nation could transform the clandestine trade from India to Europe into legitimate trade. Scott and his allies succeeded in putting this issue at the centre of the agenda by sending their memorials to the Ministry.[35] Although, at the beginning of the negotiations, the Ministry did not recognise the extent of the clandestine trade, they became more seriously concerned about this problem after receiving these memorials.[36] They argued that, because the EIC did not facilitate the remittance of trading capital but opposed it, the estimated value of remittance through the foreign channels after the conquest of Bengal amounted to £10 million.[37] In his communication to the Company, Dundas insisted that:

> Both Mr. Pitt and I are so strongly impressed with the importance of this subject [the clandestine trade] on national grounds, that we are at perfect loss, how it is possible to state with credit any part of the subject leaving that behind, ... if enclosed [letter from the persons connected with the clandestine trade] ... is refuted, it seems impossible to call the truth of the fact in question.[38]

They also asked the Ministry to include a clause in the new Charter to legalise British subjects and others residing in India or elsewhere to act for the subjects of all nations on agency.[39] Their attempts to relax the restrictions

---

[34] Marshall, *Problems of Empire*, pp. 212–3, "Hints respecting the E I Trade, 4 March, 1793".

[35] Tripathi, *Trade and Finance*, p. 28–9.

[36] Ibid.

[37] *Papers Respecting the Negotiation*, No III, Article No. XXI, The Memorial Respecting the Clandestine Trade, with the Committee's Remarks thereon.

[38] *Papers Respecting the Negotiation*, No VII, Letter from Dundas to the Chairman, 15 April 1793.

[39] *Papers Respecting the Negotiation*, No. II, Article No. VII, Copy of the Clause Proposed to be Inserted in the Impending Act for New Charter by the Agents for Persons Resident in the East Indies.

on the East India trade received additional support from the 'New Shipping Interest', led by Brough, Chapman, Fiott, etc.[40] These new shippers wanted to break through the long-term privileges of the 'Old Shipping Interest'. Given their ample evidence and strong insistence, the Ministry grew increasingly convinced that the EIC should extend its facilities for the private traders. From the viewpoint of the conservative part of the Company, notably the 'Old Shipping Interest', the change of the Ministry's mind was a surprising event. After several communications, Dundas eventually informed the Company that he would include the private traders' claim for legalising all persons residing in India to act as commercial agents in the substances of his propositions to Parliament.[41] He also suggested to the Company that it should be obliged to provide no less than 3,000 tons of shipping to the private merchants for trading with India, at a cost of £5 per ton for outwards and £15 per ton for inwards in peace-time.[42] As Webster rightly pointed out, Scott and his friends of private trade were closely linked not only to the mercantile community of the City of London but also to the insiders of the Company's affairs.[43] These facts enabled them to access prime figures of the Company and British politics more easily than others; thus, they could exercise direct and effective influence in the negotiations over the future of the Company's monopoly during the period.

Nevertheless, the private traders in India and London were not the only group that seriously challenged the Company's traditional privileges. Another significant group included those who were connected to mercantile and manufacturing activities based in provincial towns. In fact, these individuals represented a variety of economic interest groups. One such group included those with manufacturing interests who were producing goods for the Company's commodity exports to Asia, particularly woollen goods and metals. Regarding the former, although, for many years, the British textile industry had shown strong hostility towards the Company's import of Indian cotton piece goods to Europe, its export of woollen goods to China in the late eighteenth century significantly contributed to the local economy of manufacturing regions such as Devon.[44] In their

---

[40] Tripathi, *Trade and Finance*, p. 28.

[41] *Papers Respecting the Negotiation*, No IV, Article No. II, Resolution Referred to the Letter from Dundas to the Chairman.

[42] Ibid.

[43] Webster, *Twilight of the East India Company*, p. 37.

[44] H.V. Bowen, "Sinews of Trade and Empire: The Supply of Commodity Exports to the East India Company during the Late Eighteenth Century", in *The Economic History Review*, Vol. LV, No. 3, 2002, pp. 476–7.

memorial to Dundas, Exeter's manufacturers of long-ells admitted that the Company's annual exports of their goods to Asia significantly increased. Meanwhile, they also blamed the Company's large purchase of woollen goods for increased wool prices, which damaged their business with the European continent.[45] In compensation for it, these manufacturers demanded that the Company purchase their finished goods from them directly instead of buying unfinished goods and preparing and dying them in London. Norwich's manufacturers of worsted goods also asked for the Company's support to facilitate the export of their products in their petition to the Ministry.[46] Similarly, Cornwall's tin miners demanded an option to sell their products to the Company or to export them to Asia on the Company's ships and then to receive their returns in the form of bills of exchange or raw materials.[47] Overall, since these provincial manufacturers' intention was to expand their commodity exports to Asia through the EIC's trade rather than to create new channels, their claims for the opening of the East India trade were also relatively moderate.

Compared with the manufacturing interests of these regions, demands from the mercantile and manufacturing interests of Glasgow, Manchester, and Liverpool went further. In such industrial regions as Lancashire and Western Scotland, the newly growing cotton manufacturing industry experienced a series of technological innovations and improved its productivity. For instance, a contemporary writer described the development of cotton industry in Paisley, a neighbouring town of Glasgow, as follows:

> There is one encouraging circumstance ... that they had not only great advantages from the machinery invented, but also the weavers perform their operations better than the Asiatics.[48]

Consequently, by the time of the renewal of the EIC's Charter of 1793, its products were able to compete with Indian cotton piece goods of lower quality. However, the industry still could not do so with good of higher quality such as muslins.[49] The claims from Glasgow and Manchester reflected

---

[45] J. Bruce, *Reports on the Negotiation, between the Honorable East-India Company and the Public Respecting the Renewal of the Company's Exclusive Privileges of Trade for Twenty Years from March, 1794*, 1811, pp. xxxii–xxxiii, A Memorial from Merchants of Exeter to Henry Dundas, dated 9 March 1793.

[46] Ibid., pp. xlviii–xlix, A Petition from the Merchants and Manufacturers of Norwich to the Lords of Privy Council for Plantation and Trade, dated 13 March 1793.

[47] *Papers Respecting the Negotiation,* No.III, Article V, Letter from Lord Falmouth and the Other Gentlemen Interested in the Mines of Cornwall, to Mr. Dundas.

[48] *The Gentleman's Magazine and Historical Chronicle,* Vol. 61, Part 1, 1787, p. 466, "New Description of Paisley".

[49] Tripathi, *Trade and Finance*, pp. 24–5.

the transitional period of growth and development in Britain's cotton manufacturing industry.

In December 1792, the Directors of the Chamber of Commerce and Manufacturers in Glasgow sent their petition to Dundas. From their viewpoint, although good reasons for granting the monopoly to the EIC might have existed in the past, there were no longer any such reasons for it to retain exclusive trading privileges.[50] In this petition, they argued that, since the British private traders now had sufficient enterprise and capital to carry on their trade with the East Indies, they should have the right to export manufactured items and import raw materials in their own vessels.[51] At the same time, to protect the local textile industry, they argued that the Company should not import any Indian piece goods for home sale exceeding certain conditions and that the state should ban the export and use of British cotton machinery in India.[52] In addition, the manufacturers of Paisley, who were closely connected to those of Glasgow, sent a similar petition to London that criticised the Company for damaging the progress of cotton manufacturing in Britain through its imports.[53]

During the debates on the renewal of the EIC's privilege of 1793, perhaps the most active part of the provincial interests was the merchants and manufacturers of Manchester. In January 1791, the "Muslin and Cotton Manufacturers and Cotton Spinners" of the Manchester district held a meeting and made resolutions to criticise the Company's import of Indian cotton piece goods as damaging to the British manufacturers.[54] At the beginning of March 1793, they established the committee in a public meeting and sent their delegation to London to hold an interview with William Pitt (the Younger) and Dundas on 16 March 1793. In their interview, the delegates asked for the opening of the China market and exemption from all import and export duties to India as well as the reduction of the Company's freight rates for private traders to £4 or less per ton for outwards and £12 or less per ton for inwards.[55]

Moreover, Manchester's lobbying activities showed some signs of collaboration among the provincial manufacturing towns and outports for the

---

50 Bruce, *Report of the Negotiation*, pp. viii–xi, Resolutions of the Directors of the Chamber of Commerce and Manufacturers at Glasgow, on the Subject of the Trade of the East-India Company, dated 25 December, 1792.

51 Ibid.

52 Ibid.

53 Ibid., pp. xvii–xviii, Resolutions of the Manufacturers at Paisley.

54 A. Redford, *Manchester Merchants and Foreign Trade 1794–1858*, 1934, pp. 108–9.

55 Bruce, *Report of the Negotiation*, pp. xx–xxvii, Proceedings of the Merchants and Manufacturers of Manchester, on the Subject of the Trade of the East India Company.

opening of the East India trade during this period. To strengthen their claim that the EIC should provide private traders with cheaper freight rates than the rates it had suggested in the negotiations, the Manchester committee tried to build a collective view with the neighbouring merchants of Liverpool, who were also fighting for entry into the East India trade. For this purpose, these two parties communicated with each other between 1792 and 1793. The merchants of Liverpool supported Manchester's demand by affirming that they could undertake to provide shipping to private traders in peace-time at a rate of £14 per ton for outwards and inwards.[56] In another example, Thackeray and Simpson of Manchester formed a delegation with the representatives of its neighbouring towns for the British Calico and Muslin Manufacturers and held an interview with the Ministers.[57] In this meeting, the delegation made some requests to the Ministry encouraging the Company's import of cotton wools, as well as in support of banning the import of Indian piece goods.[58] Nevertheless, in terms of the size of the collaboration and the ability to form a common front against the Company's privileges, the provincial interests of this period cannot bear comparison with those of later periods. In the free trade movement of 1793, because of their too-varied demands in pursuing their own interests, the provincial interests failed to develop their campaigns into a unified nationwide movement. Therefore, the collaboration of different provincial interest groups during this period was confined to a regional level.

Regarding the government and the EIC's response to the claims of the different provincial mercantile and manufacturing interests, the Ministry and the Company accepted the claims from Manchester and Glasgow to encourage the import of raw materials from India for the domestic cotton industry.[59] The Company also made a concession to Cornish tin miners after their negotiations. The EIC agreed to export 800 tons of tin annually at the rate of £72 per ton and sell it in the markets of India or China, although it added the condition that its obligation was to be reduced to 400 tons or less unless it could achieve the stated quantity at the end of each successive four-year period.[60] In fact, in spite of their initial high expectations,

---

[56] Ibid., pp. xxiv–xxv, Letter from Thomas Earle of Liverpool to the Manchester Committee, dated 8 March 1793.

[57] *Papers Respecting the Negotiation*, No III, Article No. XIV; Bruce, *Report of the Negotiation*, pp. xx–xxvii, Proceedings of the Merchants and Manufacturers of Manchester.

[58] Bruce, *Report of the Negotiation*, pp. xx–xxvii.

[59] *Papers Respecting the Negotiation*, No III, Article No. XIV, Minute of a Conversation between Mr. Pitt, Mr. Dundas, and Several Gentlemen from Manchester.

[60] Ibid., Article No. VI, Letter from Mr. Dundas to Lord Falmouth, dated 22 March 1793.

the export of tin never became a profitable part of the Company's commerce.[61]

However, not only the Company, which always showed hostility towards any attempt to undermine its commercial privileges, but also the Ministry rejected most other demands made by these provincial interest groups. For instance, Henry Dundas rejected the assertion of Exeter's manufacturers of long-ells, as he observed that "it was impossible to bring forward that grievance, or the remedy for it, as a matter of Parliamentary arrangement".[62] He also rejected the demand of the "British Calico and Muslin Manufacturers" for the exemption of British manufacturers from all import and export duties in the East India trade on the grounds that their claim was unreasonable.[63] Moreover, Dundas ignored the claims from both Glasgow and Manchester for the prohibition of the import of Indian cotton piece goods for home sales. In the debates, he was convinced that the total ban on imports of Indian products would result in an increased possibility of smuggling into Britain, although, after 1797, the duty rates on cotton goods were rapidly increased to protect the British cotton manufacturing industry.[64] Without sufficient communication and collaboration among the different parties of provincial mercantile and manufacturing interests, their arguments for the relaxation or abolition of the Company's monopoly could not refute the consistent assertions of their opponents. Consequently, they had only a limited impact on the Ministry's decisions on the renewal of the Charter in the 1790s.

In the reform of the EIC in 1793, the intention of the government was not the total abolition of the Company's monopoly but its modification to increase the amount of trade between Britain and India to meet the demands of British commercial and manufacturing interests. The new Charter put the EIC under an obligation to provide private merchants with an annual capacity of up to 3,000 tons for their cargoes in the holds of ships at the discounted freight rates of £5 per ton for outwards and £15 per ton for inwards. From the viewpoint of the free trade advocates, this was the first monumental achievement in breaking into the Company's exclusive trade.

---

61 Bowen, "Sinew of Trade and Empire", p. 480.

62 *Papers Respecting the Negotiation*, No III, Article No. VII, Letter from Mr. Dundas to the Chairman, dated 23 March 1793.

63 Ibid., Article No. XII, Minute of Conversation between Mr. Pitt, Mr. Dundas, and Messrs. Gregg and Frodsham, Delegates from Manchester.

64 Ibid., Article No. XIV, Minute of a Conversation between Mr. Pitt, Mr. Dundas, and Several Gentlemen from Manchester; E. Baines, *History of the Cotton Manufacture in Great Britain*, 1835, p. 325.

Nevertheless, the Company was able to retain its trade monopoly with India and China. According to Philips, if one takes the situation of war with France into consideration, it was the appropriate decision to serve the best interest of the nation. In this view the renewal of monopolistic trading rights gave an advantage to Britain because the armed convoy of the Company was likely to prevent Britain's East India trade from suffering heavy losses incurred by French privateers, and this gave British manufacturers an opportunity to establish themselves in the overseas market with the supremacy of its naval power during the war period.[65]

Further Struggles and the End of the Monopoly, 1794–1833

In spite of the EIC's concessions, the renewed Charter could not succeed in satisfying those who claimed free access to the East India trade, as the traffic between Britain and the East Indies increased and the services that the Company supplied to them could not meet their demand. Therefore, the agency houses in India demanded that the Company permit the use of their own India-built-ships for their import trade to Britain. In the late eighteenth and early nineteenth centuries, this question brought about serious antagonism within the Company. Against the wishes of the Company Directors, especially those who were linked with the 'Old Shipping Interest', Wellesley, who was in office as the Governor-General of India from 1798 until 1805, supported the claims of the private merchants.[66] The rapid growth of British territories in India under his aggressive foreign policy resulted in well-known consequences for the second half of the Company's history: an increase in its debts in India and a slump in the India trade. Shusaku Imada, a Japanese scholar, pointed out the correlation between the Company's financial standing in India and the size of its 'investment' in goods for export to the United Kingdom by contrasting the period of John Shore, the Governor-General who adopted a non-intervention policy from 1793 to 1798, and the period of Wellesley, who succeeded Shore and aggressively expanded the British territories until 1805.[67] Moreover, two other factors worsened the position of the Company: a series of wars in Europe and the growing demand for free trade from the private traders and the provincial mercantile and manufacturing interests.

---

65 C.H. Philips, *The East India Company, 1784–1834*, 1940, p. 79.
66 Imada, *Pakusu Buritanika to shokuminchi Indo*, Chapter 1.
67 Ibid., pp. 43–57.

As the growth of private trade and the decline of the Company's India trade occurred before his eyes, Wellesley tried to promote private trade and give it more responsibility for British trading activities in Asia. Wellesley, who was appointed as the Governor-General thanks to his connection with the state rather than with the Company, chose such an economic policy to resolve the dilemma of the expansion of British territories and the deterioration of the Company's commercial performance.[68] Dundas and the 'Private Trade Interest' group represented by Scott within the EIC supported his attempts to extend the private traders' responsibility for the growth of the East India trade.[69]

Nevertheless, the defenders of the long-term privileges in the Company's business countered these attempts. In 1799, Jacob Bosaquent, acting on behalf the 'Old Shipping Interest', accused Scott of his own firm's involvement in illegal trading activities.[70] The opponents of free trade eventually succeeded in branding the claim of the 'Private Trade Interest' as motivated by self-interest and undermined their influence in the Company's internal politics.[71] Consequently, by 1800, the pro-monopoly group, led by Bosaquent and Charles Grant, was able to take the initiative in the Company's management and exerted their power to shape the opinions of a special Select Committee that the Court of Directors established to consider the question of the participation of India-built ships in their favour.[72] This committee recommended that the use of India-built ships should be restricted to circumstances where the Company was unable to provide a sufficient number of ships.[73] In spite of the strong defiance from the critics of the 'Old Shipping Interest', the majority of the Company's proprietors supported the committee's advice. Eventually, in the early 1800s, the private traders' attempts to introduce the regular use of India-built ships to the import trade failed.

The triumph of the conservative group in the battle against the structural reforms of the East India trade in the early nineteenth century did not mean at all that the EIC was able to overcome the problems from which the Company had suffered during the second half of the eighteenth century. The reality was different. In the debates on the introduction of the

68 Philips, *The East India Company*, p. 93. According to Philips, Wellesley (Lord Mornington) was a friend of Pitt. He had worked as an Assistant Commissioner for the Board of Control under Henry Dundas before his appointment as the Governor-General of India.

69 Imada, *Pakusu Buritanika to shokuminchi Indo*, pp. 58–60 and p. 105.

70 Webster, *The Twilight of the East India Company*, p. 45.

71 Ibid., pp. 45–6.

72 Ibid., pp. 48–51.

73 Ibid., pp. 50–1.

India-built ships into the East India trade, supporters of the 'Old Shipping Interest', such as Charles Grant, insisted that their opponents were overstating the size of the clandestine trade.[74] However, although the relaxation of restrictions on the East India trade was intended to fix the structural defects of the Company's remittance from the East Indies to Europe, the new Charter Act of 1793 obviously failed to do so. In fact, after the second half of the 1780s, especially after the outbreak of the Napoleonic Wars in 1792, American merchants became increasingly involved in the remittance of British subjects from India to Europe.[75] While many European countries were at war, American merchants took advantage of their neutral position to expand their trading activities in the East Indies. After 1796, Jay's Treaty, which Britain and the United States signed in 1794, also gave them favourable conditions.[76] Article xiii of the treaty was very ambiguous in terms of the restrictions of American trade with the East Indies. It permitted American vessels to anchor in British possessions in the East Indies virtually 'unrestrictedly' for their imports from India to the United States. This article also did not contain wording to restrict American imports from India for domestic consumption, nor did it ban circuitous trade through Europe. In regard to taxation, American ships were levied at the ports of British territories on the same terms as British ships. In addition, although coastal trade in India was prohibited to American ships, in reality, this regulation was not rigidly applied until 1801.[77]

Figures 1 and 2 show the growth of US trade between 1795–96 and 1805–06 with Bengal, where the British most successfully established their political and commercial foundation in Asia. Figure 1 shows that the values of exports from Bengal to the United States grew rapidly from approximately 1.2 million rupees to 6.1 million rupees between 1798–99 and 1800–01 and then fluctuated between approximately 3.3 million rupees and 6.7 million rupees. In Figure 2, the value of imports into Bengal shows a similar trend. In the same period, imports increased dramatically from approximately 1 million rupees to 5 million rupees and then fluctuated. However, the value of the imports from the United States tended to be higher than those from London in the first half of the 1800s. The trend of trade between the United

[74] Ibid., p. 50.

[75] Regarding the growth of the American trade with India in this period, see H. Furber, "The Beginnings of American Trade with India 1784–1812", in R. Rocher (ed.), *Private Fortunes and Company Profits in the India Trade in the 18th Century*, 1997, Chap. II. Originally published in *The New England Quarterly* Vol. 11, No. 2, 1938, pp. 235–65.

[76] Ibid., pp. 243–5.

[77] Ibid., p. 251.

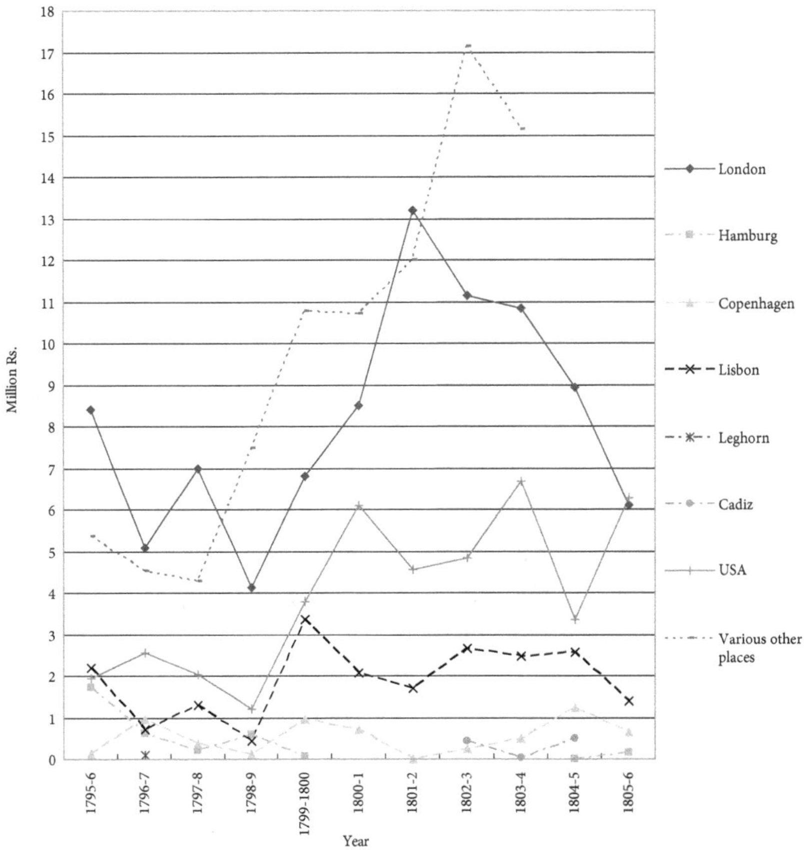

Figure 1. Exports from Bengal: Regional Distribution (1795/96–1805/06).

Source: K.N. Chaudhuri, "Foreign Trade and Balance of Payments (1757–1947)", in D. Kumar (ed.), *The Cambridge Economic History of India, Vol. 2: c.1757–c.1970*, 1983, Chap. X, p. 820, Table 10.3A. The original source is Parliamentary Papers, *Fourth Report on the Affairs of the East India Company*, 1812, Vol. VI, Appendix 47. Chaudhuri corrected the original figures from the source using the Reports 1805–06. In the creation of this graph, these corrected figures have been used instead of the original figures.

States and Bengal showed a contrast to those of ports on the European continent, which suffered from the chaos of the Napoleonic Wars. Holden Furber quoted figures reported to the Court of Directors by Charles Grant and Edward Parry, the Directors of the EIC, in 1807. According to them, between 1795–96 and 1804–05, the remittances, which are indicated by an excess of exports over imports, from Calcutta to Britain by foreign ships amounted to 135 *lacs* of *sicca rupee* (approximately £1.35 million), of which

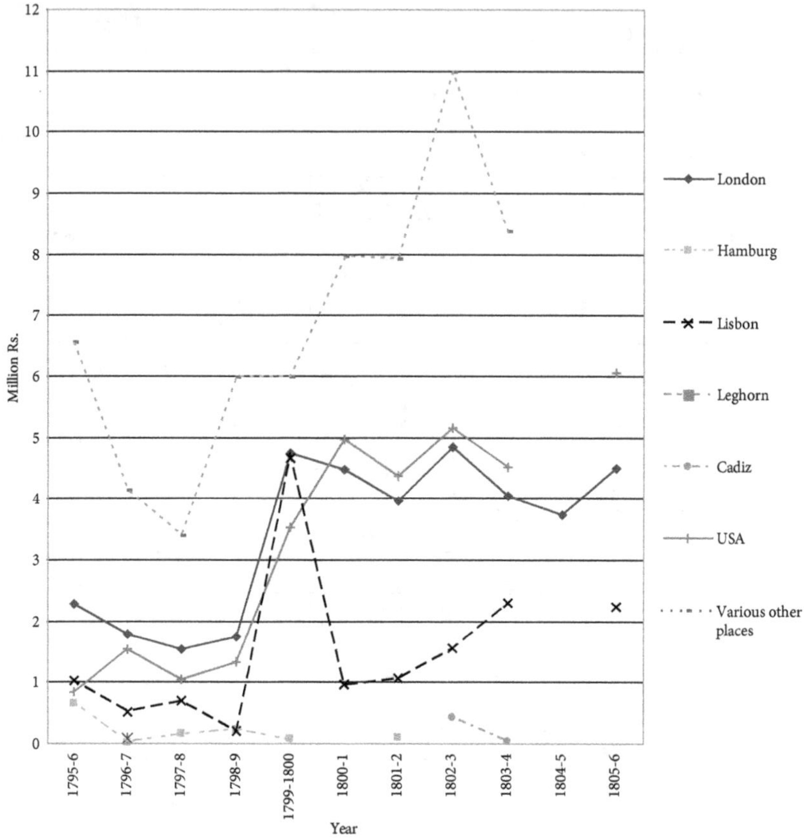

Figure 2. Imports into Bengal: Regional Distribution (1795/96–1805/06).
Source: see source for Figure 1.

59 *lacs* (approximately £0.6 million) were sent by Americans.[78] The remittance from India to Britain in foreign ships was the target of strong criticism in Britain because it provided foreign merchants with British capital to compete with the EIC in trade. In their memorials to the Board of Control, merchants and agents for private merchants in India mentioned that:

> ... from the increased and increasing demand in Europe and America for Indian commodities, the produce and manufactures of British India have

[78] Ibid., p. 260.

> increased far beyond what the Capital of the East India Company, applicable to its investment, is capable of exporting...[79]

Then, in a later part, they continued to insist that:

> ... a large and undue proportion of the Indian Trade is at present in the possession of Foreigners, the Governor General [Wellesley] distinctly asserts and adds his deliberate opinion, that unless effectual means be instantly adopted to check them, the most serious mischiefs are to be apprehended. The people who for the present seem to have been most successful in their encroachments, are the Americans, who having but little Capital of their own, and few commodities applicable to Indian markets, carry on this lucrative traffic for the most part on British Capital and Credit...[80]

The fact that Americans and others conducted illicit trade in significant amounts, even after the renewal of the Charter in 1793, clearly indicates the defects and limitations of the partially reformed trading system.

Therefore, in spite of the failure to achieve the opening of the East India trade in the 1790s, the demand for free trade increased further by the time that the Charter Act of 1793 needed to be renewed in the first half of the 1810s. The French blockade of Britain, particularly after they captured Holland, Westphalia, and the northern part of the Germanies in 1810, severely damaged British exports of manufactured goods and re-exports of American and West Indian merchandise to the European continent. The increase in political tension between Britain and the United States in a dispute over the Orders in Council and the outbreak of war between these two countries also negatively impacted those who were involved in the American trade and the manufacturing industry, which depended on raw materials from the United States. In the free trade movement at this time, provincial mercantile and manufacturing interests took the initiative. Meanwhile, private merchants in London, who had initially demanded the opening of the trade, changed their attitude in favour of the Company because they feared that the claims of the provincial interests would go too far and end the special status of the port of London.[81]

From 1793 to 1813, provincial manufacturing interests in Britain, particularly cotton manufacturers, changed their perception of the India trade. Between the late 1790s and the early 1800s, the rapid increase in customs duties on Indian cotton textiles resulted from the demands of British textile

---

79 Parliamentary Papers, *Supplement to the Appendix to the Fourth Report from the Select Committee on the Affairs of the East India Company*, 1812 (151) (182), p. 63.

80 Ibid., pp. 66–7.

81 Philips, *The East India Company*, p. 182.

manufacturers to drive them out of the British market, and this measure succeeded in doing so. After the exclusion of Indian goods from the British market and the further growth of the industry, provincial manufacturers regarded India as a market for their products. These provincial manufacturers linked up with the merchants of outports who were excluded from the East India trade, which London merchants dominated. Representatives from several manufacturing towns and outports in Britain and Ireland gathered in London in 1812 to organise their lobbying activities effectively for the abolition of the EIC's exclusive Charter and for their direct participation in the East India trade.

As a result of the more organised and more effective lobbying of the provincial interests, particularly for the opening of the import trade, the India trade was fully opened to all British subjects, although the Company was able to secure a monopoly in the trade of tea and the China trade. After 1814, those who took the initiative in the East India trade were the private traders, particularly agency houses in India. The Company's internal politics also reflected this change. That is to say, in the Courts of Directors and Proprietors, the political influence of private traders increased during the 1820s, while other interest groups were losing their presence. For instance, according to Cyril Philips, by 1826, eight Directors represented the 'Private Trade Interest' in the Court, and by 1831, seventeen out the thirty Directors (including the six men retired by annual rotation) supported this faction.[82] At the same time, during the 1820s, many prominent figures among the Directors, such as Charles Grant, Edward Parry, William F. Elphinstone, Joseph Cotton, and Jacob Bosanquet, had died or retired, and those who took over their posts were not as capable as they had been in dealing with the Company's business.[83] In fact, most of those who took the post of the Company's Chairmanship from 1822 to 1829 had no experience residing in India. Similarly, in 1831, fewer than half of the Directors had previously lived there.[84] Consequently, they had little knowledge of the actual state of India and could not exercise as significant an influence as their predecessors had on British commercial policies in the East Indies. However, this was not the only significant change in the Company and the East India trade after 1814. As the following chapters explain in detail, after the opening of the India trade, the provincial manufacturers established

[82] Ibid., p. 243.
[83] Ibid., p. 244.
[84] Ibid.

their connection with these agency houses, particularly those in London, through their trading activities with Asia.

Although the Charter Act of 1813 opened the India trade, the Company carried on its India trade for the secure channel of the remittance. The trade was no longer profitable, but the Company needed to keep the value of imports from India to Britain high. To compensate for the deficit of the India trade and to maintain the remittance, the large profits earned from the China and tea trade were crucial for the Company. At the same time, during this period, among the Indian products imported to Britain by the Company, indigo became the most important single commodity. Previously, Indian cotton piece goods had held a similar position. However, during the second half of the eighteenth and the early nineteenth centuries, through the adaption of technological innovations, the British cotton manufacturers successfully gained competitive power and excluded their Indian rivals from the European market. The development of indigo plantations in India was financed by the investment of the agency houses. However, by the end of the 1820s, indigo was oversupplied in Europe and the price declined. The economic depression in Britain also impacted trade. From 1825 to 1831, the price of indigo in London diminished by half.[85] Meanwhile, in India, its price remained high as the EIC continued to purchase the products for import from India until the Company virtually stopped the indigo trade in the season of 1830–31, which resulted in the collapse of the indigo market in Calcutta.[86] This event severely damaged the agency houses, such as the House of John Palmer & Co., and the Bengal economy as a whole. In fact, by that time, the financial foundations of these Indian agency houses were shaken by their mismanagement of trading and banking businesses, as well as by the disloyalty of partners to the firms.[87] Eventually, the failure of John Palmer & Co. in 1830 triggered a financial crisis in India, which led to a chain of bankruptcies among the agency houses in Calcutta during the first half of the 1830s.[88]

The fundamental cause of the failure of the agency houses in Calcutta was largely attributed to the termination of the Company's exclusive rights in the India trade, which caused India's unstable economic condition. The relationship between the EIC and the agency houses had been mutually

[85] K.N. Chaudhuri, "India's Foreign Trade and the Cessation of the East India Company's Trading Activities", in The *Economic History Review*, New Series, Vol. XIX, No. 2, 1966, p. 353.

[86] Ibid.

[87] A. Webster, *The Richest East India Merchant: The Life and Business of John Palmer of Calcutta 1760–1836*, 2007, Chapter 6.

[88] Philips, *The East India Company*, pp. 277–8.

supportive. In the old economic framework based on the Company's India monopoly, the agency houses almost succeeded in excluding new entrants from the 'country trade' and their other businesses, such as banking and investment in indigo planters.[89] In the meantime, in return for the Company's tolerance of their private trade within Asia, they supported it financially. However, the renewal of the Charter Act of 1813 destroyed this framework, and competition among the private merchants increased as newcomers entered the same businesses. For instance, between 1815 and 1829, the number of agency houses increased from 20 to 39.[90] In addition, the large issue of loans by the Company to wage the war against the Burmese between 1824 and 1826 also affected the performance of the agency houses. Since the agency houses needed to keep attracting the investments of their clients to finance their commercial activities, they were forced to increase interest rates, which curtailed their profits.[91] Consequently, their position in the Indian economy became unstable, which culminated in a series of bankruptcies among the agency houses.

Philips described the downfall of 'Private Trade Interest', which had maintained a strong influence over British East India policy after the opening of the India trade in 1813, creating confusion among the Court of Directors.[92] In addition, the Parliamentary Reform of 1832 undermined the Company's political influence. In the early 1830s, the Whig government made attempts to cut the expenses of the empire as a part of financial reconstruction. Before the reform, those who represented colonial interests, such as Indian nabobs and West Indian planters, often returned to Parliament from rotten boroughs, a practice that received severe criticism from the public for the typical form of 'Old Corruption'. These colonial interests were critical of the reduction in colonial expenses. Therefore, from the government's viewpoint, the abolition of rotten boroughs in the reform was partially aimed at weakening the influence of its opponents in Parliament.[93] Both the bankruptcies of agency houses and the parliamentary reform certainly curtailed the political influence of the EIC over British policy in the East Indies. However, I will demonstrate in the following

[89] A. Webster, *Gentlemen Capitalists: British Imperialism in South East Asia 1770–1890*, 1998, p. 68. Webster explains, that before the termination of the India monopoly, most of these businesses were oligopolised by the six leading agency houses.

[90] Ibid., p. 69.

[91] Tripathi, *Trade and Finance*, pp. 162–3.

[92] Philips, *The East India Company*, chap. X.

[93] M. Taylor, "Empire and Parliamentary Reform: The 1832 Reform Act Revisited", in J. Innis and A. Burns (eds.), *Rethinking the Age of Reform*, 2003, pp. 302–9.

chapters, the effective and coherent lobbying activities of provincial interests, who at this time collaborated with some of the private traders engaging in the East India trade, also significantly impacted the debates on the total abolition of the Company's monopoly. As the Charter was passed by the Parliament in 1833, the China trade was opened to all British traders, and the Company ended all trading activities. This event finally completed the long process of the Company's transformation from a commercial company to the administrative institution of India.

Conclusion

After the acquisition of *diwani*, the main concern of British imperial policy in India became the maintenance of the channel of remittance from India to Britain. Although the EIC and the state hoped to transfer some of the surplus of India-landed revenue to Britain after its territorial acquisition, the newly acquired political elements led the Company into expensive political and economic turmoil both in India and at home. The Company's insufficient facilities for remittances resulted in the supply of British capital to foreign European and American merchants. Facing these problems, after the 1790s, the EIC was gradually forced to abandon its privileges of monopolistic trade with the East Indies to maintain and to develop the channel of remittance in the structural change of the East India trade. In such circumstances, the private traders in India and London, who increased their presence not only in the East India trade but also within the Company, sought ways to break into the Company's monopolistic trade. Similarly, as a result of the Industrial Revolution, provincial interests began to advocate for the opening of the East India trade. However, in the debates surrounding the renewal of the Company's Charter in 1793, the provincial lobbyists' influence was limited due to a lack of coherent arguments and sufficient collaboration. In contrast, as Tripathi and Webster argued, the 'Private Trade Interest' within the Company, represented by David Scott, was able to exert a direct and effective impact on the negotiations with the state.

In spite of the relaxation of the Company's monopoly, after 1793, the capacity that the Company could provide to the private traders in the 'regulated monopoly' was still insufficient, and the clandestine trade conducted by foreign flags also continued. As a result, although the pro-monopoly groups of the Company effectively denied the private traders' attempt to use India-built ships regularly during the late 1790s and early 1800s, the demand for the opening of the East India trade had developed further by the early 1810s. The campaigns of the provincial merchants and manufacturers in opposition to the renewal of the EIC's Charter in 1812 and 1813 developed under such conditions. After the opening of the India trade in 1814, private traders, particularly the agency houses in India, took the initiative in the Company's internal politics as well as in the East India trade. Nevertheless, at the same time, the partial abolition of the Company's monopoly destroyed the previous framework of the East India trade, in which the private traders were actually protected from competition. The increase in competition led to the failure of the Calcutta agency houses in the financial crisis that occurred during the early 1830s. This incident weakened the Company's voice further, whilst the provincial lobbyists could effectively claim free access to Asia in the debates over the renewal of the Charter between 1829 and 1833. Eventually, the Company's monopoly was totally abolished.

The following chapters will examine, in the debates on the renewal of the Charter between 1812 and 1813 and between 1829 and 1833, how different provincial manufacturing towns and outports organised unified national campaigns for direct access to the East Indies and the extent to which they could exert influence on the Charter negotiations.

CHAPTER TWO

CHALLENGING THE COMMERCIAL GIANT: THE GLASGOW EAST INDIA ASSOCIATION, 1812–1813

Introduction

This chapter examines the lobbying activities of provincial mercantile and manufacturing interests in Glasgow between 1812 and 1813. With the approach of the expiry of the East India Charter, both the EIC and their opponents started lobbying. The Glasgow East India Association (EIA), organised by mercantile and manufacturing interests in Glasgow, was one of a number of provincial lobbying groups opposed to the EIC's monopoly, along with similar organisations in the outports of Liverpool and Bristol and in the manufacturing towns of Manchester, Birmingham, and Sheffield.

Like other recent works on British imperialism, studies on the formation of its imperial policies in the East have been influenced by the 'gentlemanly capitalist thesis' of Cain and Hopkins and tend to devalue the political influence of provincial interests. Regarding the opening of the India trade in 1814, Webster argued in his 1990 thesis that the government's concerns, based on its economic strategy for resolving the problem of inflation and securing raw materials during the period, were more significant than the provincial interests' lobbying.[1] Certainly, in his recent work, he presented the lobbying activities of the provincial mercantile and manufacturing interests more positively, but his analysis focused more on the roles of the private traders in the metropolis and in Asia.[2] Case studies in this and subsequent chapters will analyse how the Glasgow EIA organised an effective and influential campaign and advocated for free access to Asian markets.

These chapters will also assess the contribution of Scots to the formation of Britain's imperial policy by examining the lobbying activities of the Glasgow EIA. The significance of this association is that this lobbying group

[1] A. Webster, "The Political Economy of Trade Liberalization: The East India Company Charter Act of 1813", in *The Economic History Review*, New Series, Vol. XLIII, No. 3, 1990, p. 417.

[2] A. Webster, *The Twilight of the East India Company: The Evolution of Anglo-Asian Commerce and Politics 1790–1860*, 2008, Chapter 3.

was one of the early efforts of Scottish overseas merchants and nascent manufacturers to gain access to the overseas markets from which they had been excluded in the early nineteenth century. Moreover, at the national level, the association succeeded in collaborating effectively with other UK lobbying groups for free trade.

The main primary sources for analysing the members of the Glasgow EIA and its lobbying activities are the Glasgow East India Association Minutes and Correspondence.[3] These records show how the merchants and manufacturers of Glasgow attempted to influence parliamentary decisions on the renewal of the East India Charter by co-operating with other associations sharing similar interests all over Britain and Ireland during the first half of the nineteenth century. Supplementing these documents, contemporary articles from the *Glasgow Herald* and official documents of correspondence and proceedings in the negotiations between the Directors of the EIC and the Ministers, which were published in the form of pamphlets by the Company's supporters and its opposition, have been used, along with other literature.

The Growth and Peculiar Status of Glasgow

Before the eighteenth century, Glasgow was a local religious and commercial centre in the west of Scotland and already held a significant position in the coastal and the Irish trade among Scottish towns. However, it was only after the 1740s, when Glasgow's tobacco trade with the American colonies began to prosper, that the town obtained a truly important status in British overseas trade. The tobacco trade was one example of the Scottish contribution to the expansion of British overseas trade. Glasgow's tobacco trade developed rapidly between the 1740s and the first half of the 1770s. Between 1741 and 1752, Scottish imports of tobacco increased from 8 million to 21 million lbs., and in 1758, exceeded those of London and other English outports.[4] In 1771, Scottish imports reached 47 million lbs.[5]

---

[3] Glasgow East India Association Committee Minute Book 1812–1813 (MS891001/1, Glasgow Mitchell Library); Correspondence Incoming 1812–1813 (MS891001/3, Glasgow Mitchell Library); Correspondence Outgoing 1812–1814 (MS891001/12, Glasgow Mitchell Library).

[4] T.M. Devine, "The Golden Age of Tobacco", in T.M. Devine and G. Jackson (eds.), *Glasgow, Vol. I, Beginning to 1830*, 1995, p. 140.

[5] Ibid.

The pattern of the tobacco trade was that of a re-export trade to the European continent.[6] Devine pointed out that raw cotton used in the initial development of the cotton industry during the late eighteenth century was mainly imported from the Caribbean, not from North America.[7] Therefore, the importation of tobacco was not directly connected to domestic economic activities in Glasgow and other parts of Scotland. Moreover, although several 'Tobacco Lords' of Glasgow were involved in the establishment of such banks as the Ship Bank (in 1749), the Arms Bank (in 1750), and the Thistle Bank (in 1761) in Glasgow, direct investment by the banks in industrial sectors was not a decisive element in the industrialisation of the city.[8] However, because consumer goods such as linen and woollen goods were exported by tobacco merchants from Scotland to the American colonists, the contribution of their export trade to domestic industry was not irrelevant. At the same time, some of the tobacco traders who purchased estates became directly involved in mineral mining. Although the conversion of capital from the tobacco trade to the industrial sector did not happen to a significant degree in Glasgow, the trade made some contribution to Glasgow's peculiar economy, in which its overseas trade and manufacturing industry were closely interwoven.

The collapse of the tobacco trade during the American War of Independence in the 1770s did not end the Glasgow merchants' engagement in overseas trade. During this period, the West Indies became a hub of clandestine trade between the United Kingdom and the United States, and Glasgow's trade with that region grew rapidly. In terms of its share, in 1781, the West India trade accounted for 21% of the total official value of exports from Scotland, 42% by the end of the eighteenth century, and 65% in 1813.[9] As noted above, the West India trade contributed more significantly to the early development of the Scottish cotton industry than the American tobacco trade by supplying vital raw materials to the

6 For instance, in 1771, when the import of tobacco reached its peak, approximately 47.2 million lbs. of tobacco were imported to Scotland, and 45.6 million lbs. were re-exported to the European continent, mainly to France, Holland, Denmark, and Norway. See H. Hamilton, *Economic History of Scotland in the Eighteenth Century*, 1963, pp. 416–9.

7 Devine, "The Golden Age of Tobacco", p. 171; Hamilton, *Economic History of Scotland*, pp. 412–3.

8 Discounting of bills was the more common method for their involvement in the industry. The colonial traders also preferred purchasing lands with profits from their commercial activities rather than investing in the manufacturing industry. R.H. Campbell, "The Making of the Industrial City", in T.M. Devine and G. Jackson (eds.), *Glasgow, Vol. I, Beginning to 1830*, 1995, p. 188; Devine, "The Golden Age of Tobacco", p. 172.

9 Campbell, "The Making of the Industrial City", p. 192.

industry and providing the manufacturers with a necessary market for their goods.

During the second half of the eighteenth century, Glasgow prospered as a commercial centre but also experienced the rapid development of the manufacturing industry. As happened south of the border, industrialisation led to the growth of Scotland's urban population during this period. In 1801, the population of Glasgow was already approximately 77,000; by 1821, the number nearly doubled, and it reached 202,000 in 1831.[10] This rapid expansion of the city resulted mainly from the inflow of labour from outside the city, such as the Highlands and Ireland.

In the 1780s and 1790s, the centre of the development of the Scottish cotton industry was the countryside of Lanarkshire, Renfrewshire, Dunbartonshire, Stirlingshire, and Ayrshire because the mills needed water-power, but Glasgow's merchants provided a great deal of capital for these mills. Although the main source of funding for the development of the Scottish cotton industry was the capital accumulated within the textile industry, the connection of Glasgow's colonial merchants, especially the West Indian traders, with the industry during this phase was not negligible.[11] With the adoption of steam power after the 1790s, the cotton spinning industry became concentrated in Glasgow and Paisley.[12] The dramatic increase in the importation of raw cotton indicated this rapid growth of the Scottish cotton industry. The import of raw cotton was 137,160 lbs. on the eve of the American War of Independence, 1,757,504 lbs. in 1790, and amounted to 11,114,640 lbs. by 1812.[13] To the cotton textile industry in Glasgow, looking for new markets and securing stable sources of raw cotton for its expanding production were significant concerns. For Glasgow's cotton manufacturers, India was a very promising market as well as a source of raw material.

In terms of heavy industry, the modern production of iron in Scotland developed with the increase of demand for iron in Britain during the Seven

---

[10] B.R. Mitchell, *British Historical Statistics*, 1988, pp. 26–7.

[11] Regarding the internal accumulation of capital within the cotton industry, see Devine, "The Golden Age of Tobacco", p. 170. In terms of the connection between the West India trade and the cotton industry, for instance, Robert Dunmore, who was involved in the tobacco trade and in the West India trade, held a partnership with the Buchanan Brothers and founded cotton mills in Balfron, Stirlingshire, in 1790. He was also involved in the Duntocher Cotton Wool Company of Dunbartonshire in 1788 through his partnership with James Dunlop. S.G. Lythe and J. Butt, *An Economic History of Scotland*, 1975, p. 167.

[12] In 1839, out of 192 mills in Scotland, 98 were located in Glasgow. See Lythe and Butt, *An Economic History of Scotland*, pp. 185–7.

[13] J. Butt, *The Industrial Archaeology of Scotland*, 1967, pp. 18–9.

Years' War (1756–63). However, the Scottish iron industry before 1830 developed slowly. From 1788 to 1830, output increased by approximately 30,000 tons, whilst, between 1830 and 1840, it rose by more than 200,000 tons.[14] Compared to the development of the cotton industry, the iron industry, which later became one of the engines of Scotland's economic growth, was less successful before 1830.

As a consequence, the success of Glasgow's merchants in the American tobacco trade and in the West India trade helped Scotland to expand its commercial activities to the Atlantic Rim during the second half of the eighteenth century. At the same time, domestically, their activities contributed to the economic prosperity of the city. Although significant capital transfer from the tobacco trade to the Scottish cotton industry did not occur, the colonial trade created demand for local manufacturers' products. Moreover, the initial development of the cotton industry was largely dependent on the importation of raw materials from the West Indies, and several West Indian merchants of Glasgow held stock in the industry. As a result of the continuing prosperity of its mercantile interests and the newly growing manufacturing industry, represented by the cotton industry during this period, Glasgow had a more diversified economic structure than other major provincial towns such as Liverpool, where foreign trade and related commercial businesses dominated its economy, and Manchester and Birmingham, both of which were dependent on manufacturing industries. As will be illustrated in the rest of this chapter, the nature of Glasgow's economy influenced its lobbying activities in opposition to the renewal of the EIC's Charter.

Problems, Dissatisfaction, and the Foundation of the Glasgow EIA

The Charter Act of 1793 allowed British private merchants, who had been excluded from the East India trade on the grounds of the Company's privileges for a long time, to trade with India under certain conditions. However, most private merchants and manufacturers, including those of Glasgow, were not satisfied with this relaxation and demanded more comprehensive freedom to pursue the East India trade. In Glasgow, for instance, the Directors of the Chamber of Commerce and Manufacturers complained

[14] Mitchell, *British Historical Statistics*, p. 28.

about the 1793 regulation in their resolution.[15] This resolution indicated that, first, in spite of the relaxation of the restriction on the trade in 1793, private traders were allowed to trade only within the Company's territories in India. They were still excluded from direct trade with the rest of the subcontinent under native powers and from trading with other countries and areas between the Cape of Good Hope and the Straits of Magellan, which included China. Second, space on the ships provided by the Company for the products of these private merchants was limited, expensive, and inconvenient, which limited profits from the trade. Third, because their cargoes had to be transported by the Company's ships both inward and outward, the private merchants lacked flexibility in their trade. For example, the Report of the Committee of Chamber of Commerce & Manufactures stated that:

> ... the merchant who wished to export was obliged to apply before the 30th of August for freightage of the goods which he meant to ship in the month of March or April of the following year; in the fifteen days after the application, he was bound to pay or secure to the Company the freight of these goods which were not to be shipped till six months afterwards; and if, by the end of October, he did not deliver to the Company a list of the different kinds of his goods, and the quantities of each kind, the freight became forfeited.[16]

In addition to these conditions, since all British subjects had to receive the Company's permission to live within the area of its monopoly, a private merchant was unable to send his agents or servants there freely to manage his concerns.[17] Thus, private merchants not only needed to decide on the types of exported goods and their quantities long before their shipment but also had difficulty obtaining up-to-date and accurate information about demand for their goods in the East. The import trade from India was in a similar position. As a result, private merchants were forced to take risks in estimating demand or lose commercial opportunities. These private merchants believed that they could hardly succeed in their trade with the East Indies under such restrictive conditions.

In resolutions, the merchants and manufacturers of Glasgow also criticised the condition of the East India trade that, "by the Act 37th of the same Reign (George III), c.57, the Privilege of trading to those countries, although

---

[15] The resolutions passed by the Directors of the Chamber of Commerce and Manufactures of Glasgow, held on 14 February 1812, in *Glasgow Herald*, 17 February, "Trade to the East Indies".

[16] *Glasgow Herald*, 2 March 1812, "Report of the Committee Chamber of Commerce & Manufactures", p. 1.

[17] Ibid.

denied to British subjects, is permitted to Foreign Nations in amity with his Majesty".[18] This contradictory condition made those who were excluded from the East India trade envious, and many critics of this 'misconduct' in economic policy believed that the flourishing of American merchants in the East India trade at the expense of the profits of British subjects partly resulted from British investment in American merchants, as discussed in Chapter 1. Their capital could have contributed to Britain's hegemony over this trade if it had been invested in their own commerce rather than with foreigners under conditions of free trade.[19]

Therefore, those who were dissatisfied with the Company's monopoly in the East India trade regarded the expiration of the Charter on 1 March 1814 as another chance for them to obtain free entry into the trade. Early in 1812, the question of the renewal of the Company's Charter began to be discussed seriously in Glasgow, as in other parts of the British Isles.[20]

The leader of the free trade movement in Glasgow was its merchants and manufacturers. In February 1812, at the meeting of the Chamber of Commerce of Glasgow, Kirkman Finlay, James Dennistoun, James Hopkirk, Francis Garden, James Robertson, David Connell, Alexander Campbell, James Buchanan, James Buchanan, Jr., James Ewing, and Dougald Bannatyne were appointed to a committee "to consider and report what steps ought to be taken upon the approaching expiration of the East India Company's Charter".[21] The Magistrates and Council also named John Hamilton (the Lord Provost), Andrew Templeton (a Merchant Baillie), James Black, Kirkman Finlay, Archibald Newbigging, and Samuel Hunter (all Councillors) to a committee for the same purpose.[22] The fact that these two institutions representing Glasgow's local economy and politics began to consider lobbying against the renewal of the EIC's Charter indicated the significance of this issue for the commercial elite. The two committees were the direct antecedents of the Glasgow EIA. The Glasgow EIA's incoming correspondence contains a letter from Thomas Attwood, a High Bailie of Birmingham, dated 21 February 1812, in which he wrote that:

> ... to request that we will urge to your Committee the propriety of their immediately obtaining private letters from different merchants of Glasgow,

---

18 Ibid., 17 February 1812, "Trade to the East Indies", p. 1.

19 Anon., *Letters on the East India Monopoly, Originally Published in the Glasgow Chronicle, with Addition and Correction*, 1812, pp. 22–3.

20 Committee Minute Book 1812–13, 29 October 1813, "Report of the Glasgow Committee to the Subscribers, for the Object of Obtaining a Free Trade to India and China", p. 65.

21 *Glasgow Herald*, 10 February 1812.

22 Ibid.

> addressed to other correspondents in the manufacturing districts of Scotland, particularly in the towns round Glasgow, pressing the necessity of holding meetings in each town to propose petitions against the East India Monopoly.[23]

This was one of the earliest contacts between provincial towns that urged them to organise the national campaign. During this period, the free trade supporters of Birmingham sent similar letters not only to all its neighbouring towns but also to Liverpool, manufacturing towns in Northwest England, Bristol, Edinburgh, Dublin, and other Irish towns.[24] As a result, Birmingham, Bristol, and Liverpool had already decided to send a deputation to London in April.[25] Compared with these towns, the start of Glasgow's lobbying was delayed, but the Chamber of Commerce and Manufacturers of Glasgow and the Magistrates and Councillors presented their petitions to Parliament on 19 and 25 March, respectively.[26] This indicates that they had already prepared their petitions prior to the establishment of the Glasgow EIA.[27]

The establishment of the Glasgow EIA was intended to unify and to more efficiently organise Glasgow's lobbying for free trade with the East Indies. The Chamber of Commerce and Manufacturers and the Magistrates and Council of Glasgow called a general meeting of merchants and manufacturers on 23 March 1812 in the name of the Lord Provost. It passed several resolutions.[28] The main points of the resolutions were: (1) the inexpediency and prejudice of the Charter; (2) the unfairness of the Charter for the exclusion of British ships from the East India trade and legal navigation of foreigners; (3) the determination of their resistance against the renewal of the Company's monopoly by the use of every legal and constitutional means; (4) their objection to any regulation confining the trade to the port of London; (5) the preparation and submission of their petitions to Parliament; and (6) the appointment of a committee [the General Committee of the Glasgow EIA] for the preparation of the petitions and the collection of subscriptions for this purpose. From that time onward, the committee appointed by the resolutions played a central role in this movement.

[23] Incoming Correspondence 1812–13, Letter from Thomas Attwood, dated 21 February 1812, letter no.1. It seems that "Your Committee" in his letter was one of those two committees, most likely the committee of the Chamber of Commerce.

[24] Ibid.

[25] Ibid.

[26] *The Parliamentary Debates*, Vol. XXII, 19 March 1812.

[27] Ibid., 25 March 1812.

[28] Committee Minute Book 1812–13, 23 March 1812, "Resolution of a General Meeting", pp. 1–2.

Economic Interests and Political Status of the Members of Glasgow EIA

The Glasgow EIA was founded to break the commercial dominance of London merchants over the East India trade. Therefore, before analysing the debates over the renewal of the Company's Charter, it is necessary to understand what types of economic interest groups were involved in this association. Assessing the characteristics of those involved in the association's lobbying activities can also give clues as to how the Glasgow EIA formed its lobbying strategies and organised its campaign. For this purpose, first, the characteristics of the members of the General Committee of the association will be examined. Although the committee took the initiative in the free trade movement of Glasgow, its activities reflected demands from the subscribers to the association. Therefore, it is also worth understanding the interests of the subscribers as a group.

To identify the characteristics of the Glasgow EIA's committee and subscribers, biographical information on those individuals has been collected. Some of the basic sources are the matriculation books of the Merchants' House of Glasgow, J.R. Anderson's *The Burgesses & Guild Brethren of Glasgow 1751–1846*, and Glasgow Postal Directories. The first two sources contain similar information, such as an individual's occupation, his father's name and occupation, and, in *The Burgesses & Guild Brethren*, the names of his wife and her father can sometimes be found.[29] Although, as will be explained later, these sources present a problem with respect to the definition of 'merchant' or 'merchants', they provide useful basic information for cross-referencing purposes. To extend the biographical information from the data, this study has used several near-contemporary publications.[30]

Appendix I shows the names of members of the General Committee and the secretary, those of firms in which members had an interest, and descriptions of these companies. The General Committee consisted of 46 people through almost all of the period from 1812 to 1814.[31] Most were leading

---

[29] J.R. Anderson, *The Burgesses & The Guild Brethren of Glasgow 1751–1846*, 1935; Merchants' House of Glasgow Matriculation Books (T-MH-17 Glasgow City Archives); *Glasgow Post Office Directories*, 1812–14.

[30] For example, G. Stewart, *Curiosities of Glasgow Citizenship*, 1881; J. MacLehose, *Memoirs and Portraits of One Hundred Glasgow Men*, 1886; A. Thomas, *The Old Country Houses of the Old Glasgow Gentry*, 1878.

[31] Only Andrew Reid was named a member of the Committee about a week after the foundation of the Glasgow EIA, and Alexander Oswald died on 8 June 1813. See Committee Minute Book 1812–13, 31 March 1812, p. 8; SC36/48/8 (Scotlandspeople) the list of inventories of Alexander Oswald, dated 18 March 1814.

businessmen in the city in terms of the size of the firms in which they had an interest and their personal wealth. Because the Chamber of Commerce and Manufacturers and the Magistrates and Councillors took the initiative to establish the association, it was a natural outcome that most of those who had previously been appointed to the committees of these two distinct public bodies retained their posts in the newly established General Committee. Except for James Buchanan, Jr., all of the members of the Chamber of the Commerce and Manufacturers committee were elected to the new committee. From the committee of the Magistrates and Councillors, four of six members—John Hamilton (Lord Provost), James Black, Kirkman Finlay (who had also been on the committee of the Chamber of Commerce and Manufacturers), and Archibald Newbigging—were appointed.

From Appendix I, it is clear that the economic interests of the General Committee were varied: the West India and American tobacco trade, cotton spinning and manufacturing, sugar refining, iron manufacturing, and so on. Nevertheless, two main economic interests can be identified among the committee members. The first notable characteristic is the presence of a significant number of Glasgow's Atlantic traders—that is, American and West Indian merchants, especially the latter. This interest group was already well organised with social and political connections. In 1807, "the Planters and Merchants in Glasgow interested in the trade with the British West Indies" established the Glasgow West India Association (WIA) for "the common good, and benefits which would naturally arise by their united action in all cases associating the West India Trade".[32] John Gordon was appointed as the chairman of the association; Robert Dennistoun, Francis Garden, Alexander Campbell, and Robert Bogle junior were directors; and James Ewing was the secretary.[33] In fact, as shown in Table 1, which lists the General Committee members who also subscribed to the Glasgow WIA and their West Indian firms, all of these main figures of the Glasgow WIA were members of the General Committee of the Glasgow EIA. Moreover, fourteen names among the General Committee members (including the aforementioned merchants) were identified as having made individual subscriptions to the Glasgow WIA, and at least two committee members had stock in the companies listed on the company subscriptions.[34]

[32] Abstract of the Minute Book of the Glasgow West India Association, Minutes (MS891002, Glasgow Mitchell Library), Vol. 1, p. 1.

[33] Ibid., p. 8.

[34] Ibid., Company and Individual Subscriptions, pp. 6–8.

This indicated the involvement of powerful pressure group which promoted a different branch of overseas trade in the Glasgow EIA.

Even when the West India trade held a dominant position in Glasgow's economy (although to a lesser extent than the American tobacco trade, and it lasted for only a short period), those Glasgow merchants who engaged in this trade were looking for new opportunities to diversify their business and to spread their business risks. The West India trade, which depended largely on climatic influence, was a naturally risky business, but the effects of the American War of Independence and the Napoleonic Wars on the West Indian economy further increased its risks.[35] A series of bankruptcies among major West Indian firms actually happened during this period.

Table 1. The General Committee members who subscribed to the Glasgow WIA and their West Indian firms.

Name	Company
Robert Bogle	Robert Bogle Jun. & Co.
James Buchanan	Dennistoun, Buchanan & Co.
Alexander Campbell	John Campbell Sen. & Co.
Colin Campbell	John Campbell Sen. & Co.
David Connell	David & James Connell
Adam Crooks	Leitch & Smith
Robert Dennistoun	G. & R. Dennistoun & Co.
James Ewing	James Ewing & Co.
Francis Garden	Francis Garden & Co.
John Gordon	Stirling, Gordon & Co.
Robert Hagard	
(John Hamilton)	John Hamilton & Co.
(James Hopkirk)	Hopkirk, Cunninghame & Co.
John McCaul	
Charles Stirling	Stirling, Gordon & Co.
Alexander Wighton	Watson, Wighton & Co.

Note: A name in brackets means that he has been identified as a member of the Glasgow WIA from a company subscription.

Source: Appendix I and the list of subscribers to the Glasgow WIA in the Minute Book of the Glasgow West India Association.

35 S.G. Checkland, "Two Scottish West Indian Liquidation after 1793", in *Scottish Journal of Political Economy*, 1957, Vol. 4, pp. 127–43; T.M. Devine, "An Eighteenth-Century Business Elite: Glasgow-West India Merchants, c. 1750–1815", in *Scottish Historical Review*, Vol. 57, 1978, p. 50.

Alexander Houstoun & Co., which handled between one-third and one-half of sugar cargoes imported to the Clyde in the 1770s and 1780s, went bankrupt in 1795. Other major failures included R. Bogle & Sons in 1772; Robert Dunmore in 1793; McNeil, Stewart & Co. in 1802; and John McCall & Sons in 1819.[36] In addition, as early as 1807, when the slave trade on which the West Indian economy significantly relied was banned in the British colonies, the anti-slavery movement seems to have cast doubt on the promise of the West India trade. The West Indian merchants' desire for diversification in their trading activities and the spreading of their business risks in the wartime period can explain their significant attendance in the General Committee of the Glasgow EIA.

In the movement against the renewal of the East India Charter, free trade supporters at both the national and the local levels took into consideration the interest of the West Indian merchants. On 22 April 1812, the General Deputation of provincial manufacturing towns and outports, which gathered in London for their lobby, passed the motion of Richard Spooner, representing Birmingham's interest, and seconded by Kirkman Finlay, that:

> ...in endeavouring to promote a free trade to the East, it is the opinion of this Meeting that due care should be taken to prevent any measures being adopted, which may prove prejudicial to the West India or manufacturing interests...[37]

From the fact that Finlay seconded the above motion, it is clear that the interests of the Glasgow EIA were consistent with those of the General Deputation in this respect. At the meeting of the Glasgow EIA's Sub-Committee of Correspondence on 18 December 1812, "the danger which might rise from a free inspection of East India Sugars, and their interference with that produced by our West India Colonies in the home market" were placed on the agenda. The committee recommended that the delegation to London suggest and enforce the best-calculated means to protect the West India trade without imposing undue restraints on the importation of Asian products.[38]

Although, among the Glasgow EIA's minutes and correspondence letters during the period, only a few refer directly to the interest of the West Indian traders, their interest certainly influenced the association's policy. In Moss's

---

36 Ibid.

37 Committee Minute Book 1812–13, Instruction to London Deputation, dated January 1813, p. 32.

38 Ibid., 18 December 1812, p. 25.

research on Birmingham's free trade movement, because the town's economy was based mainly on the manufacturing industry and its campaigners represented it, he failed to identify the West Indian interests as one of the key players in the national campaign.[39] At the national level, the interest of the West Indian merchants was embodied by the establishment of different duty rates between East and West Indian sugar. After the opening of the India trade, the West Indian sugar interests succeeded in maintaining their advantage over their East Indian counterparts, as the duty was 27s. per cwt on the former and 37s on the latter.[40] This arrangement was reasonable for the West Indian interests, who also joined the Glasgow EIA's campaign. The Glasgow EIA and other similar provincial associations during this period lobbied for the removal of restrictions imposed on the East India trade, but these events indicated that the provincial lobbyists needed to sacrifice their East Indian interests in favour of the existing economic interests in the provincial towns. In the long term, this arrangement worked negatively for the East Indian interests. As the later chapters will show, fewer West Indian merchants actually entered the East India trade after 1814 than the West Indian interests that subscribed to the association, and most of them remained West Indian merchants. In the 1820s and the 1830s, the West Indian interests and the East Indian interests conflicted with each other over the equalisation of the sugar duties.

Another significant economic group indicated in Appendix I included those with interests in the manufacturing sector, especially in the cotton industry. Many held stocks in overseas trade. This reflected the duality of the city's economic activities, which was different from that of other major provincial towns. Of the 47 members of the General Committee plus the secretary at the table, at least 28 members were directly related with several kinds of manufacturing industries. At least 21 held stocks in cotton spinning and manufacturing and other textile businesses, such as cloth manufacturing and linen drapery. Among the individuals and firms listed in Appendix I, for instance, in the New Lanark Cotton Company from 1812 to 1814, Robert Dennistoun took four shares (£28,800 in value); Alexander Campbell took three shares (£21,000); Colin Campbell took three shares; and Robert Owen took ten shares (£70,000) out of the total 26 shares.[41]

39 D.J. Moss, "Birmingham and the Campaigns against the Orders in Council and East India Company Charter 1812–1813", in *Canadian Journal of History*, Vol. XI, Issue 1, 1976, pp. 173–88.

40 C.H. Philips, *The East India Company*, 1784–1834, 1940, pp. 250–1.

41 I. Donnachie, *Robert Owen: Owen of New Lanark and New Harmony*, 2000, p. 102.

Kirkman Finlay, Archibald Buchanan, and John Gordon were the partners of James Finlay & Co., another famous cotton manufacturing firm. In 1800, of the firm's stock totalling £65,000, Kirkman Finlay held £16,000, the house of Leitch & Smith held £10,000, Alexander Gordon held £2,000, and John Gordon held £8,000.[42] In its cotton manufacturing business the firm bought the Ballindalloch mills on the Endrick in 1798, the Catrine mills on the Ayr in 1801, and the Deanston mills on the Teith in 1806.[43] In the operation of these mills Kirkman Finlay exploited his family connection with the Buchanan cousins. James Buchanan was a close friend of Sir Richard Arkwright, and his younger brother, Archibald, had trained under Arkwright and obtained the know-how to operate cotton mills before he entered the firm of James Finlay & Co.[44]

In the early 1810s, Britain was suffering from a general economic depression, and Glasgow and its surrounding areas were no exception. This coincided with the intensification of the Napoleonic Wars. After the Battle of Trafalgar in 1805, Napoleon shifted his tactics against Britain from direct military invasion to economic warfare. He assumed that the dominance of French merchants and manufacturers over the continental economy and the reduction of Britain's bullion reserves and inflation would make Britain's financial support to its foreign coalitions more difficult. To achieve these goals, he attempted to block Britain's manufacturing goods and colonial re-exports to the European continent.[45] In November 1806, he issued the Berlin decree, which prohibited vessels from the United Kingdom and its colonies from entering any ports controlled by France and its satellite countries. Under the Milan decrees of November and December of 1807, the restrictions were extended to the confiscation of British or British-borne goods carried by neutral vessels that had called at British ports before entering territories under French control.[46] British exports to the continent were further limited in 1810, when France annexed Holland, Westphalia, and the northern German territories and defeated Austria, which shut

[42] James Finlay & Co. Balance Book, 1789–1800 (UGD91/1/4/1/3/1 Glasgow University Archives).

[43] C. Brogan, *James Finlay & Company Limited: Manufacturers and East India Merchants, 1750–1950*, 1951, Chapter X and XI.

[44] Ibid., p. 6 and pp. 61–2.

[45] G. Ellis, *The Napoleonic Empire*, 2003, pp. 110–2. While Napoleon attempted to prohibit British exports to the European continent, its imports were less restricted because France needed to obtain cash. For instance, grain was largely exported from France to Britain during the bad harvest of 1810.

[46] Ibid.

the door on British manufactured products. The history of James Finlay & Co. shows how Kirkman Finlay made successful efforts to break the economic blockade by establishing a commercial network over the European continent during the war.[47] Nevertheless, Glasgow's local economy suffered an economic depression because of the dislocation of overseas trading activities.

At the same time, the relationship between the United Kingdom and the United States gradually deteriorated after the issuing of the Orders in Council of 1807, which insisted that ships of neutral countries, including the United States, trading with Europe call at British ports. The Orders and the Milan decrees put US vessels in a difficult position, as they had to risk detention or confiscation by either Britain or France.[48] The Americans strongly opposed these regulations and retaliated with the Embargo Act and the Non-Intercourse Act and eventually declared war against Britain in June 1812. Thus, during this period, Glasgow's cotton manufacturers needed to seek new markets for their products and a stable supply of raw materials.

One of their attempts to solve the problem involved the diversification of their trade to other countries and regions. Nevertheless, the end of speculative trade with South America, the West Indies, and the Iberian Peninsula worsened the difficulties of British manufacturers in 1810.[49] Kirkman Finlay knew the economic situation of Glasgow very well because he had been a director and the chairman of the Chamber of Commerce, and he was engaging in both manufacturing and mercantile business. He commented in 1811 on the considerable depression in Glasgow and its neighbouring manufacturing districts since the end of 1810:

> I really cannot say exactly, but as compared with 1809 and the former part of 1810, which were years of uncommon and unnatural extent; the falling off must have been very considerable, and the falling off must have been very considerable if there had been no impediment to the trade; but the falling off is certainly very considerable from those causes… The trade was at the worst probably, about the month of May and June 1811, and probably July; but from that period it has gradually, but very slowly continued to improve.[50]

---

47 Brogan, *James Finlay & Company Limited*, Chapter III. According to his testimony in the Select Committee, the company had about 700 correspondents on the Continent in 1803. See Ibid., p. 18.

48 H. Hamilton, *The Industrial Revolution in Scotland*, 1966, pp. 134–5.

49 E.F. Heckscher, *The Continental System: An Economic Interpretation*, 1922, pp. 176 and 239–40.

50 Brogan, *James Finlay & Company*, p. 21.

Although the economic condition of manufacturers in Glasgow showed a little improvement after the middle of 1811, the recovery was still very slow, and Britain's long-term war with France negatively impacted trade with the European continent around the period when the Glasgow EIA was established in 1812. Glasgow's cotton and other manufacturing interests wanted to seek new overseas markets in the East Indies.

The urban middle class was concerned that unemployment and the low wages of the working class, who were engaged in the rapidly growing manufacturing industry, could result in social unrest in the city and surrounding areas. The petition of merchants and manufacturers of Glasgow argued that:

> ... it is of the utmost importance to secure the peace of the community, by affording full work and fair wages to operative classes ... the skill, industry and capital of the manufacturing are inadequately occupied and consequently a part of the population remains unemployed.[51]

They hoped that the opening of the East India trade would improve demand for their manufacturing goods and secure raw materials, as well as solve the problems of unemployment and low wages in the manufacturing industry, which would help to maintain public order during the difficult time of war.

Previous historical studies have pointed to different motives for which provincial manufacturing towns and outports joined the free trade campaign. For instance, according to Moss, Birmingham's manufacturers had no difficulty collaborating with those of Liverpool, Bristol, Plymouth, Glasgow, and Sheffield. However, in the campaign, only Birmingham and Sheffield aimed to obtain the new export market, and the rest of the towns wanted to take London's share of the East India commerce and shipping.[52] Meanwhile, Webster explained that:

> Birmingham industrialists and Liverpool merchants saw India as a potential market, while Hull, Bristol, and Plymouth wanted a share in the shipping and import trade of the E.I.C.[53]

Nevertheless, Glasgow's case indicates that even within one city lobbyists' motives for joining the campaign were different. Due to the city's economic structure, the Glasgow EIA represented both commercial interests that wanted to enter a branch of foreign trade where the London interest had a

[51] Committee Minute Book 1812–13, Petition "to the Honourable the Commons of the United Kingdom", p. 28.
[52] Moss, "Birmingham and the Campaigns", p. 180.
[53] Webster, "The Political Economy of Trade Liberalization", p. 405.

monopoly and manufacturing interests that were looking for a new market for their manufactured goods.

In terms of local politics, members of the General Committee held several significant offices. Table 2 lists the Magistrates and Town Council of Glasgow during the Glasgow EIA's campaign; names in italic type indicate the committee members. As mentioned previously, John Hamilton (Lord Provost/Councillor), James Black (Councillor), Kirkman Finlay (Lord Provost/Councillor), and Archibald Newbigging (Baillie of the River and Firth of Clyde/Councillor) transferred from the committee of the Magistrates and Councillors into the General Committee. In addition to

Table 2. List of the Magistrates & Town Council of Glasgow (1811–14).

Offices	1811–12	1812–13	1813–14
Lord Provost	*John Hamilton*	*Kirkman Finlay*	*Kirkman Finlay*
Merchant Baillies	John Gaithrie Joshua Heywood Andrew Templeton	Joshua Heywood Charles S. Parker William Leckie	Charles S. Parker Samuel Hunter *William Dalgleish*
Trades Baillies	Robert Ferrie Robert Tennent	Robert Tennent William Rodger	William Rodger *Archibald Newbigging*
Dean of Guild	*Daniel Mackenzie*	*Daniel Mackenzie*	John Guthrie
Deacon Convener	*Basil Ronald*	*Basil Ronald*	Walter Ferguson
Treasure, Councillors ex officiis	Nicol Brown	Robert Austin	John Berry
Master of Works, Councillors ex officiis	Richard Smellie	Richard Smellie	
Baillie on the River and Firth of Clyde	William Leckie	*Archibald Newbigging*	Andrew Templeton
Depute do.	Samuel Hunter	James Burns	Joshua Heywood
Principal Baillie of the Barony of Gorbals	William Rodger	*William Dalgleish*	Robert Hood
Resident Baillies	Robert Jamieson Arthur Barclay	Thomas Lancaster James Cross	David Niven *Ebenzer Richardson*
Baillie of Provan	John Morison	John Morison	John Morison
Baillie of Port-Glasgow	Archibald Falconer	David Johnston	
Visitor of Maltmen	Hugh Tennent		
Councillors from the Merchant	*James Black*	George Rutherfurd	Joshua Heywood
	William Glen	*Henry Monteith*	John Guthrie

(*Continued*)

Table 2. (*cont.*)

	George Rutherfurd	John Berry	*John Hamilton*
	Henry Monteith	John Guthrie	William Eccles
	John Berry	*John Hamilton*	*James Dennistoun*
	William Eccles	William Eccles	Andrew Templeton
	James Dennistoun	*James Dennistoun*	William Leckie
	Samuel Hunter	Andrew Templeton	*Daniel Mackenzie*
	Charles S. Parker	Samuel Hunter	John Ryburn
	William Leckie	*William Dalgleish*	*Robert Dennistoun*
	Kirkman Finlay	*Daniel Mackenzie*	*John More*
	William Dalgleish	John Ryburn	
Councillors from the Trades	Robert Austin	Robert Ferrie	Robert Tennent
	Walter Ferguson	William Brand	John Graham
	William Brand	John Graham	William Mirrlees
	John Graham	William Mirrlees	James Cleland
	William Mirrlees	*Archibald Newbigging*	John Machen
	Archibald Newbigging	James Cleland	James Burns
	William Rodger	John Machen	Robert Hood
	James Cleland	James Burns	*Basil Ronald*
	John Machen	Robert Hood	Robert Jamieson
	James Burns	*Basil Ronald*	William Mitchell
	Robert Hood	Robert Jamieson	James Hunter

Note: Names in italic type indicate that they were members of the General Committee of the Glasgow EIA.
Sources: *Glasgow Herald*, 11 October 1811, 16 October 1812, and 15 October 1813, "List of the Magistrates & Towns Council of Glasgow".

these men, Daniel MacKenzie (Dean of Guild/Councillor), Basil Ronald (Deacon Convener/Councillor), William Dalgleish (Merchant Baillie/ Principal Baillie of the Barony Gorbals/Councillor), Ebenzer Richardson (Resident Baillie), James Black, Henry Monteith, James Dennistoun, Robert Dennistoun, and John More (all Councillors) were also appointed to the committee. Many other members of the General Committee later held such offices at some point in their lives. For example, committee members who had experience holding the office of Lord Provost were James Black (elected in 1808, 1809, 1816, and 1817), Henry Monteith (in 1814, 1815, 1818, and 1819), Robert Dalgleish (in 1830 and 1831), and James Ewing (in 1832). In addition, some of the committee members were elected as MPs. Apart from Finlay, who represented the city in the Parliament during the second half of the campaign, Henry Monteith, James Ewing, and James Oswald served as MPs in the 1820s and the 1830s. This indicated the strong connection between the Glasgow EIA and the centre of local politics. In his work, Moss identified Richard Spooner and Thomas Attwood, who led Birmingham's lobbying group, as members of the council of Birmingham, and the latter was the High Bailiff at that time.[54] This connection enabled the association to obtain full support from the local corporation easily and to exploit its authority, as the examples of the petition from the Magistrates and Councillors to Parliament and the Lord Provost's attendance at the General Deputation showed.

In terms of number, the General Committee was dominated by businessmen who belonged to the Merchants' House. In pre-reform Glasgow, this institution held significant power in local politics as a result of the long-term contribution of overseas trade to the economic development of the city.[55] Of the 46 members of the General Committee plus the secretary, 35 men were members of the Merchants' House, only 3 were from the Trades' House, and another 9 did not belong to either institution or are unknown. The apparent dominance of the Merchants' House over the Trades' House does not mean that the political influence of those who engaged in domestic industry was weak. By the early nineteenth century, following the rapid growth of the city and its economy, the occupational status of burgess membership did not accurately describe the type of business they actually conducted there.[56] Many overseas merchants who belonged to the Merchants' House had developed their interest in the rapidly-developing manufacturing industry in the process of diversifying their business, and their interests were well represented in local politics.

Appendix II contains the list of subscribers to the Glasgow EIA, the sums of their payments in the first and second subscriptions, and the descriptions of their main businesses. The table has been created from the Glasgow business directories. Some care is necessary in using this contemporary source. In the Glasgow business directories (and in other sources), both individuals and companies are very often described as 'merchant' or 'merchants'. In the descriptions of the subscribers' businesses quoted from the directory, out of 145 individual and company subscribers, 35 are described

---

54 Moss, "Birmingham and the Campaigns", p. 175.

55 I. Maver, "Politics and Power in the Scottish City: Glasgow Town Council in the Nineteenth Century", in Devine, *Scottish Elites*, 1994, Chap. 5.

56 Ibid., p. 101.

as 'merchant' or 'merchants', and they are the largest group in terms of the descriptions of their businesses. According to Stana Nenadic, in nineteenth-century Glasgow, 'merchant', especially 'overseas merchant', was regarded as an occupation with high prestige.[57] At the same time, occupational titles describing manufacturing sectors were less prestigious in the contemporary city than they may have been in other British industrial towns.[58] Moreover, many of Glasgow's Atlantic traders held both mercantile and manufacturing interests. For these reasons, in Glasgow, various types and sizes of businesses often used the titles 'merchant' and 'merchants'—that is to say, not only very wealthy foreign traders but also small shopkeepers and even manufacturers described themselves as 'merchants'. For example, in the directories, James Finlay & Co. is described as 'merchants', although Kirkman Finlay's firm was known as one of the most successful cotton manufacturing companies in Scotland at that time.

To address this problem, additional information from the sources used for Appendix I supplements the descriptions of the subscribers' businesses from the business directory, although the information in the table is still incomplete. Conversely, it is reasonable to say that occupational titles other than 'merchant' and 'merchants' in the directory can be regarded as indicating the main businesses of the listed individuals and companies. Taking this point into consideration and then looking at the table, we can recognise that the types of businesses in which the subscribers were engaged varied. The range of activities was similar to those in which the Glasgow EIA's General Committee were involved: the West India trade, the American trade, and other overseas trade, cotton spinning and manufacturing, iron manufacturing, banking, and so on.

If Appendix I and Appendix II are compared, it becomes clear that many of the General Committee members or their firms paid more for subscriptions than others did. For example, Table 3, created based on these appendices, shows the relationship between the subscribers who paid more than £15.15s to the Glasgow EIA and the General Committee members. Of the 25 subscribers on the list, 15 were committee members themselves or their firms. Because subscriptions were voluntarily collected, it can be said that the members of the committee were not only those who

[57] S.S. Nenadic, "The Structure, Value and Influence of the Scottish Urban Middle Class: Glasgow, 1800 to 1870", unpublished PhD thesis, University of Glasgow, 1986, pp. 57–8.

[58] Ibid.

were most economically and politically powerful but also those eager for the opening of the East India trade in the city.

As their presence was remarkable in the General Committee, the Atlantic traders, especially the West Indian merchants, were again a significant group among the subscribers to the Glasgow EIA. Out of 145 individual and company subscribers, at least 23 were identified as West Indian and American merchants. Moreover, among the 52 subscribers paying more than £10 at least 22 engaged in trade with the West Indies and the United

Table 3. The relationship between the subscribers who paid more than £15.15s to the Glasgow EIA and the General Committee members.

Name of Subscribers	Names of the General Committee Members
James Finlay & Co.	A. Buchanan, K. Finlay, J. Gordon
Henry Monteith & Co.	H. Monteith
New Lanark Co.	C. Campbell, R. Dennistoun, R. Owen
John Campbell, Sen. & Co.	A. Campbell, C. Campbell
Dennistoun, Buchanan & Co.	J. Buchanan, J. Dennistoun [possibly]
Stirling Gordon & Co.	J. Gordon, C. Stirling
William Stirling & Co.	W. Stirling
Leitch & Smith	A. Crooks
John McIlwham	
Findlay, Duff & Co.	
William Scott & Co.	
G. & R. Dennistoun & Co.	R. Dennistoun
Corbett, Buchanan & Co.	
Blair, Steven & Co.	
Neilson & Hunter	
Alexander & James Crum	J. Crum
D. & J. Connell	D. Connell
Douglass, Brown & Co.	
James Ewing	J. Ewing
Thomas & James Edgar	
J. & G. Buchanan	
John McCaul	J. McCaul
John McCall & Co.	J. McCall
M & J. Preston	
Hopkirk & Cunningham	J. Hopkirk

Source: Created from Appendices I and II.

States. Half of the 26 subscribers who paid more than £15 were Atlantic traders. In value, Atlantic traders contributed £373.16s. of the total subscriptions of £1410.19s. (including £315 from the Chamber of Commerce and Manufacturers). Therefore, the contributions of the Atlantic traders, especially the West Indian merchants, were greater than the average in terms of the number of subscribers and the size of their subscriptions. As the involvement of a large number of Atlantic traders in the General Committee showed, this also indicated that the East India question mattered more to this economic interest group than to others.

Meanwhile, at least 53 subscribers are identified as holding their main economic interests in several types of manufacturing industries and businesses related to them.[59] (See Appendix II.) At least 21 subscribers among them were definitely engaged mainly in cotton/linen manufacturing industry and its related businesses. This figure may be a minimum: Many subscribers whose businesses described as 'manufacturer(s)' and 'merchant(s)' in the postal directories and some with unknown businesses also appear to have been cotton/linen manufacturers.

In the first and second rounds of subscriptions, the top three subscribers were leading cotton manufacturers in Scotland: James Finlay & Co., Henry Monteith, Bogle & Co., and the New Lanark Cotton Company. In the General Committee, shareholders of all three companies were included. Apart from the Chamber of Commerce and Manufacturers, which subscribed £315 in these two subscription collections, the total subscription of £155.10s made by Kirkman Finlay's James Finlay & Co. was exceptional. Although Finlay and his firm operated both mercantile and manufacturing businesses, like many West Indian merchants, his business was more strongly connected with the spinning and manufacturing of cotton (and trade with the European continent) during this period than many of the other leading mercantile families and their firms. According to his testimony in Parliament his cotton manufacturing business employed approximately two to three thousand people, a figure matched by the number of employees at the New Lanark mills.[60] Henry Monteith of Henry Monteith, Bogle & Co., was the third son of James Monteith, a weaver in Anderston. He was involved in his father's business and became one of the most successful cotton manufacturers in Scotland. As an extensive cotton manufacturer, he engaged in cotton spinning, weaving, and bleaching and later

[59] Here, "businesses related [to manufacturing industries]" include such businesses as 'cotton-brokers' and '(cotton/iron) warehouses'.

[60] Brogan, *James Finlay & Company*, p. 17; Donnachie, *Robert Owen*, p. 98.

extended his business to turkey red dyeing and calico printing.[61] Most of the big subscribers who had paid in the first subscription collection, including many West India magnates, reduced their payments by half in the second collection or did not make any payment, while the three cotton textile firms increased their subscriptions or paid the same amounts in the second collection (with the exception of the Chamber of Commerce and Manufacturers). As will be explained in the following section, the timing of the second collection was not favourable to the lobbyists, as the public had started to lose interest in the East India question. Excluding the subscription from the Chamber of Commerce and Manufacturers, the collection of the second round of subscriptions amounted to £427.2s., and subscriptions from these top three firms reached £149; in other words, they paid more than one-third of the total subscriptions. Since they did not reduce their subscription amounts in the second collection, it is clear that the leading cotton manufacturers remained the keenest part of the anti-monopolist group in Glasgow throughout the campaign period.

As a consequence, those appointed to the General Committee were the most notable businessmen and politically prominent figures in Glasgow. In particular, several members of the committee had interests in the local cotton manufacturing industry as well as in the West India trade. Therefore, the Glasgow EIA represented the interests of local 'merchants' with long experience in foreign trade with the West Indies and the United States who were seeking new opportunities to expand their trade to the East Indies. It also represented local 'manufacturers' who were experiencing difficulty in their exports to Continental Europe due to Napoleon's economic blockade and looking for alternative markets. The group of subscribers showed a similar range of economic interests. Both mercantile and manufacturing interests largely supported the lobbying activities of the Glasgow EIA. The earlier part of this chapter has already referred to Finlay's enthusiasm for the campaign against the renewal of the East India Charter, but along with him, some other leading cotton manufacturers showed great eagerness for free trade.

Methods of Lobbying Activities

The main activities of the Glasgow EIA in opposition to the renewal of the EIC's Charter for its monopoly in the East India trade consisted of:

[61] G. Stewart, *Curiosities of Glasgow Citizenship*, 1881, p. 113–4.

(1) collecting signatures for petitions and subscription money from the citizens of the city, (2) printing circulars and pamphlets and writing letters, which were forwarded to cities and towns all over the United Kingdom, and publishing resolutions and other related articles in the newspapers, and (3) sending a deputation to London to collaborate with other delegates from all over the United Kingdom to lobby the Ministry and MPs. This section will describe the first two activities. Then, the following section will examine the lobbying activities of their deputation in London because their activities were more complicated than those of the other two, and it seems easier to understand their activities and influence when they are described in the context of the course of the debates over the renewal of the Charter.

The Glasgow EIA needed to collect as many signatures for the petitions as possible to prove that its activities represented the collective opinion of the citizens of Glasgow in opposition to the renewal of the East India Charter. At the same time, to maintain its lobbying activities, the association had to secure financial resources. Its lobbying activities relied totally on the voluntarily subscribed money, which was the weakest point of the association. From 1812 to 1813, determining how to secure financial resources was one of the association's prime concerns.

Although two members were appointed to "a committee for the special purpose of procuring subscriptions to defray the expenses" in the first meeting of the General Committee on 24 March 1812, the Glasgow EIA recognised that "the subscription of the petitions to Parliament, proceeded very slowly" and decided to extend the number of the sub-committee members to eleven.[62] After the extension of the sub-committee, the organisation started to collect subscriptions at local banks and counting houses.[63] The association also set up the opportunity to collect signatures from the public for petitions to Parliament in the Tontine Coffee Room and at other locations.[64] Furthermore, subscriptions from Port-Glasgow, which amounted to £73.19s, were added to the Glasgow EIA's funds.[65]

However, as the Report of the Sub-Committee of Correspondence dated 23 April 1812 described, the organisation's lobbying activities, especially sending its delegates to London, involved heavy expense.[66] Determining

---

[62] Committee Minute Book 1812–13, 31 March 1812, pp. 6–7.

[63] Ibid., 2 April 1812, p. 9.

[64] Ibid.

[65] Ibid., p. 52. Cash from Archibald Falconer, a Baillie of Port-Glasgow (£3.19s), is included in this amount.

[66] Ibid., 23 April 1812, p. 12–3.

how to meet such expenses was often on the agenda of the association's meetings. To collect subscriptions more efficiently, the association divided the members of the Sub-Committee of Subscriptions into groups of five and gave the list of potential subscribers to each group to take a different area or class of residents.[67] Regarding the second collection of subscriptions the secretary remembered in his letter nevertheless that "… I before signified to you the backwardness experienced among almost all classes of people here when subscription was proposed…"; the collection of subscriptions was again not at all an easy task for the Glasgow EIA.[68] On 1 March 1813, the sub-committee decided to postpone the collection of subscriptions because, at the time, "the subscriptions for the Russia sufferers" was progressing and they wanted to avoid interrupting this activity.[69]

The Glasgow EIA made some attempts to break through this difficult situation. The members resolved to divide the city into five districts, and each division of the Sub-Committee of Subscriptions would be in charge of one district and set the date for the collection of subscriptions in advance.[70] Moreover, the General Committee decided that each of those who attended this meeting would subscribe half the amount of his former subscription and that those attendees would also encourage absent members and former subscribers to do so.[71] In spite of such encouragement for subscriptions, only one-third (33 of 95) of the first subscribers, excluding the Chamber of Commerce and Manufacturers, made second subscriptions, and some of the members of the sub-committee or their firms did not subscribe money because they lost interest. As a result, their subscriptions amounted to just £313.10s. Significant contributions from James Finlay & Co. and the Chamber of Commerce and Manufacturers, which doubled their previous subscription amounts (from £52 to £105 and £105 to £210, respectively), enabled the association to raise a total amount of £637.2s, so they were able to sustain their lobbying activities.[72]

The Glasgow EIA's financial sources, which depended largely on voluntary subscriptions, were thus unstable, and it faced the problem of collecting subscriptions for its lobbying during the campaign. Nevertheless,

---

67 Committee Minute Book 1812–13, 27 November 1812, p. 24.

68 Outgoing Correspondence 1812–14, Letter to Charles Stirling and James Oswald dated 16 March 1813, letter no. 45.

69 Committee Minute Book 1812–13, 1 March 1813, p. 35.

70 Ibid., pp. 35–6.

71 Ibid., 2 March 1813, p. 36.

72 Ibid., p. 57.

thanks to the strong efforts of certain Glasgow businessmen, the association could financially maintain its lobbying activities.

To rouse public opinion in Glasgow and other Scottish towns and persuade influential politicians to join its movement against the renewal of the EIC's Charter, the Glasgow EIA instructed Archibald Buchanan, its secretary, to send several letters to those concerned with the debate and to print circulars and pamphlets. During this period, Glasgow was the centre of the free trade campaign in Scotland. Following the letter from Thomas Attwood of Birmingham, in which he urged Glasgow to persuade its neighbouring towns to present their petitions against the East India monopoly to Parliament, the Glasgow EIA's Sub-Committee of Correspondence ordered the secretary to print a "circular; together with Resolution of General Meeting [held two days ago], and forward copies to every Towns of United Kingdom of any note … and the Noblemen and Members of Parliament…" on 25 March 1812.[73] These influential politicians to whom the association sent its circulars and resolutions included the Marquis of Douglas, the Duke of Montrose, the Marquis of Lansdowne, the Marquis of Wellesley, the Earl of Bathurst, the Earl of Liverpool, the Earl of Lauderdale, Viscount Melville, Lord Dundas, Lord Archibald Hamilton, Spencer Perceval, George Rose, Thomas Turton, Bart, and another nine MPs.[74] This is an example of the provincial interests' attempts to lobby influential politicians for support. In his article, Webster identified the Board of Trade as one of the main players in the government's decision on the renewal of the Company's Charter, but he failed to show evidence for the provincial lobbyists' contact with the Board of Trade.[75] However, the list of politicians included the President and Vice-President of the Board, the Earl of Bathurst, and George Rose. This is clear evidence of the communication between the Board and the provincial lobbyists.

The names of the towns to which Glasgow EIA's secretary sent the letters and the copies before the summer of 1812 are unknown. However, as the economy of Glasgow's neighbouring towns such as Paisley and Port Glasgow had close ties with the city, their interests were almost identical to those of Glasgow. Between March and June, several neighbouring towns of Glasgow (Paisley, Port Glasgow & Newark, Kilmarnock, Renfrew, Dumbarton, Lanark, and Rutherglen) presented their petitions to Parliament.[76] In addition, Greenock, which was a main port for Western Scotland and had

---

[73] Committee Minute Book 1812–13, 25 March 1812, pp. 3-2–4.

[74] Outgoing Correspondence 1812–14, Letter to Marquis of Douglas dated 28 March 1812, letter no. 2.

[75] Webster, "The Political Economy of Trade Liberalization", p. 407.

[76] *The Parliamentary Debates*, Vol. XXI–XXIII.

large interests in overseas trade, had already sent its petition to Parliament in February 1812, before the Glasgow EIA started its lobbying. During the period, approximately 55 UK towns and regions submitted petitions against the renewal of the Charter. Scottish towns apart from Glasgow and its surrounding areas included Kirkcaldy, Dundee, Arbroath, Leith, Edinburgh, Perth, Dumfries, Dunfermline, Stirling, Montrose, Linlithgow, and Aberdeen. Taking into consideration the fact that 22 of the 55 places that petitioned Parliament were in Scotland, the significance of the Scottish free trade movement during the period is evident.

Prior to and after the opening of the new Parliament in the winter of 1812, the Glasgow EIA again delivered letters and circulars to other Scottish burghs, such as Peebles, Paisley, and Lanark, to encourage new petitions or deputations to London.[77] During the campaign, none of its neighbours dispatched a deputation to London along with Glasgow, but Paisley, Port Glasgow, Newark, Greenock, and Rutherglen did submit petitions to Parliament.[78]

Printed pamphlets and circulars often accompanied the letters. Printed forms of protest were conventional among the middle class in Britain for more than a century, and in the debate over the renewal of the East India Charter, the publication of pamphlets was one lobbying activity that both the EIC and their opponents widely employed.[79] According to Philips, in 1812 and 1813, more than 30 pamphlets were published criticising the Company's monopoly.[80] One of the most widely circulated pamphlets against the renewal of the East India Charter published in Glasgow during the period was *Letters on the East India Monopoly*.[81] During their stay in London, Glasgow's deputation asked Mr. Watson, the editor of the *Edinburgh Correspondent*, to print 1,000 copies of the pamphlet, and sent them to London in April 1812. The Glasgow EIA ordered a further 200 copies in 1813 and 300 in 1814 after the new Charter was passed in Parliament.[82]

Resolutions of the General Meeting were also often published in Glasgow's newspapers, such as the *Glasgow Courier* and the *Glasgow Herald*,

---

[77] Incoming Correspondence 1812–13, Letter to James Kerr dated 22 November 1812, letter no. 28, to John Orr, Chief Magistrate of Paisley, 27 November 1812, no. 30, and to Provost Lanark, 19 January 1813, no. 34.

[78] *The Parliamentary Debate*, Vol. XXIV. At this time, other Scottish cities and towns that presented petitions were Edinburgh, Perth, Montrose, Dumfries, and Elgin.

[79] S. Nenadic, "Political Reform and the 'Ordering' of Middle-Class Protest", in T.M. Devine (ed.) *Conflict and Stability in Scottish Society 1780–1850*, 1990, Chapter 4, pp. 68–9.

[80] Philips, *The East India Company*, p. 182.

[81] Anon., *Letters on the East India Monopoly, Originally Published in the Glasgow Chronicle, with Additions and Corrections, Second Edition*, 1812.

[82] Committee Minute Book 1812–13, pp. 51, 59–60 and 84–5.

and in papers in Edinburgh and even London.[83] Payment for pamphlets, the publication of resolutions and other forms of advertisement was the second-largest category in the Glasgow EIA's expenditures, exceeded only by the expenses for its deputation to London.[84] Together with sending its deputation and petitions to London, the Glasgow EIA's activities were not confined to the local area; rather, the association played a major role by using these lobbying networks to spread throughout the United Kingdom.

Glasgow's Deputation and Negotiations for Free Trade

The Glasgow EIA prepared its petition to Parliament while communicating with similar public bodies throughout Britain, such as those in Liverpool and Birmingham. According to the resolution of the General Committee of 24 March 1812, it decided to send John Hamilton, Kirkman Finlay, and Robert Dennistoun as the deputation to London at the beginning of April. These men were part of the General Deputation with other delegates from principal cities and towns of the United Kingdom that lobbied Parliament to oppose the renewal of the EIC's Charter.[85] The General Committee gave the deputation to London a letter of instruction for negotiation with the government.[86] This instruction was based on the resolutions of the General Meeting held on 23 March 1812 and had three main objects: (1) the entire abolition of the EIC's commercial monopoly in trade with India, China, and other countries and areas, which were specified in the Charter; (2) freedom of residence in India, China, and other countries and areas for their agents or servants; and (3) the removal of restrictions confining both exports from and imports to the port of London.

Before gathering in London, the representatives of the provincial manufacturing towns and outports already had some positive expectation of the opening of the Indian trade through their knowledge of several communications between the Company's Directors and Ministers.[87]

[83] Ibid., 25 March 1812, p. 3-2–4. Other newspapers were the "[Glasgow] Chronicle, Journal, Packet & Scotchman, the Edinburgh Courant, Correspondent & Caledonian Mercury, the London Times, Day, Courier, Globe, Traveller & Morning Chronicle".

[84] The total expenses of the association for their activities amounted to £1778.18s.3d.; £303.17s.7d. was paid for the publications, and the costs for their deputation to London amounted to £1279.6s.84d. See Committee Minute Book 1812–13, pp. 51–2 and 59–60.

[85] Committee Minute Book 1812–13, 24 March 1812, "Resolution of the Committee", p. 3.

[86] Ibid., "Meeting of the Glasgow Committee on 31 March 1812", pp. 6–8.

[87] Outgoing Correspondence 1812–14, 3 March 1812, Letter to T. Attwood Esq. High Bailiff of Birmingham.

Although in a 1800 communication relating the renewal of the Charter Henry Dundas had expressed his satisfaction with the "propriety of continuing a monopoly of the trade in the hand of the East India Company", the government's attitude towards the renewal of the EIC's Charter gradually changed by 1812.[88] In 1808 and 1809, Robert Dundas, Henry's son and the President of the Board of Control, pointed to the necessity of an enlargement of private trade with British India and proposed the admission of private merchants into the India trade under necessary regulations.[89] In a communication between the Board of Control and the Company, Robert Dundas confirmed that:

> ... it is now ... the fixed intention of His Majesty's Government, to withhold their concurrence from any proposition which might be submitted to Parliament for continuing to the East India Company their privileges of exclusive trade on their present footing.[90]

In commercial terms, the Company and the British government had already agreed upon the continuity of the China trade and the opening of the export trade from outports to India at this point, whilst it appeared that the import trade from India would be confined to the port of London.[91] According to Philips, the pressure of the agency houses and London merchants forced the EIC to recognise the necessity of the relaxation of the Company's monopoly, and before the debates over the new Charter began, the Chairmen of the EIC privately agreed with the Ministry to support the opening of the export trade to India.[92] Regarding the opening of the export trade, the lobbying of some of the gentlemanly capitalists, and their nexus—in other words, the private trading interests in London and the East—played a more significant role than the provincial mercantile and manufacturing interests. This devalues the influence of the provincial lobbyists on national politics. Nevertheless, as we will see below, the London

---

88 An Impartial Reporter, *The Preliminary Debate at the East India House, January, 5th, 1813*, Appendix No. XII, pp. 59–61, "Extract of a Letter from Lord Melville to the Chairman Dated 2nd April, 1800".

89 The East India Company, *Correspondence and Proceedings in the Negotiation for a Renewal of the East India Company's Charter*, 1812, pp. 6–11, No. 4, "Letter from the Rt. Hon. Robert Dundas to the Chairman and Deputy Chairman Dated 28th December 1808" and p. 39, No. 8, "Letter from the Right Honorable Lord Viscount Melville to the Chairman and Deputy Chairman, Dated the 17th December 1811".

90 Ibid., pp. 49–51, No. 10, "Letter from the Right Honorable Lord Viscount Melville to the Chairman and Deputy Chairman, Dated 21st March 1812".

91 Ibid., No. 11, "Hints Submitted to the Consideration of the Right Honourable Lord Melville by the Deputation of the Court of Directors, 4 March 1812, and his Lordship's Observations Thereon, Dated 21 March 1812".

92 Philips, *The East India Company*, p. 181.

interests' attitude in the debates over the renewal of the Charter after April 1812 indicated that they did not wish for further relaxation of the East India trade beyond the opening of the export trade. The real debates between the provincial merchants and manufacturers and the London mercantile interests were over the remaining restrictions.

In April, the General Deputation of the provincial manufacturing towns and outports that gathered in London started lobbying for the abolition of the EIC's trading monopoly, and during the session of the Houses of Parliament, they continued their negotiations with the Ministry. On 10 April, Glasgow's deputies held a meeting with Spencer Perceval, the Prime Minister, for the first time.[93] In this interview, the deputies found that there still remained the chance of changing the government's intention to confine the import trade to the port of London if they could show evidence of secure collection of public revenues from the customs duties on imports at local ports. The deputies wrote in their correspondence to Glasgow:

> ... we suppose the Committee will consider the gaining this point as the virtual accomplishment of our wishes, and that consequently our time and attention ought to be particularly directed to remove these objections.[94]

Therefore, the possibility of the secure and efficient collection of public revenues at outports became the main question in the commercial aspects of the renewal of the Charter.

On 15 April, the members of the General Deputation held an interview with Perceval, Robert Dundas, and Lord Buckinghamshire.[95] These three statesmen were the key figures in the debates over the renewal of the Charter. The details of this meeting are unknown because a letter dated 16 April, in which the deputies informed the association on the details of the interview, is unfortunately missing. However, according to other communication between them, they must have discussed the collection of the revenues in outports again; in reply to the deputies' letter of 16 April, the association's secretary informed them that the association had just found a person who could give complete information on the collection of revenues at the local port.[96] In their interview, Dundas raised objections to the opening of the China trade and the import trade from India to the outports.[97] However, when Dundas was appointed to the Admiralty in a cabinet

---

93 Incoming Correspondence 1812–13, 10 April 1812, letter no. 7.

94 Ibid.

95 Ibid., 15 April 1812, letter no. 9.

96 Ibid.; Outgoing Correspondence 1812–14, 20 April 1812, letter no. 14.

97 Incoming Correspondence 1812–14, 15 April 1812, letter no. 9.

re-shuffle, Lord Buckinghamshire took over his office. Therefore, in spite of Dundas's objections, the result of the meeting was very positive towards the General Deputation. Finlay expressed his satisfaction two days after the interview, as he had received the strong impression that the sentiments of MPs in both Houses were in their favour.[98] As a result of these interviews with the Ministry the provincial mercantile and manufacturing interests understood that they needed to provide the Ministry with their evidence.

These men's opponents also strongly lobbied the Ministry for their own interests. The Company defended restriction of the import trade from India to the port of London by arguing that, because its public auctions determined the values of commodities accurately under the present system, the revenue of *ad valorem* duties could be fairly collected.[99] Nevertheless, unlike a public auction in one place, private sales elsewhere would hinder the ascertainment of the values of these goods because the market values would be different among the ports, which could result in fraud.[100] Their arguments received support from London's mercantile community, which held interests in the sale of East India piece goods. As mentioned previously, the London mercantile interests originally supported the opening of the East India trade. However, according to Philips' explanation, as they faced the strong lobby organised by the provincial interests, they changed their position and supported the Company to protect their advantages over the outports.[101] On 21 April, the London merchants, represented by Thomas Brown, held a meeting in the City and sent their petitions to Perceval for the confinement of return cargoes to the port of London and requested an interview with him.[102] While they pointed out the advantages of the long-established system of duty collection at the port of London, they also warned that cotton manufacturers in Glasgow, Manchester, and other manufacturing towns would need to compete directly with the Indian cotton pieces if they were imported to the outports.[103] They clearly showed their opposing position against the provincial interest groups.

To convince the Ministers, the General Deputation called those who were familiar with the details and could bear witness to information on the

98 Ibid., 17 April 1812, letter no. 10.

99 Anon. *Letters on the East India Monopoly*, 1812, pp. 82–94.

100 Ibid.

101 Philips, *The East India Company*, p. 182.

102 Liverpool Papers (British Library, Add. MSS. 38410), f. 72, Petition to the Right Hon. Spencer Perceval dated 25 April 1812 and Resolutions passed at a meeting of the buyers and other interests in the sale of East India piece goods, held in the City of London, dated 21 April 1812.

103 Ibid.

secure collection of revenue at the local ports under free trade. They also presented their scheme for the collection of duties.[104] For instance, because Glasgow did not have a witness with this knowledge, the General Committee sent to London Archibald Falconer, the chief magistrate of Port Glasgow, where the customs house revenue was collected.[105] He arrived in London on 26 April to assist the General Deputation.[106]

As explained, the Glasgow EIA sent its letters and the copies of resolutions to several influential politicians, including the President and the Vice-President of the Board, at the end of March 1812, before it sent the deputy to London. Webster also referred to George Rose's sudden intervention in the issue of the renewal of the Company's Charter on 3 April 1812. If the provincial lobbyists' contact with the Board of Trade in March and Rose's intervention are taken into consideration, it is reasonable to argue that the provincial lobbyists succeeded in persuading the Board to intervene on the issue. The records of the Glasgow EIA showed that the provincial mercantile and manufacturing interests continued to lobby the Board of Trade. On 13 April, the General Deputation had a meeting with Rose.[107] In this meeting, Rose said that:

> He had read with very great attention every written and printed paper which had been sent to him, that although he had opinions they led him to investigate farther and to induce him to wish more discussion of the subject, at the same time while he thought the Trade of India would be open, he said that the Company should not have an exclusive right to the trade of China.[108]

These records showed that provincial merchants and manufacturers strongly lobbied the Board of Trade and that their information persuaded Rose, who had said that "the whole subject [the renewal of the Charter] is new to me" in his communication in early April, to form his favourable attitude towards the opening of the East India trade.[109]

However, regarding the reasons for opening the India trade, Webster placed more emphasis on the government's economic strategy to "combat inflation and secure essential supplies of cheap raw materials, thus helping to maintain social stability" than on the provincial interest groups'

---

104 Committee Minute Book 1812–13, 28 April 1812.

105 Ibid., 23 April 1812; Outgoing Correspondence 1812–14, Letter to Archibald Falconer Esq., 20 April 1812.

106 Incoming Correspondence 1812–13, 27 April 1812, letter no. 13.

107 Ibid., 13 April 1812, letter no. 8.

108 Ibid.

109 Bathurst Papers (British Library, Loan 57), Vol. 5, 3 April 1812, Letter from G. Rose, which was passed to Lord Bathurst through Robert Dundas.

influence.[110] Nevertheless, social stability and securing alternative sources of raw materials were also demands of the provincial mercantile and manufacturing interest groups. Provincial middle-class men were more sensitive to the instability of local society than any others because they employed a large number of workers. In fact, in the three midland counties of England, the Luddites had destroyed more than one thousand stocking frames by February of that year, and a considerable number of properties were also damaged in the Northern manufacturing counties of England in social unrest.[111] Many petitions from the provincial interests expressed their concern about the working class' economic distress.

At the same time, the provincial interests also sought stable sources of raw cotton because of the deterioration of the political relationship between Britain and the United States as we saw before. In his letter to the Earl of Clancarty, who succeeded the Earl of Bathurst as the President of the Board of Trade, John Gladstone, who represented the Liverpool interests in the General Deputation in London at that time, strongly insisted that the American raw cotton imported to the United Kingdom should be replaced by Indian cotton.[112] What Webster called "the government's economic strategy" was, in fact, a response to the demands of the provincial mercantile and manufacturing interests, who suffered from depressed economic conditions in wartime. In consequence, the influence of the provincial interests on the Board of Trade should not be devalued.

On 27 April, Glasgow's deputation communicated to their hometown their optimistic views because they were indirectly informed that "the strong point will be the China trade and that all others will be cancelled probably with little difficulty".[113] In fact, on the same day, following the meeting between the deputation of the EIC and the Ministry, Lord Buckinghamshire notified the EIC of the government's opinion that the import trade should not be confined to the port of London.[114] By this time, the government and the Company held different views regarding the effects of the opening of the import trade to the outports. The EIC thought that:

> It appeared in the conference [held on the 25th of April] ... with the Chancellor of the Exchequer and your Lordship [Lord Buckinghamshire], to be his opinion that checks could be devised to prevent an indefinite extent of smuggling

110 Webster, "The Political Economy of Trade Liberalization", p. 417.

111 F.O. Darvall, *Popular Disturbances and Public Order in Regency England*, 1969, p. 209.

112 S.G. Checkland, *The Gladstones, A Family Biography 1764–1851*, pp. 73–4.

113 Incoming Correspondence 1812–14, 27 April 1812, letter no. 13.

114 The East India Company, *Correspondence and Proceedings*, p. 80, No. 14, "Minutes of a Secret Court of Directors Held on Tuesday, the 28th, April, 1812" and p. 81, No. 15, "Letter from

> tea, ruinous to the Company, which we fear from opening the outports to the India trade.[115]

The Company strongly opposed this sudden change, and the General Court of Proprietors passed a resolution stating that "this court has learnt with deep concern and surprise, that His Majesty's Ministers have been induced to change the view".[116] The General Deputation maintained direct access to the key figures of national politics. On 9 May 1812, its deputies had another interview with Perceval and Lord Buckinghamshire.[117] In this meeting, Perceval confirmed to them that he had given his consent to the opening of the import trade from the East Indies to the major ports of the country.[118]

However, the Ministry did not intend to lay any bills before Parliament immediately.[119] At the time the government's priority was resolving problems related to the Napoleonic Wars, especially those of the Orders in Council, against which the provincial commercial and manufacturing interests also lobbied strongly.[120] Moreover, Perceval was assassinated by John Bellingham on 11 May 1811. For these reasons further progress of the measure was suspended. Eventually, the General Deputation was dissolved and each deputy returned home.[121] Consequently, the General Deputation's lobby, through its direct access to key figures in national politics—including Perceval, the Earl of Buckinghamshire, and George Rose—and the support from their hometowns, succeeded in changing the Ministry's opinion regarding the opening of the import trade to the outports in spite of the objections of London's mercantile community.

---

the Right Honorable the Earl of Buckinghamshire to the Chairman and Deputy Chairman Dated 27th April, 1812".

115 Ibid., pp. 84–5, No. 16, "Letter from the Deputation to the Right Honorable the Earl of Buckinghamshire, Dated 29th April, 1812".

116 The East India Company, *Correspondence and Proceedings*, "Resolution of a General Court of Proprietors, Held on Tuesday 5 May 1812".

117 Liverpool Papers, ff. 81–2, 12 May 1812, Minutes of Conversation, at Interview with the Right Honourable Spencer Perceval, and the Right Honourable the Earl of Buckinghamshire; Philips, *The East India Company*, p. 184. In March 1812, Lord Buckinghamshire succeeded Robert Dundas as the president of the Board of Control.

118 The minutes of the interview state, "In answer to the Enquiry of the Deputation Mr. Perceval said, that the letter addressed by Lord Buckinghamshire to the Chairman and Deputy Chairman of the Court of Directors, dated April 27, 1812, was written with his concurrence and contained the sentiments of His Majesty's Government" and also "That it had not been decided to what parts the ships from India shall be allowed to return, but the principal ports of England, Ireland and Scotland, would certainly be included".

119 *The Parliamentary Debates*, Vol. XXIII, 5 May 1812, pp. 41–2.

120 Moss, "Birmingham and the Campaigns", pp. 173–88.

121 Committee Minute Book 1812–13, 29 October 1813, pp. 66–7.

Communications between the Board of Control and the EIC in November and December 1812 indicated that the opening of the import trade from the East Indies to the outports had already been decided in May, although the government thought that some modifications that would confine the import trade to those ports with adequate facilities would be necessary.[122] The claims of the provincial manufacturing towns and outports were supported by the answers of the surveyor of the King's Warehouse and his Assistant to queries on the possible increase of fraud and smuggling to the United Kingdom under the condition of free trade with the East Indies.[123] Most of the officers supposed that the opening of the East India trade would increase smuggling to the country but that it would not increase more than the growth of the entire East India trade. At the same time, they suggested that it would be necessary to confine the trade to the major outports that had proper facilities, such as Liverpool, Bristol, and Glasgow. Moreover, in his letter dated 24 December, the Earl of Buckinghamshire referred to the effective lobbying of the provincial manufacturing towns and outports:

> They [the provincial interests] urged their claim to an equal participation in the general trade to India, and their conviction, that the ground upon which the exclusion in favour of the port of London was defended, viz. the additional danger of smuggling, could not be supported, and they were satisfied that the alleged danger might be obviated by revenue regulation. They also entered largely into the subject of the China trade, contending strenuously against the renewal of the Company's Charter; and stated their reasons for believing that measures might be adopted by which that trade could be opened, without injury to the revenue, and without hazarding the continuance of the intercourse with the Emperor of China's dominions.
>
> The importance attached to these representations, induced His Majesty's Government to revise the arrangement which had been in contemplation; and although they did not see cause, under all the circumstances bearing upon the question, to alter the opinion they had entertained, of the propriety of continuing the existing restrictions upon the commercial intercourse with China, and of preserving to the Company the monopoly of tea trade, they nevertheless felt, that the merchants belonging to the outports

122 An Impartial Reporter, *The Preliminary Debate at the East India House*, p. 41, Appendix No. I, "At a Select Committee of Correspondence, the 27th, November 1812" and p. 42, Appendix No. II, "Letter from the Chairman and Deputy Chairman to the Right Honorable the Earl of Buckinghamshire, Dated 28th, November 1812".

123 Parliamentary Papers, *Minutes of Evidence Taken before the Committee of the Whole House, and the Select Committee on the Affairs of the East India Company*, 1812–1813, pp. 339–56.

> had established a claim against an absolute restriction of the import trade to the port of London.[124]

He admitted the provincial lobbyists' claims regarding the extension of the import trade to outports, although he thought it would be proper for the Company to maintain its monopoly in the China trade. In fact, the provincial lobbyists regarded his statement as the triumph of their campaign. Referring to the Earl of Buckinghamshire's decision, they noted that:

> ... [the] ability and zeal of the Deputation of last year have produced a decided conviction on the minds of his Majesty's Ministers with regard to the propriety of permitting to the Outports a free exercise of the Import and Export Trade with India...[125]

In September 1812, Parliament was dissolved and a general election was held. From the constituency of Glasgow and other Clyde burghs, Kirkman Finlay was elected. The difficulty of Birmingham's manufacturing interests in the debates over the Orders in Council may indicate the significance of having a Parliamentary member who directly represented the provincial interests.[126] Like Glasgow, before 1832, Birmingham was not a single constituency but formed a country constituency of Warwickshire with other neighbouring towns. Nevertheless, the MP for Warwickshire disrupted the Birmingham interests' campaign by making unfavourable remarks in Parliament. Men whom Philips identified as the more prominent members in the first General Deputation were Gladstone, Brackenbury, Littledale, and Wainwright from Liverpool; Macadam and Schonswar from Bristol; Broadley from Hull; Spooner from Birmingham; and Loudon from Edinburgh.[127] Among these leading members, only Kirkman Finlay became an MP. In the House of Commons he played an important role in opposition to the renewal of the Company's exclusive Charter.

The provincial mercantile and manufacturing interests used their network again. With the approach of the new session's opening, the Glasgow EIA prepared new petitions to Parliament and appointed Robert Dennistoun, Charles Stirling, and James Oswald as its new deputation to London. This was in response to a request from the Liverpool Committee to reassemble the General Deputation, although only Stirling and Oswald actually left for London. The new deputies received similar instructions to

---

[124] An Impartial Reporter, *The Preliminary Debate at the East India House*, p. 47, Appendix No. IX, "Letter from the Right Honorable the Earl of Buckinghamshire to the Chairman and Deputy Chairman of the East India Company, Dated 24th, December 1812".

[125] Committee Minute Book 1812–13, January 1813, p. 33.

[126] Moss, "Birmingham and the Campaigns", pp. 184–5.

[127] Philips, *The East India Company*, p. 182.

those for the previous deputation from the General Committee, i.e., to insist on: (1) their equal participation in the East India trade, (2) the residence of their agents and servants in India, (3) the opening of the China trade, (4) the safety of state revenue from the customs duties collected at the outports, and (5) the extension of export and import to the outports.[128] The two men represented Glasgow in the General Deputation in London until March 1813. After the government's opinion shifted to the opening of the import trade to the outports, the China trade became the main agenda in the negotiation between the General Deputation and the Ministry, although they still needed to further discuss other topics such as the restriction on the size of ships for the trade with the East Indies, as their interview with Lord Liverpool indicated.[129] The provincial interests succeeded in raising this topic for discussion in their individual meetings with the Ministry and in Parliament, but their lobbying efforts yielded little success.

After March of the two deputies only Oswald remained in London to continue lobbying for his home town.[130] However, he expressed a desire to return to Glasgow in April for personal reasons, and in spite of the General Committee's request he left London before the end of April.[131] Following his resignation, the Glasgow EIA lost its representative in the General Deputation, so it was urgent for the organisation to appoint a replacement. Eventually, with James Ewing's appointment to the deputation on 2 May 1813 Glasgow had a voice in the General Deputation again.[132] Nevertheless, during the absence of Glasgow's deputy Kirkman Finlay was still in London as a representative for the city in Parliament and maintained correspondence with the association.[133]

On 23 March 1813, Lord Castlereagh introduced the question of the Charter's renewal in the House of Commons and moved resolutions towards that end. The main points were that the Charter, including the exclusive right for the China trade, should be renewed, but the relaxation of the India trade should be allowed for the opening of both import and export trade between the outports and India.[134] By the end of the month, the General Committee of Glasgow was very pessimistic about the opening of the China trade, including the tea trade. Therefore, the committee

128 Committee Minute Book 1812–13, January 1813, pp. 31–2, letter to Robert Dennistoun, Charles Stirling, and James Oswald, Esquires.
129 Incoming Correspondence 1812–13, February 1813, letter no. 24.
130 Committee Minute Book 1812–13, 29 March 1813, p. 39.
131 Ibid., 15 April 1813, p. 43; Incoming Correspondence, 1812–13, 24 April 1813, letter no. 33.
132 Committee Minute Book 1812–13, 2 May 1813, p. 44.
133 Incoming Correspondence 1812–13, 29 April 1812 and 3 May 1813, letter no. 34.
134 Committee Minute Book 1812–13, 29 October 1813, pp. 67–8.

gave its consent to the deputation to seek the possibility of shortening the duration of the Company's monopoly to seven or ten years.[135] In terms of the China trade, the Board of Control maintained its consistent opinion in opposition to these claims during the debates in spite of the provincial interests' strong lobby and George Rose's support of opening the China trade. Regarding this point, Sir George Stauton's advice influenced Buckinghamshire's opinion. His experience as a supercargo at Canton and familiarity with the conditions of the China trade convinced Buckinghamshire to adopt his opinion for the continuity of the Company's monopoly in this trade.[136] In the Select Committee, the EIC called a number of witnesses in the next two months to argue for the danger of opening the East India trade. The facts given by those who were called from a number of positions of the Company's service were often biased in favour of the Company's arguments. Nevertheless, in spite of their bias towards the Company, these testimonies failed to convince the Ministers and Parliament of the advantages of continuing the EIC's exclusive privilege in the India trade. Correspondence between the General Committee and its deputies to London implied that although they regretted that the China trade would not be open to the outports, they were optimistic about the influence of their evidence on the Parliamentary decision, and they often thought that some testimonies practically supported free trade.[137] Although, in the following two months, approximately 50 witnesses were called to the Committee of the Whole House and the Select Committee, the Ministry's opinion remained the same.

While the General Deputation prepared evidence to support its claims, after May they began to fear that the final decision over the renewal of the Charter might be postponed until another session.[138] They knew that as the economic conditions of the country gradually improved the question of the Charter attracted less attention from the public than before.[139] Lord Castlereagh also wished to finish the debate in the current session since the Ministry wanted to concentrate on the war and suggested that the General Deputation not call their witnesses.[140] Therefore, the provincial lobbyists

---

[135] Ibid., 29 March 1813, Meeting of the General Committee.

[136] Philips, *The East India Company*, p. 186; Webster, "The Political Economy of Trade Liberalization", p. 412.

[137] Ibid., p. 409; Outgoing Correspondence 1812–14, 24 April 1813, Letter to Robert Dennistoun.

[138] Ibid., 7 May 1813, Letter to Kirkman Finlay Esq.

[139] Ibid., 24 May 1813, Letter to James Ewing Esq.

[140] Committee Minute Book 1812–13, 29 October 1813, pp. 68–9; Philips, *The East India Company*, pp. 188–91.

decided not to give their evidence in order to settle the East India question swiftly.[141] On 31 May, the House of Commons passed the resolutions. On the one hand, the first and second resolutions empowered the EIC to continue the administration of British territories in India and to keep the exclusive trade with China for another twenty years. On the other hand, the third resolution allowed the free entry of all licensed British merchants to the India trade.[142] Before the end of the session the bill was finally placed before Parliament. After several discussions and modifications the new bill passed both Houses, and royal assent was granted on 21 July 1813.

The Report of the Glasgow Committee summarised the commercial terms of the new Charter.[143] First, after the expiration of the old Charter on 10 April 1814, all British subjects equipping themselves with ships of 350 tons or more were to be legally permitted to participate in commercial intercourse with countries beyond the Cape of Good Hope eastward under the licence granted by the Court of Directors of the EIC, with the exception of the China trade, from which private traders were to be excluded. Second, with regard to the trading articles, the importing of tea by private merchants remained forbidden, and the outports were allowed to import commodities manufactured of silk, hair, and cotton wool only for the purpose of re-export. Third, the same duties were imposed on the Company's commodities as on private traders, and the Company was to keep books at home and in India to show the separation between its political and commercial affairs. Moreover, the EIC was required to submit the accounts to Parliament every year for examination and to place all duties on its goods to the debit of the commercial branch. Fourth, without the consent of the Board of Control, the appropriation of part of the revenue to commercial purposes was forbidden. All residents in India were subject to the Company's local governments. Finally, Parliament was reserved the power to alter the bill for proper reasons, and the Charter Act was to last for twenty years. Compared with the previous Charter, most of the terms were favourable to provincial merchants and manufacturers in Britain. Although they failed to convince the government of the merits of opening the China trade, the reversal of the Ministry's decision on the opening of the import trade to outports was a result of their successful lobbying, and this was their triumph over London's mercantile society.

---

141 Outgoing Correspondence 1812–14, 28 May 1813, Letter to James Ewing Esq.

142 Philips, *The East India Company*, p. 190.

143 Committee Minute Book 1812–13, 29 October 1813, pp. 70–2.

After James Ewing returned to Glasgow at the end of October 1813, the subscribers of the Glasgow EIA held a General Meeting on 2 November.[144] This was the last major event of the association in the early 1810s. At this meeting, the members celebrated the abolition of the Company's monopoly in the India trade and offered their thanks to Kirkman Finlay for representing the city in Parliament and to the members of the deputation and the secretary.[145] Also at this meeting, a new committee was created "for attending to the progress of the Bill to be introduced in the next session of Parliament, for regulating the important subject of the circuitous trade to and from India, and to communicate with other Committees"; Robert Dennistoun, Charles Stirling, James Buchanan, John More, David Connell, Henry Monteith, James Ewing, and James Oswald were appointed to the posts.[146] Unfortunately, the activities of this committee are unknown. However, what is clear is that after the opening of the India trade in 1814, some Glasgow merchants started trade with the East Indies. For instance, Kirkman Finlay sent his first ship, named the 'Earl of Buckinghamshire', from the Clyde to Bombay directly in 1816; then, in the following year, he sent the 'George Canning' to Calcutta.[147] Nevertheless, as will be explained in the next chapter, Glasgow's East Indian interests failed to maintain their association. As a result, after the opening of the India trade, their lobbying was inactive until 1829.

Conclusion

This chapter has examined the Glasgow EIA and its lobbying activities in the early 1810s. The organisation represented both the mercantile and manufacturing interests of Glasgow, especially among the members of the General Committee and the subscribers to the association. The presence of those involved in the West India trade and the cotton spinning and manufacturing industry, which dominated the economic activities of the city and its neighbouring areas, was remarkable. On the one hand, the involvement of various different economic interests in the campaign indicated that the lobbying activities were widely supported by the business elite of the city. On the other hand, the case of the West Indian merchants, who demanded

144 Committee Minute Book 1812–13, 2 November 1813, pp. 78–9.

145 Ibid.

146 Ibid.

147 J. MacLehose, *Memoirs and Portraits of One Hundred Glasgow Men*, Chapter 21.

protection for their existing trade at the expense of the East India trade during the campaign, shows that the provincial interests had some divisions. Nevertheless, it is difficult to argue that such divisions critically affected the provincial lobbyists' ability to organise their campaign. They formed effective groups and their lobbying was influential enough.

Before the lobbying activities of the General Deputation in London began in April 1812, the continuation of the monopoly in the China trade had already been agreed upon as a result of negotiations between the EIC and the Board of Control. The Ministry had also decided to remove the restriction that prevented vessels from leaving UK ports other than London for the East Indies. After their initial negotiations with the Ministry, the Glasgow deputation and other provincial towns and outports recognised that the Ministry would change its opinion if they could prove that the opening of the import trade to the outports would not negatively impact the secure and efficient collection of customs duties. Therefore, they set this topic as their main target and strongly lobbied the Ministry. In the debates over this subject they were able to exercise their influence strongly enough to persuade the Ministry to change its opinion. In the face of strong lobbying from the provincial interests, Lord Buckinghamshire decided that the import trade would be opened to the outports and admitted their influence in his communication with the Company. In this issue the influential lobby of the provincial interests contrasted with the incompetence of London's mercantile society. The records of the Glasgow EIA also show clear evidence that the provincial interests strongly lobbied the President and Vice-Presidents of the Board of Trade to persuade them to support their claims. Consequently, from Buckinghamshire's statements and the provincial lobbyists' influence on the Board it is clear that the Ministry's change of opinion regarding the import trade from India was a result of the strong lobby organised by the provincial interest groups.

During the Parliamentary sessions of 1812 and 1813, the contribution of Glasgow to the free trade campaign was significant. Although the Glasgow EIA made attempts to encourage other Scottish towns to join the campaign, its activities were not confined to Scotland. The association sent letters to influential politicians, whilst their resolutions and pamphlets were widely circulated across the whole country. The Glasgow EIA's close communication with other major provincial towns also helped the organisation to create its campaign strategies. In London, the deputation of the Glasgow EIA formed the General Deputation with those from several other towns and strongly lobbied the Ministry and the Parliament. The Glasgow EIA was undoubtedly one of the most active institutions in the campaign.

CHAPTER THREE

STRUGGLING FOR LUCRATIVE TRADE: THE GLASGOW EAST INDIA ASSOCIATION, 1829–1833

Introduction

After the renewal of the EIC's Charter of 1813, the East Indian interests in Liverpool, Manchester, and other towns in North England organised further lobbying activities in the 1820s, such as petitioning Parliament for the equalisation of the duties levied on East Indian sugar and West Indian sugar. Meanwhile, Glasgow's interests were relatively inactive. However, their lobbying was revived by the foundation of the new Glasgow EIA in 1829, five years before the expiry of the Charter. Unlike the previous Glasgow EIA of 1812–13, the new association was a permanent organisation established to promote free trade in the East Indies. That is to say, the association wrestled not only with the EIC's attempts to renew the Charter but with several other problems that British merchants and manufacturers were facing in this branch of overseas trade. These problems included the equalisation of duties levied on East and West Indian sugar and the heavy duties imposed on British manufactured goods in the Dutch possession of the island of Java. The organisation continued its activities after the eventual renewal of the EIC's Charter in 1833.

In terms of the opening of the China trade and the end of the EIC's commercial branch in 1834, Michael Greenberg and other historians have emphasised the influence of commercial and manufacturing interests in provincial manufacturing towns and outports, especially those in Lancashire, as in the case of the opening of the India trade two decades earlier.[1] These historians argued that the industrialists' need to find new export markets for their manufactured goods and the increasing demand for raw materials resulting from their expanded production capacity after the Industrial Revolution encouraged them to exert more pressure on the Company's China monopoly. Nevertheless, more recently Cain and

[1] M. Greenberg, *British Trade and the Opening of China 1800–42*, 1961, p. 179; D. Eyles, "The Abolition of The East India Company's Monopoly 1833", unpublished PhD thesis, University of Edinburgh, 1955, p. 304.

Hopkins have emphasised a non-industrial element. These two historians contended that the merchants of both London and India, rather than Manchester's manufacturers, were seeking opportunities to develop their trade in Southeast Asia and the Far East, and exerted decisive pressure to abolish the Company's monopoly in the China trade.[2] Huw Bowen also stressed that the unprofitability of the EIC as a commercial organisation predated the abolition of its monopoly. In contrast, Webster supported Tripathi's explanation regarding the provincial merchants and manufacturers' more effective lobby during the 1829–33 campaign compared to the previous one.[3]

The free trade campaign from 1829 to 1833 was not a simple movement organised solely by provincial mercantile and manufacturing interests. Nevertheless, it is also incorrect to regard the opening of the China trade as the sole product of the gentlemanly capitalists of London and their nexus. The records indicate not only that John Crawfurd, a former EIC servant and a Scottish Orientalist, acted as a general agent for the interests of the private merchants in the East Indies in the free trade movement, but also that the provincial lobbyists collaborated with some gentlemanly capitalists in London during the campaign.

The Re-establishment of the Glasgow East India Association

The renewal of the Company's Charter in 1813 represented a mixture of success and failure of the lobbying organised by Glasgow and other provincial merchants and manufacturers. Under the new Charter of 1813, all British merchants were permitted to trade with both the Company's and natives' territories in India after 10 April 1814. However, the Company succeeded in retaining its privileges in the trade of tea and in the China trade. As a result, although the EIC continued its trade with India, it specialised in the China trade, which still produced large profits. The growth of national income in which industrial sectors played a prime role and the increase in the urban population in the provincial manufacturing towns became the key factors

---

[2] P.J. Cain and A.G. Hopkins, *British Imperialism: Innovation and Expansion 1688–1914*, p. 325.

[3] A. Tripathi, *Trade and Finance in the Bengal Presidency 1879–1833*, 1979, pp. 198–9; A. Webster, "The Strategies and Limits of Gentlemanly Capitalism: The London East India Agency Houses, Provincial Commercial Interests, and the Evolution of British Economic Policy in South and South East Asia 1800–1850", in *The Economic History Review*, New Series, Vol. LIX, No. 4, p. 749.

in the growth in the consumption of tea in Britain during this period.[4] Figure 3 shows the Company's profit and loss on the India and China trade in the 15 years after the renewal of the Charter. During this period, the profit gained from the China trade oscillated between approximately £760,000 in 1822–23 and £1.4 million in 1814–15; the average profit was just above £1 million per year. Meanwhile, the Company's India trade deteriorated.[5] With the exception of 1824–25, the trade operated at a loss after 1820–21, which in 1828–29 amounted to approximately £555,000. Merchants in Glasgow and other outports were excluded from the lucrative tea trade. Adam Smith and other classical economists made arguments on free trade stating that the system of freely moving prices under free economic conditions could be beneficial for consumers.[6] From the viewpoint of free trade supporters the Company's exclusive trading right for its tea trade was against the interest

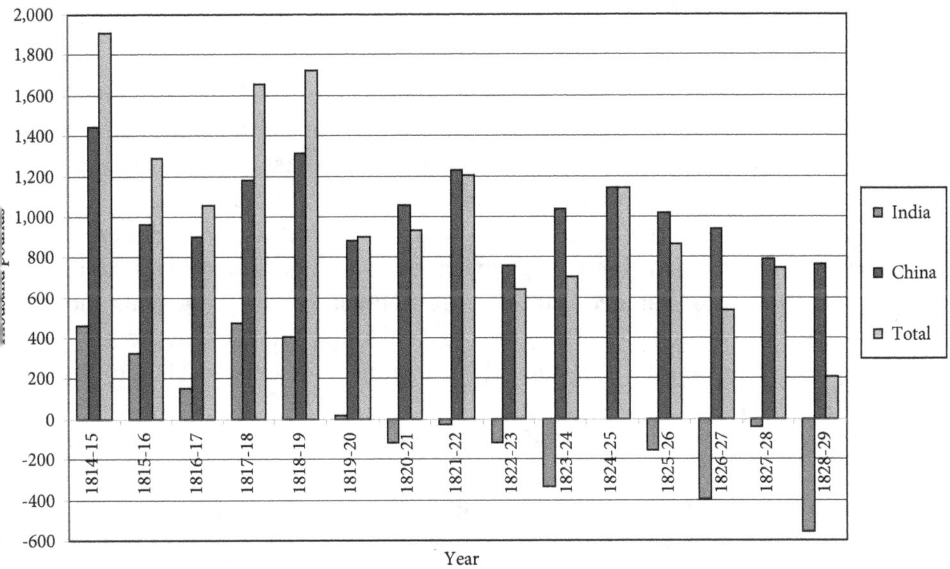

Figure 3. Profit and Loss of the EIC on the India and China Trade between 1814–15 and 1828–29

Source: British Parliamentary Papers, *Minutes of Evidence Taken before the Select Committee on the Affairs of the East India Company; and also an Appendix and Index, II. Finance and Accounts – Trade, 1832*, Appendix No. 3, p. 45.

[4] J.R. Ward, "The Industrial Revolution and British Imperialism, 1750–1850", in *The Economic History Review*, New series, Vol. XLVII, No. 1, 1994, pp. 44–65.

[5] Regarding the EIC's trade with India and China during this period, see also H.V. Bowen, *The Business of Empire: The East India Company and Imperial Britain, 1756–1833*, 2006, pp. 252–9.

[6] P. Mathias, *The First Industrial Nation: An Economic History of Britain 1700–1914*, 1969, p. 201.

of all consumers in the United Kingdom. They believed that the state's interference in the East India trade by granting a Charter of exclusive trade to the Company resulted in higher prices on imported commodities.

Moreover, the EIC needed to transfer capital from India to Europe in the form of its 'investment' in Chinese products to settle its financial obligations in England, especially payments of dividends to the proprietors and interest on debts derived from the administration of India. Such operations of the Company became the target of criticism. Before the previous renewal of the Charter of 1813, Lord Lauderdale had denounced the fact that the Company determined the quantity of exports from India based on the amount of money that its servants wanted sent home with no consideration for the state of the European market.[7] Similarly, J.R. McCulloch critically described the EIC as a "Company which carried a sword in the one hand, and a ledger in the other– which maintains armies and retails tea".[8]

During this period, tea was the single most important commodity for the Company to operate the system of international financial transfer between Europe and Asia, and those who were opposed to the Company thought that political considerations distorted its price, which harmed the interests of all British subjects. At the same time, some contemporaries expected that the opening of the China trade would give private traders an effective means of sending their returns from India, in which they faced great difficulty resulting from the Company's need to process government remittances. McCulloch argued that the institution that managed the remittance to England was not necessary and that bills of exchange could entirely replace the remittance through the medium of 'investment' in Chinese products.[9]

In addition to the import of tea, many British manufacturing interests regarded China as a potential market for their own manufactured goods. Before he accepted an executive position in the Company James Mill, who followed the views of Adam Smith, had argued that:

> ... it would, indeed, be a matter of astonishment, if the acuteness and ardour of private adventurers should not find means of producing commodities to the taste of every people in the world who have enough to give for them.[10]

---

[7] J. Maitland [Lord Lauderdale], *An Inquiry into the Practical Merits of the System for the Government of India under the Superintendence of the Board of Controul*, 1809, p. 137.

[8] D.P. O'Brien, J. *R. McCulloch: A Study in Classic Economics*, 1970, p. 340.

[9] Ibid., p. 341.

[10] W. Barber, *British Economic Thought and India 1600–1858*, 1975, p. 134.

In the first sixteen years after the opening of the Indian trade, Indian exports in the hands of private traders (an average of £5,451,452 per year) overwhelmed the EIC (an average of £1,882,718 per year).[11] Traditionally, the Directors of the Company and their supporters defended their exclusive trade with the East Indies by arguing that they could expect little increase in British exports to the East Indies, even if the trade was opened to all British subjects, because the local demand for British products was already satisfied by the Company's exports. Nevertheless, as a result of the growth of British exports to India after 1814 and the American merchants' success in this trade, this argument became less convincing.

The opening of the India trade to British private traders in 1814 created new East Indian interests in outports, although some private traders had already engaged in 'country trade' or used the limited facilities provided by the Company.[12] However, in Glasgow, those who had interests in the East India trade failed to organise themselves to lobby the state for their own interests before the end of the 1820s. It is very difficult to determine why they failed to organise their lobbying during this period. However, one probable reason was Kirkman Finlay's gradual withdrawal from Glasgow's affairs during the same period.[13] He had been a key figure in the previous free trade campaign. Nevertheless, he lost his parliamentary seat for the Clyde burghs in 1818 and was elected for Malmesbury, Wiltshire. He also bought a property in Cowal, Argyll, and developed the land there. Although he became President of the Chamber of Commerce again in 1823 and 1824, he was less active in both the commercial and political affairs of the city than he had been during the 1810s. Another reason was simply that the East India trade for Glasgow was not as significant as it was for Liverpool. The lack of statistical data on Liverpool's overseas trade does not allow us to directly compare these two cities during this period. Nevertheless, some clues are available from the London EIA's reports of the 1830s and 1840s.[14] In terms of British ships that entered from the East Indies, Liverpool counted 126 ships in 1836, just a few years after the opening of the China trade, whilst the total number of British ships to the Clyde, Leith, and other

[11] R. Dutt, *The Economic History of India under Early British Rule*, 1956, p. 293.

[12] J.G. Parker, "Scottish Enterprise in India, 1750–1914", in R.A. Cage (ed.), *The Scots Abroad: Labour, Capital, Enterprise, 1750–1914*, 1985, Chap. 7.

[13] C. Brogan, *James Finlay & Company Limited, Manufacturers and East India Merchants, 1750–1950*, 1951, pp. 28–9.

[14] The London East India Association, *Reports of the Committee of the East India Association*, 1838, pp. 27–8; The London East India Association, *The Fifth Report of the Committee of the East India Association*, 1841, pp. 25–6.

British locations (excluding London, Bristol, and Hull) in 1839 was still only 25. Similarly, with respect to the number of British ships that cleared for the East Indies in the same period, the former counted 172 ships and the latter 96 respectively; this trend continued in the later period.

As Charlton's work and the following chapters describe, Liverpool's East Indian merchants and Manchester's manufacturers, whose interests were represented by their own EIA and Chamber of Commerce, were more active than Glasgow's East Indian interests.[15] In particular, Liverpool played a central role in debates over trade with the East Indies during the 1820s, such as the abolition of the limitation of the tonnage of ships for the trade and the equalisation of duties on East Indian sugar and West Indian sugar. Moreover, the inactivity of Glasgow's East Indian interests contrasted strikingly with their West Indian counterpart, which organised powerful lobbying efforts against the abolition of slavery during the same period. According to traditional historical views, slavery and the slave trade were linked to such English ports as Bristol and Liverpool, but Iain Whyte's work illustrated that the Glasgow WIA, which he described as "the most powerful group representing slaving interests outside London", lobbied for their own interests in national debates over the abolition of slavery.[16] Nevertheless, as the expiration of the Charter approached five years later, it was essential for Glasgow's East Indian interests to organise a lobbying group to promote their trade effectively.

Kirkman Finlay remained a leading figure in the lobbying activities in Glasgow against the renewal of the EIC's Charter in the late 1820s and early 1830s. In the 1810s and 1820s he was the President of the Chamber of Commerce in the city, so he was in a position to be influential. On 16 April 1829, Finlay and eight other businessmen of Glasgow gathered to hold a meeting at the Tontine Hotel to discuss the foundation of the new Glasgow EIA.[17] A public meeting of those who had an interest in free trade with India and China took place on 22 April.[18] In his speech at this meeting, Finlay reiterated a strong preference for free trade by referring to Adam Smith and heavily criticised the Company's monopoly for its old-fashioned

[15] K. Charlton, "Liverpool and the East India Trade", in *Northern History*, Vol. VII, 1972, pp. 56–63.

[16] I. Whyte, *Scotland and the Abolition of Black Slavery, 1756–1838*, 2006, p. 146.

[17] The Glasgow East India Association Committee Minute Book 1829–1847 (MS89001/2, Glasgow Mitchell Library), 16 April 1829, p. 1. The other eight participants in the meeting were Charles Todd, Rowan Ronald, James Anderson, William Graham, Hugh Cogan, James Buchanan, John Weighton, and Andrew Tennant.

[18] Ibid., 22 April 1829, pp. 1–3.

mercantilist character and prohibitive nature.[19] In this meeting the attendants resolved to form an association for the protection and furtherance of the general interests of the East India trade and to call the East Indian interests of the city and its neighbourhood to become its members.[20] The Glasgow EIA was officially funded by 32 gentlemen who signed up as members.[21] To achieve the purposes of this association, it was decided to establish a general fund by requiring an entry subscription of five guineas and an annual subscription of half a guinea from each member.[22]

In the meeting Finlay also referred to his receipt of a letter from the Liverpool EIA.[23] The association of Liverpool had expressed its intention to send a deputation to London in May to discuss with other deputations the proper means of opposing the renewal of the EIC's Charter.[24] The Liverpool EIA had been arranging for a meeting with the Duke of Wellington through its MP, William Huskisson, who held the office of the President of the Board of Trade at that time, and invited other deputations to attend.[25] The receipt of the letter from Liverpool indicated that the communication between Glasgow and Liverpool played an important part in the re-establishment of the Glasgow EIA. Finlay shared the Liverpool businessmen's opinion that it was proper to persuade the government to give its early attention to the subject of the renewal of the Company's Charter and to make a case for the total abolition of its monopoly to the Ministers.[26] The meeting supported his view and resolved that the East Indian interests of Glasgow claim the total abolition of the EIC's trading monopoly with their use of every proper and constitutional means and that they were willing to collaborate with other mercantile bodies organised for the same purpose. They appointed Alexander Garden, the Lord Provost of Glasgow, and Robert Dalglish as their deputies to London.[27] Later, Robert Douglas Alston, George Stirling, and James Ewing joined them.[28] On 6 May, a committee of eighteen members was appointed and the offices of a chairman, a deputy chairman, and a treasurer and secretary were established to manage the affairs of the association. At the next day's meeting, Finlay and James A. Anderson were

---

19 *Glasgow Herald*, 24 April 1829, "East India Trade".
20 Committee Minute Book 1829–47, p. 1.
21 Ibid., p. 3.
22 Ibid., p. 2.
23 Ibid.
24 Ibid.
25 M. Greenberg, *British Trade and the Opening of China 1800–42*, pp. 181–2.
26 *Glasgow Herald*, 24 April 1829, "East India Trade".
27 Committee Minute Book 1829–47, p. 2.
28 Ibid., 28 April 1829, p. 4.

unanimously elected as the chairman and deputy chairman, respectively, and William P. Paton, who had deep knowledge of the East India trade through his own experience of residing in the Malay Archipelago, was chosen as secretary and treasurer.[29] With the appointment of these office-holders, the organisation was fully established to begin its lobbying activities against the renewal of the EIC's Charter and to deal with other aspects of the East India trade in earnest.

The Economic Interests and Political Status of Members of the Re-established Glasgow EIA

To understand the characteristics of its members as a group and how these characteristics influenced their lobbying strategies, it is essential to analyse the economic interests and political status of the Glasgow EIA's members. Appendix III contains a list of the 146 members of the Glasgow EIA between 1829 and 1833, their occupations, and the firms in which they had interests. As explained in Chapter 2, the short-lived Glasgow EIA of the previous campaign consisted of the city's mercantile and manufacturing interests. This table indicates that the economic interests of the members of the re-established Glasgow EIA were also varied. Nevertheless, it also shows that the association had some different characteristics from the previous organisation.

First, according to the information obtained from shipping advertisements in the *Glasgow Courier*, *100 Glasgow Men*, the records of the Glasgow WIA, and other sources, 23 members of the new Glasgow EIA were engaged in overseas trade. The records of the Glasgow WIA and other sources concerning James Finlay & Co. and Dennistoun, Buchanan & Co. also identified another 6 members as foreign traders. Therefore, in total, at least 29 members of the Glasgow EIA were clearly engaged in foreign trade and shipping businesses. Among them, 14 members were involved in the East India trade. Although the information in Appendix III is limited and there is a possibility that the number of known overseas traders, particularly the East Indian traders, could increase based on further research, the table demonstrates that, whilst many of the foreign traders and shipping interests of the association were engaged in the East India trade, the destinations of their trade were not confined to this area. They were also involved

[29] Ibid., 7 May 1829, p. 8; *Glasgow Herald*, 8 May 1829, "East India Monopoly".

in other branches of foreign trade, including the West Indies, South America, British North America, the United States, and Europe. This proves the existence of varied foreign trading and shipping interests within the association. The members' varied trading destinations reflected the diversification of Glasgow's foreign trade during this period.

During the 1812–13 campaign, the West Indian interests had been one of the largest economic interest groups that lobbied for the end of the East India and China monopoly in Glasgow and influenced the association's strategies. Nevertheless, while such mercantile firms as James Finlay & Co. and Walter Buchanan's Buchanan, Hamilton & Co. engaged in the East India trade, the presence of the West Indian interests in the trade and in the new association was limited. The records of the Glasgow WIA contain the names of the West Indian merchants who attended at general meetings, annual general meetings, and meetings of its directors. Compared with Appendix II, in which at least 22 company and individual subscribers for the previous Glasgow EIA can be identified as members of the Glasgow WIA, among those who attended these meetings of the Glasgow WIA from 1823 to 1834 (nearly 50 names can be identified), only James Bogle, Arthur Connell of D. & J. Connell and later A. & J. Connell, James Ewing and William Mathieson of James Ewing & Co., and George Scheviz were on the list of members of the new Glasgow EIA. Appendix III shows that, apart from these individuals, James Buchanan of Dowanhill and his son, James, also comprised one of the leading West Indian firms in the city and were partners of Dennistoun, Buchanan & Co., which also engaged in the East India trade through Buchanan, Brown & Co.[30]

There were some reasons why only a small number of the West Indian merchants actually engaged in the East India trade after the opening of the India trade. The first reason was that the motives of the West Indian merchants for attending the previous campaign were the hardships they experienced during the disruption of the West India trade caused by the Napoleonic Wars. Although at the beginning of Glasgow's previous campaign its West Indian interests were one of the groups that most seriously pursued the opening of the East India trade, when economic conditions improved after the second half of 1812, Kirkman Finlay and some other cotton manufacturers remained the keenest part of the city's free trade movement rather than those who were involved in the West India trade.

[30] Minute Book of Dennistoun, Buchanan & Co. Glasgow 1806–42 (MS Murray 605, Glasgow University Special Collection Department), 14 February 1825.

The second reason was the different nature of the East India trade compared to the West India trade. For instance, according to one of the testimonies given at the Select Committee:

> ... a ship which would go from Liverpool to the West Indies, and bring a good and sufficient cargo from thence, could not convey indigo, silk and saltpetre, with advantage to the ship-owner, on the terms at which the East India Company now engage that class of shipping ... although a small leak would in no degree be detrimental to a West Indiaman, it may create a very considerable loss to a ship that has an East India cargo on board.[31]

Without altering the vessels themselves or their outfits, vessels employed for the West India trade were not suitable for the East India trade, which had longer shipping routes and required more time. The West Indian interests also needed to obtain knowledge and to establish trading networks to enter the East India trade, which the Company had monopolised for many years. Checkland's work indicated that John Gladstone, who had established himself as a prominent West Indian merchant, entered the East India trade in 1814, but after the initial expansion of trade he struggled to make a profit in the Indian market, in spite of his ability to reduce risks in the longer-distance trade with the East Indies.[32] These cases involved Liverpool, but the principles also applied to Glasgow. These may have partly prevented Glasgow's West Indian interests from entering the East India trade to an extensive degree.

Third, the East Indian and West Indian traders showed the incompatibility of their interests after the opening of the India trade. Although the old Glasgow EIA had made attempts to defend the West Indian interests as well as to promote free trade in the East Indies between 1812 and 1813, the new association did not do so. In fact, at the national level, the East Indian interests and the West Indian interests had prolonged disputes over the equalisation of customs duties between East Indian and West Indian sugar during the 1820s and the 1830s. The annual report in 1824 by the Chairman and Directors of the Glasgow WIA stated that:

> Uniting with the party of Mr. Wilberforce they [the East India opponents] have struck a blow at the vital interests of the [West Indian] colonies and threatened their very existence with the most indefatigable industry they

[31] Parliamentary Paper, *Minutes of Evidence Taken before the Committee of the Whole House, and the Select Committee on the Affairs of the East India Company, 1813. 24 November 1812–22 July 1813. Vol. VII*, p. 397.

[32] S.G. Checkland, "John Gladstone as Trader and Planter", in *The Economic History Review*, New series, Vol. VII, No. 2, 1954, pp. 217–22.

> circulated statements through the whole country representing the conduct of the planters in the most hideous light denouncing the cultivation of sugar though the medium of Negro labor and calling on the whole people of Britain to come forward and petition the legislature, for the immediate improvement and ultimate emancipations of the slaves.[33]

The West Indian interests in Glasgow showed strong opposition to the alteration of the duty on East Indian sugar for home consumption, and they condemned the East Indian interests for their connection with the anti-slavery movement for this purpose. In consequence, the interests of the East Indian traders deviated from those of the West Indian traders after the renewal of the Company's Charter of 1813.

Consequently, in Glasgow the majority of the West Indian merchants did not have serious interests in the East India trade during this period, in spite of their significant participation in the previous free trade campaign. In Liverpool's case, Charlton, who explained the involvement of the West Indian interests—particularly John Gladstone—in lobbying against the renewal of the Company's Charter, insisted that:

> The campaign of the Liverpool merchants to 'free' the East India trade is an important part of the port's history, showing its ability to diversify its interests when a traditional one [the West India trade] was lost…[34]

In Glasgow's case, although the opening of the India trade in 1814 and of the China trade in 1834 diversified Glasgow's overseas trading activities, it does not seem that its West Indian traders actually exploited or tried to exploit opportunities presented by the abolition of the Company's commercial privileges.

In contrast to Glasgow's West Indian merchants Table 4 shows that the cotton manufacturing interests and their nexus kept a position as one of the major economic interest groups in the re-established association. Among the members of the association, at least 45 members—in other words, nearly one-third of the total—were obviously engaged in cotton manufacturing and its related industries, including spinning, weaving, calico-printing and bleaching, and yarn warehouses. However, their number was almost certainly much greater. Based on a comparison between the number of those who were involved in the cotton manufacturing and related businesses and that of other manufacturing businesses, we can

---

33 Abstract of the Minute Book of the Glasgow West India Association (MS891002, Glasgow Mitchell Library), Vol. 3, "Annual Report by the Chairman & Directors of the West India Association", dated 15 January 1824, pp. 481–2.

34 Charlton, "Liverpool and the East India Trade", p. 54.

Table 4. Manufacturing interests in the Glasgow EIA, 1829–33.

Categories	Number
Cotton manufacturing and related industries	45
Other manufacturing industries	8
'Manufacturer(s)'	24
'Merchant(s)'	26
Unknown	23
Others	20
Total	146

Note: The category of 'Cotton manufacturing and related business' includes spinners, weavers, calico-printers and bleachers, pullicate manufacturers, yarn warehouses, dyeworks, cotton works, calenderers, and their equivalents, plus the members of Ellis, Bleaymire & Co. Yarn warehouses are regarded as belonging to this category because the warehousemen provided their yarn to hand-loom weavers in the putting-out system. 'Other manufacturing businesses' include saddlers, engineers, drysalters, wholesale woollen drapers, and their equivalents. 'Manufacturer(s)' include those who are identified just as 'manufacturer(s)', but when their businesses are known, i.e., when they belong to the first two categories, they are excluded from this category. 'Merchant(s)' include those who are identified just as 'merchant(s)', but those who belong to the first three categories, i.e., those who were clearly engaged in some kind of manufacturing industries, are excluded. 'Others' include foreign traders, shipping agents, bankers, accountants and writers, wholesale stationers, and other occupations, but those who belong to the above categories are excluded.

Source: Created from Appendix III.

estimate that a large majority of 24 members identified just as 'manufacturer(s)' were also engaged in these businesses. In addition, some of those who are identified just as 'merchant(s)' and some of those that this research has failed to identify must have belonged to these businesses. Therefore, approximately one-half of the association's members were probably involved in cotton manufacturing and its related industries.

The attendance of a large number of the cotton manufacturing interests in the re-established association can be explained by their significant involvement in the East India trade during this period. After the partial opening of the East India trade in 1814, the exports of British manufacturing goods to India increased, contrary to the Company's arguments. Goods produced in the provincial manufacturing towns were largely sent to the East upon consignment by the London agency houses that specialised in the export of goods, as well as provincial mercantile houses such as James Finlay & Co.[35] These agency houses provided such financial arrangements

[35] Webster, "The Strategies and Limits of Gentlemanly Capitalism", p. 747; Records of James Finlay & Co. Ltd., December 1818–December 1854, Book of overseas consignments of stock-monetary value and account (University of Glasgow Archives, UGD91/1/5/5), p. 21.

as advances to the manufacturing interests. The system of advances was particularly significant to those in Glasgow. According to George G. de H. Larpent's testimony before the Select Committee on Manufactures, Commerce and Shipping:

> ... a very large proportion, probably to the extent of three-fourths, is conducted in that manner [advance by agency houses to manufacturers]... I believe from what I have seen of our own operation, that taking advances is not the system there [Manchester] to any considerable extent; at the same time, I believe that their shipments have not been upon so large a scale as the Glasgow ones.[36]

It is difficult to ascertain whether or not all members of the association who were involved in the cotton textile industry actually consigned their goods to the East. Nevertheless, there is some evidence of the involvement of the members of the association in trade to the East Indies. One of these manufacturing firms in Glasgow was Ellis, Bleaymire & Co. Septimus Ellis and William Bleaymire, both members of the Glasgow EIA, were among its partners. The firm, which was liquidated in the early 1830s, manufactured cotton goods at a Bankton mill and exported them to Calcutta, Bombay, and Singapore, as well as to Lima and Trinidad.[37] Another example was the firm of Archibald McIndoe & Co., merchants and calico printers, in which Archibald McIndoe and Francis Brand were partners, as Appendix III shows. The bankruptcy records of the firm of 1836 include information on the consignment of its shawls and handkerchiefs to Canton and the location of the firm's supposed creditors in Singapore, Calcutta, and Batavia, which indicated the firm's large engagement in the East India trade.[38] A. & J. Connell, which manufactured cotton and linen goods at a factory in Anderston, also consigned its goods to agents in London and Liverpool for export to the East.[39] Such evidence supports Webster's emphasis on Scottish manufacturers' connection with the London agency houses. He referred to Thomas Speir and his brother Robert, who were partners in the manufacturing firm of R. & T. Speirs. Robert was an original member of the Glasgow EIA, and the brothers held a close connection with the London-based agency house, Cockerell, Trail & Co., which engaged extensively in the East India trade.[40] In addition, Appendix III shows that

---

36 Parliamentary Papers, *Minutes of Evidence before the Select Committee of the House of Commons on Manufactures, Commerce and Shipping*, 1833, Vol. VI, p. 142.

37 Scottish Record Office, *Court of Session Productions c.1760–1840*, c.1987, p. 461.

38 Ibid., p. 502.

39 Ibid., p. 503.

40 Webster, "The Strategies and Limits of Gentlemanly Capitalism", pp. 14–5.

thirteen members of the association who registered as 'foreign merchants' with Merchants' House engaged in manufacturing businesses. It is likely that they were also involved in the East India and other foreign trade.

In consequence, the list of the re-established Glasgow EIA's subscribers indicates that the organisation represented the city's various economic interest groups, which reflected the contemporary Glasgow economy based on foreign trade and manufacturing. This was similar to the previous association's characteristics. Nevertheless, whilst the activities of Glasgow's foreign merchants and shipping interests that subscribed to the Glasgow EIA's membership were not confined to the East Indies but extended to various countries and regions, the West Indian interests, which had played a major role in the previous campaign, became a minor factor in the re-established association. Meanwhile, among the manufacturing interests in the Glasgow EIA, the cotton manufacturing interests and their nexus occupied the most significant position. Before 1814, goods produced by Glasgow's manufacturers may have been exported by the EIC or in the limited cargo space allocated to private merchants. After the opening of the India trade many manufacturing interests in Glasgow developed the trading pattern of consigning goods to the East Indies through the agency houses. As a result, whilst the East India trade became more significant to Glasgow's manufacturing interests than it had been in any previous period, as Webster argued, this also created a connection between the provincial manufacturing interests and the mercantile interests in London. Therefore, the presence of a large number of such manufacturing interests implies that there was a connection between the Glasgow EIA and a part of London's mercantile society.

In political terms members of the Glasgow EIA held significant positions in the local council, as they had done in 1812 and 1813. Appendix IV shows that during the free trade campaign all Lord Provosts (Alexander Garden, Robert Dalglish, and James Ewing) were members of the association. Moreover, members of the association occupied many positions in the Merchants' House. That is to say, 7 of the 15 baillies and approximately half of all councillors elected from the Merchants' House were Glasgow EIA members. A large number of the Glasgow EIA's members served on the Magistrates and Town Council, which enabled the association to obtain the local authority's support easily. For instance, to determine the propriety of sending a petition to Parliament, the members called a public meeting in the name of the Chief Magistrate on 5 May 1829.[41] Consequently, the

[41] *Glasgow Herald*, 8 May 1829.

petition sent from Glasgow would be claimed to represent the wish of all Glasgow inhabitants rather than that of the particular interest group.

The influence of the Glasgow EIA's members was not limited to local politics. As will be explained later, the association succeeded in having representatives in Parliament as a result of the victories of James Oswald and James Ewing in the general election of 1832, as Kirkman Finlay had done during the 1812–13 campaign. The strong support of the local authority and the city's MPs, who were involved in national politics, helped the association organise its lobbying activities effectively.

The Lobbying Activities of the Glasgow EIA from 1829–33

From 1829 to 1833, the Glasgow EIA employed similar means to those of the previous movement to promote its free trade arguments. Among the different lobbying activities, this section will explore its subscription activities and its use of letters, printed circulars, and pamphlets. The next section will analyse the activities of the Glasgow EIA's deputation in London in collaborating with other East India associations and their supporters.

The Achilles heel of the previous Glasgow EIA's lobbying activities in opposition to the renewal of the EIC's Charter was its financial resources since it was largely dependent on voluntary subscriptions from the public. In contrast, the financial resources of the free trade movement from 1829 to 1833 came mostly from the entry and annual subscriptions of its membership, plus a general fund raised for "the especial purpose of opposing the renewal of the EIC's Charter".[42]

To raise the general fund for its lobbying activities, the association collected an entry subscription of five guineas from new members, as well as an annual subscription of half a guinea from all existing members.[43] At the end of March 1830, 137 members were counted as members of the association.[44] Based on the number of members the association must have raised £719.5s. from the entry subscriptions in the first year. From the entry subscriptions the sum of 300 guineas was transferred to a general fund set up for "the especial purpose of opposing the renewal of the East India Charter".[45] By the time of the first Annual General Meeting, the amount of

42 Committee Minute Book 1829–47, 9 February 1830, p. 22.

43 Ibid., p. 2 and 6 May 1829, p. 6.

44 Ibid., 25 March 1830, "Report from the Committee of the Glasgow East India Association", p. 32.

45 Ibid., 10 February 1830, p. 23.

subscriptions reached approximately £1,500, and during this meeting the attendees also raised "a considerable sum".[46] With such resources, the Glasgow EIA could afford nearly every year to send a deputation to London, whose large expenses were paid from the fund. In July 1830, a meeting of the subscribers to this fund approved the use of £300 of it to defray some of the expenses for the return of W.W. Whitmore, one of the most active free trade supporters, to the House of Commons. Clearly, the association was able to procure enough subscription money to maintain its lobbying activities.[47] In general, the Glasgow EIA's subscription campaign went relatively well, securing stable financial sources. This reflected its membership of gentlemen, who were willing to pay the entry and annual subscriptions with a clear sense of purpose.

As the free trade interests of Glasgow had done in the previous movement, the Glasgow EIA employed a number of letters, circulars, and pamphlets as its main vehicles to lobby against the renewal of the EIC's exclusive Charter. To exchange information and opinions, the Glasgow EIA regularly communicated by letter with provincial manufacturing towns and outports in England, particularly with Liverpool, and less frequently with Newcastle, Manchester, and so on. As the centre of the free trade movement in Scotland one of the main tasks of the organisation at this time was again to stir up the public opinion of other Scottish towns against the EIC.

In early 1830, the Liverpool EIA urged provincial manufacturing towns and outports to send petitions to Parliament so that Parliament might be prepared to give a three-year advance notice to the Company at the earliest possible time in 1831.[48] Following strong advice from Liverpool the Glasgow EIA decided to petition Parliament and to persuade the authorities of other Scottish towns to do so by exploiting the personal connections of individual members. For this purpose, the following members agreed to undertake this task: J. Buchanan of Dowanhill (to Perth, Port Glasgow, and Dundee), J.A. Anderson (to Greenock), J. Davidson (to Stirling), J. Muir (to Hamilton), J. Wright (to Lanark), R. Gray (to Dumbarton and Rutherglen), W. Graham (to Dumfries), and J. Fleming (to Montrose, Banff, and

[46] Ibid., 25 March 1830, p. 34; *Glasgow Herald*, 26 March 1830.

[47] *Glasgow Courier*, 29 July 1830, "East India Meeting".

[48] Records of the Glasgow East India Association, Correspondence Incoming 1829–1830 (MS 891001/4, Glasgow Mitchell Library), 21 January 1830, letter no. 26. According to the enactment, the EIC's Charter could not be terminated before 11 April 1834, and to terminate its Charter, three-year notice was required. Therefore, giving notice to the Company on 10 April 1831 was most favorable to the free trade advocates.

Stonehaven).[49] Furthermore, in April 1830 J. Buchanan, J.G. Hamilton, and A.G. Speirs agreed to use their connections to convince the Counties of Dumbarton, Renfrew, and Lanark to petition.[50]

Among the three counties mentioned above, in the case of the County of Renfrew, the association used its close connection with free trade interests in Greenock. The County of Renfrew decided to hold a public meeting on 24 April to consider the propriety of petitioning Parliament about the China trade.[51] In this meeting Mr. Bayne, one of the Magistrates of Greenock, and Mr. Speirs put forward a motion to prepare a petition and transmit it to Parliament. Eventually, this motion was passed, and a petition was prepared and submitted to Parliament.[52] In the case of the County of Lanark, the Glasgow EIA arranged an interview with Lord Belhaven, the Convener of the County of Lanark, on the subject of petitioning Parliament. Although I was unable to find any records of this meeting, the result of the meeting between the representatives and the Convener must have been favourable to the association because the monopoly of the EIC was eventually discussed in the general annual meeting of the Commissioners of Supply for the county, and thereupon it was resolved to petition both Houses of Parliament.[53] For the County of Dumbarton, James Buchanan of Dowanhill made contact with his friend, Mr. Dennistoun of Dennistoun, in April 1830.[54] Dennistoun replied to him that he and his friends would make their best efforts to bring the subject of petitioning Parliament before the annual meeting of the County of Dumbarton at the end of April 1830.[55] At the same time, Dennistoun advised Buchanan to suggest that the deputy chairman or the secretary of the Glasgow EIA send a letter to Sir James Colquhoun, the Convener of the county, to address him on the matter.[56] Eventually, the association received a "favourable letter" from Colquhoun.[57] Although the County of Dumbarton did not send its petitions to Parliament, the association's efforts succeeded in urging the merchants and manufacturers of the

---

49 Committee Minute Book 1829–47, 25 February 1830, p. 27 and 2 March 1830, p. 28.

50 Ibid., 7 April 1830, p. 40; Renfrew County Council Commissioners of Supply Minutes 1819–1830 (CO2/1/5, Glasgow City Archives), No. 13, 24 April 1830.

51 *Glasgow Courier*, 27 April 1830.

52 Journal of the House of Commons, Sess. 1830, p. 472.

53 Lanark County Council, Commissioners of Supply Minutes (CO1/1/13, Glasgow City Archives) 30 April 1825 to 30 April 1835, No.13, 30 April 1830.

54 Incoming Correspondence 1829–30, 13 April 1830, letter no. 78.

55 Ibid.

56 Ibid.

57 Records of the Glasgow East India Association, Correspondence Outgoing 1829–1836 (MS 891001/13), 19 April 1830.

county to pay attention to this subject and to appoint a committee to "watch over the proceedings of Parliament".[58]

In addition, while J. Buchanan was negotiating with members of the County of Dumbarton, the latter suggested to him that the Glasgow EIA should contact not only the Convener of the County of Dumbarton but also that of every county in Scotland.[59] In a special meeting of the directors of the association held on 15 April, they fully discussed the propriety of this proposal but rejected the advice.[60] Although the details of the discussion were not recorded, due to the geographical adjacency of Glasgow and the three counties and the economic and personal connections between them, they thought that it would be more efficient and effective to confine their efforts to these three counties. Among a number of petitions against the EIC's monopoly sent to the House of Commons, its Journal of 1830 recorded no petitions from Scottish counties except from the Counties of Renfrew and Lanark.

In consequence, the Glasgow EIA's communications with other Scottish towns and counties reveal the existence of the provincial lobbyists' network in Scotland based on their personal connections during the free trade campaign of 1829–33. The Liverpool EIA's advice on petitioning Parliament was spread to other Scottish towns through the Glasgow EIA. The association was a hub of Scotland's free trade movement. This section shows examples of how effectively the organisation persuaded its neighbours to join the campaign. Although the Glasgow EIA might have missed an opportunity to mobilise more support from distant counties, the association was able to exercise its influence on neighbouring counties.

Between 1829 and 1833, the provincial lobbyists employed newspapers, printed circulars, and pamphlets to exchange information and ideas with other associations all over the United Kingdom and to rouse public opinion. In general, the association used newspapers and circulars to provide other lobbying groups and the public with information about the proceedings and important resolutions of special and monthly meetings of the Glasgow EIA's directors and of public meetings held by the Glasgow citizens on the opening of the East India Trade. Conversely, the association received a number of circulars and pamphlets from other EIAs, especially the Liverpool EIA, often to redistribute them all over Scotland. For instance, in January 1830 the association received 250 copies each of the resolutions

58 Committee Minute Book 1829–47, 20 May 1830, p. 42.
59 Incoming Correspondence 1829–30, 13 April 1830, letter no. 78.
60 Committee Minute Book 1829–47, 15 April 1830, p. 41.

of the Liverpool Committee, passed on 18 January 1830, of a statement of the reasons favouring the complete free trade with India and free settlement there as well as the opening of the China trade, and of the funds and financing of the EIC for the purpose of its use.[61] In addition, newspapers were employed for the purpose of advertising public meetings to the inhabitants of the city in advance, and pamphlets were distributed by the association.

Although Philips explained in his work that the provincial lobbyists' pamphlet campaign during this period was not comparable in size, virulence, and effectiveness to that of 1812–13, it was still one of the most important vehicles for the free trade interests to express their ideas to the public.[62] Although in Britain several authors produced pamphlets, in which they criticised the economic and political systems operating under the Company's Charter, the contribution of John Crawfurd to the free trade movement of this period was most remarkable, and the publication and distribution of his pamphlets were fully supported by the Glasgow EIA and other associations.

John Crawfurd was a famous Scottish Orientalist who had originally been employed in a medical post in the Indian Army by the EIC and then resided in several places in India and Southeast Asia, including India's Northern Provinces, Penang, Java, Siam, Cochin-China, Singapore, and Burma before returning to England in 1827.[63] In spite of his long service to the Company he was a strong advocate of free trade in the East Indies. For instance, when he was a resident of Singapore from 1823 to 1826, he contributed significantly to the negotiations for a treaty with the Malay rulers to secure Britain's permanent possession of Singapore in 1824, which Webster called the "products of an attempt to bolster the Bengal export economy [which the agency houses and other British private merchants dominated]".[64] After returning to his homeland, Crawfurd put himself at the centre of the free trade movement and criticised the EIC's privileges in the trade with the East Indies. As his career shows, Crawfurd did not have

---

61 Committee Minute Book 1829–47, 27 January 1830, p. 20.

62 Philips, *The East India Company*, pp. 288–9; Charlton, "Liverpool and the East India Trade", pp. 55–72; Greenberg, *British Trade and the Opening of China*, p. 289.

63 E.C.T. Chew, "Dr. John Crawfurd (1783–1868): The Scotsman Who Made Singapore British" [http://www.scholars.nus.edu.sg/landow/post/singapore/history/chew/chew11.html, accessed 10 May 2005]; K.N. Chaudhuri, *The Economic Development of India under the East India Company 1814–58*, 1971, p. 15.

64 Ibid.; A. Webster, "British Export Interests in Bengal and Imperial Expansion into South-east Asia, 1780 to 1824", in B. Ingham and C. Simmons (eds.), *Development Studies and Colonial Policy*, 1987, Chap. 4, p. 167.

significant commercial interests in the East India trade but was a philosophical challenger of the Company. He had a racial view of European superiority and believed that the introduction of free trade and colonisation by the British could aid the progress of civilisation in the East Indies.[65] In the General Deputation lobbying in London, he acted as a representative of the free trade interests in Calcutta, which paid his annual salary of £1,500.[66]

Originally, his instructions from Calcutta were concerned mainly with political aspects of the Company's affairs. Nevertheless, when he was called to the Select Committee for the investigation of the China trade in 1830, he expressed in regard to the interests of the inhabitants of Calcutta that:

> I have no recollection whatever of any mention being made in my instructions, public or confidential, of the China question; but I have no doubt that the China question is also embraced in them.[67]

Furthermore, the records of the British merchants of Calcutta show their interest in the commercial aspect of the renewal of the Company's Charter. On 15 December 1829, according to a request of 114 British and native inhabitants to James Calder, the Sheriff of Calcutta, the town held a public meeting "for the purpose of petitioning Parliament to throw open the China and India Trade, and to prove, on the expiration of the existing Charter of the East India Company, for the unfettered application of British skill, capital and industry, to the commercial and agricultural resource of India".[68] Although for British private traders in India the equalisation of duties on East Indian and West Indian sugar was more significant than it was for some free trade supporters in the United Kingdom, particularly those of manufacturing towns, these two groups had the same main purposes in their lobbying—that is, the opening of the China trade and the removal of legal restrictions on the residence of British subjects and their acquisition of land. In this General Meeting, they decided to prepare petitions to both Houses of Parliament and transmit them to J. Crawfurd, their "general agent", to deliver the petitions to the important Parliamentary members.[69]

---

65 For information on his racial view of European superiority, see J. Crawfurd, *History of Indian Archipelago*, 1820 and *Journal of an Embassy from the Governor-General of India to the Court of Siam and Cochin China Exhibiting a View of the Actual State of Those Kingdoms*, 1828.

66 Incoming Correspondence 1829–30, 15 May 1829, letter no. 9; *Report of Select Committee on the Affairs of the East India Company and the Trade between Great Britain and the East Indies and China 1830*, 1970, pp. 295–312.

67 Ibid.

68 *Report of the Proceedings at a General Meeting of the Inhabitants of Calcutta, on the 15 December, 1829*, c.1829.

69 Ibid.

In June 1829, the Central Committee on the East India and China Trade, which had been set up in Liverpool, decided to publish Crawfurd's pamphlet, *A View of the Present State and Future Prospects of the Free Trade and Colonisation of India*, and 5,000 copies were distributed to Liverpool, Manchester, Glasgow, Bristol, Birmingham, Leeds, and Crawfurd himself.[70] 500 copies were allocated to the Glasgow EIA at an expense of £25, and 200 of them were distributed to the city's major booksellers.[71] To promote its sale, advertisements for this pamphlet were inserted in various newspapers, and some of the remaining copies were forwarded to other Scottish towns and ports, such as Paisley and Greenock.

In this pamphlet, Crawfurd argued that:

> A thorough freedom of commercial intercourse between the European and Indian dominion of the Crown, and an unrestricted settlement of Englishmen in India, are the grand and essential instruments for improving our Eastern Colonies, and rendering them useful to the mother country.[72]

After his brief descriptions of the growth of free trade and the stagnant condition of the Company's trade with India after the opening of the India trade in 1814, Crawfurd gave several examples of the "evil effects of the existing system" by analysing the staple articles of trade between the United Kingdom and India.[73] For example, he argued that the value of woollen exports from Britain to India and China by the EIC declined by 49 per cent from £1,064,222 in 1814 to £539,732 in 1827, although his claim was actually exaggerated because the figures he quoted were in nominal values.[74] According to Davis's calculation, the real price of woollens went down by about 25 per cent between 1814–16 and 1824–26, due to technological improvements and higher productivity in the industry.[75] Therefore, in terms of volume, the decline of woollen exports by the Company seems to have been less significant than Crawfurd argued. Nevertheless, free trade supporters expected that a potentially larger demand for British woollens existed in China, especially the northern part, than in India and Southeast Asia because of its cooler and drier climate. Crawfurd argued that this inability of the Company to supply its woollen products to China provided

70 Incoming Correspondence 1829–30, 13 June 1829, letter no. 13.

71 Committee Minute Book 1829–47, 20 August 1829.

72 J. Crawfurd, *A View of the Present State and Future Prospects of the Free Trade & Colonization of India*, 1829, p. 1.

73 Ibid., p. 6.

74 Ibid., p. 8

75 R. Davis, *The Industrial Revolution and British Overseas Trade*, 1979, p. 23.

commercial rivals with the opportunity to deprive the British of their market.[76]

Another example was the production of cotton wool in British India. Of the average annual consumption of cotton wool of 198 million lbs. in the United Kingdom in 1827 and 1828, 142 million lbs. were imported from the United States, while only 12 million lbs. came from India.[77] Crawfurd criticised the dependence of British manufacturers on staple goods from a rival country and stressed the necessity of substituting India for the United States as a stable supplier of raw cotton. He concluded that the introduction of European skills, enterprise, and capital to India was the chief remedy for this unfavourable situation and blamed the inability of many Indian commercial crops, with their inferior quality, to compete with the products of other countries in the international markets under the existing regulations, which prevented the British from holding lands in India and investing capital freely.[78] In 1833, the Glasgow EIA showed further support to Crawfurd; a special meeting of the association decided to have 600 copies of Crawfurd's work, *Notes on the Settlement or Colonization of British Subjects in India*, which had been sent to Charles Grant, the President of the Board of Control, printed at its expense.[79]

Crawfurd also took a critical attitude towards the state of the Company's monopoly in the China trade. In another work, *Chinese Monopoly Examined*, for instance, he compared the EIC's sales price of tea with the American sales price and claimed that British subjects had been paying nearly twice as much as those who had purchased in the American market from 1819 to 1829. In other words, they made unnecessary payments totalling over £1.7 million to the Company per annum during the period.[80]

For the opposition to the EIC Crawfurd's extensive knowledge of the East Indies and experience there were invaluable. We can see his deep involvement in the free trade movement of this period and strong influence on it in a number of the communications with the Glasgow EIA. Nevertheless, his significant contribution to the provincial merchants and manufacturers' lobbying for the abolition of the EIC's monopoly has received little

[76] Crawfurd, *A View of the Present State*, p. 8.

[77] Ibid., p. 26.

[78] Ibid., p. 40. During this period, British subjects were permitted to hold land only in the towns of Calcutta, Madras, Bombay, Prince of Wales's Island (Pulo Penang), Singapore, and Malacca.

[79] Although the Special Meeting decided to publish 600 copies, the account of the Association indicates that 200 copies were actually printed at an expense of £26.5s. in 1833.

[80] J. Crawfurd, *China Monopoly Examined*, 1830, p. 87.

attention from historians compared with his activities in Southeast Asia. Glasgow's lobbyists' outgoing and incoming correspondence reveals that, apart from its members and the Liverpool EIA, Crawfurd was the person with whom the Glasgow EIA communicated most frequently during the debates over the renewal of the EIC's Charter. This Scottish man played a significant role in the formation of the provincial interests' lobbying strategies.

During the campaign, while Crawfurd was very favourably regarded by members of the Glasgow EIA, the association showed a different attitude towards James Silk Buckingham, another famous Orientalist at that time, who was the editor of such journals as *The Oriental Herald* and *The New Quarterly Review*. Philips described him as one of the most influential free trade advocates for provincial manufacturing towns and outports during the period. However, he actually failed to obtain full support from the Glasgow EIA, although his lectures were warmly welcomed by the public in the city and many other places in Scotland.[81] The association's minute book and its correspondence with James Silk Buckingham show that they had different opinions regarding the abolition of the EIC's administrative functions.

After years of international travel, Buckingham settled in Calcutta and established the *Calcutta Journal*. His fierce criticism of the EIC in the paper eventually resulted in his exclusion from India by the Company in 1823.[82] After his return to England, he continued to speak out against the Company in his publications and his lectures. In January 1829, Buckingham started his lecturing tour and went all over Britain in the next three years. On 2 August, he arrived in Glasgow and began his lectures the next day.[83] The appearance of a series of his lectures in local newspapers and two extra lectures that he held showed his popularity in Glasgow.[84] Nevertheless, the majority of the members of the Glasgow EIA considered it unnecessary to support him as the association, although it did subscribe to *The Oriental Herald*, of which Buckingham was an editor.[85] On the one hand, some members of the association supported Buckingham. For instance, A.G. Speirs and Laurence Hill attended his lectures and praised him.[86] On the

---

81 Philips, *The East India Company*, p. 289.

82 Ibid.

83 J.S. Buckingham, *History of the Public Proceeding on the Question of the East India Monopoly*, 1830, p. 31.

84 *Glasgow Herald*, 10, 13, and 24 August 1829; *Glasgow Courier*, 8, 11 and 15 August 1829.

85 Committee Minute Book 1829–47, 16 July 1829, p. 15.

86 *Glasgow Herald*, 10 August 1829, "Mr Buckingham's Lectures".

other hand, other members of the association, such as Finlay, did not think so highly of him. Finlay described him as follows:

> Mr. Buckingham who is beyond all compassion, the most confident and impudent Charlatan that has ever appeared in this Country. At the same time I think he has been of some use by enlisting many of the most noisy and ignorant in the [?] and we should not act wisely if we rejected their aid because they are brought forward by a selfish, vain and vengeful Pretender ... I shall myself take his Review although I believe that like all his other publications, it will not contain much that is valuable and bring little that can be depended on.[87]

In November 1829, Buckingham informed the Glasgow EIA of the launch of his new journal, *The New Quarterly Review*, and asked the members to support the promotion of its sales. He proposed to the association his plan to reduce the posting costs of his journals by sending a packet of letters to each of the EIAs across the country, from which they could deliver the journals to their immediate neighbouring areas.[88] The members of the association rejected this proposal, as they told him that they thought it was proper to avoid entangling their activities as the associated body with those of any private individuals if they were not supported by the Central Committee in Liverpool.[89] More importantly, on the instructions of Finlay, the secretary to the Glasgow EIA wrote to him that:

> ... your objects and those of the Assoc[iatio]n cannot be made a common course of. You are opposed to the East India Comp[an]y. The Assoc[iatio]n merely object to their Monopoly, you deprecated the Government of the Comp[an]y & the mode of its administration in India. The Assoc[iatio]n meddle not at all with the Government, neither praising nor condemning it, objecting merely to its union of Sovereign and Mercantile character and to its exclusive rights...[90]

This reply clearly reflected the personal opinion of Finlay, as his correspondence with the secretary shows.[91] His view was supported by the majority of the members of the Glasgow EIA.[92] Whilst Buckingham was interested in the political aspects of the East India question, the association showed little concern about it. Buckingham strongly criticised this attitude of the Glasgow EIA towards the debates over the renewal of the EIC's Charter.

87 Incoming Correspondence 1829–30, 25 November 1829, letter no. 25.
88 Ibid., 17 November 1829. letter no. 21.
89 Outgoing Correspondence 1829–36, 4 December 1829, letter no. 9.
90 Ibid.
91 Incoming Correspondence 1829–30, 25 November 1829, letter no. 25.
92 Buckingham, *The Question of the East India Monopoly*, p. 31.

He called the intention of the association an "imagined modification" and argued that:

> The leaders in this Association were gentlemen who seemed to think it quite possible to carry the measure of opening the trade to India and China, and entirely destroy the exclusive commercial Monopoly, and yet leave the Government of India in the hands of the East India Company. They were for Free Trade only, but not for Colonization; as if it were possible for the benefit of the one to be fully reaped without the admission of the other; and they were for taking away the trading character of the India Company only, and leaving them all the revenues, patronage, and political power they possess; as if it had not been shewn, beyond all possibility of doubt, that the latter could not be supported by them at all, without profits derived from their Monopoly on Tea; and that on this issue they must all stand or fall together.[93]

It is clear that the Glasgow EIA had a different attitude towards the two celebrated Orientalists. On the one hand, the association gave its full support to publishing Crawfurd's pamphlets and distributing them to Glasgow and its neighbourhoods. This was due largely to Crawfurd's personal influence on the provincial lobbying groups. His deep knowledge of the East Indies, his experience there, and his analysis and arguments for the complete abolition of the EIC's monopoly in the East India trade and for general free trade led him to establish his firm position in the free trade movement. On the other hand, although Philips and Eyles stress Buckingham's contribution to the provincial mercantile and manufacturing interests' free trade movement, in fact, he failed to obtain the Glasgow EIA's full support because of the members' different views on how they should treat an issue over the administrative function in India in their free trade campaign, as well as his personal character.[94] Although Buckingham wanted to link the provincial lobbyists' campaign with the EIC's political issues, the Glasgow EIA was not interested in it. With respect to the admiration for Buckingham's personal activities to promote free trade in the East Indies, there was a division between the public and the Glasgow EIA as an associated body in the city. Compared with Crawfurd, who contributed to the provincial interests' lobbying strategies, the significance of Buckingham's role in the free trade movement was that he could stir up public opinion through his popular lecturing tours and publications.

In addition, apart from the publications of John Crawfurd's works, to "enlighten the public as to the complete freedom of the East India trade", the Glasgow EIA obtained some of 1,000 copies of the substance of a speech

93 Ibid.

94 Eyles, "The Abolition of the East India Company's Monopoly 1833", pp. 198–9.

of W.W. Whitmore and distributed them in Glasgow.[95] In March 1831, acting on advice from the Liverpool EIA, the Glasgow EIA also decided to receive from London 500 copies of an article on the China trade, J.R. McCulloch's "Observations on the Influence of the East India Company's Monopoly on the Price and Supply of Tea", from the *Edinburgh Review* and distributed them all over Scotland.[96]

The Glasgow Deputation and the Proceedings of the Debate on the Charter

Following the resolution of the public meeting of 22 April 1829, the Glasgow EIA sent a deputation to London to organise a joint campaign with deputations from other provincial manufacturing towns and outports. The deputation consisted of Alexander Garden and Robert Dalglish; later, Robert Douglass Alston, George Stirling, and James Ewing joined them.[97] From the free trade advocates' viewpoint, the timing of the beginning of their lobbying for the complete opening of the East India and China trade was favourable, as Parliament had not only just finished the Catholic question but the prevailing distress of commercial districts at that time also enabled them to claim the necessity of new overseas markets for British manufactured goods.[98]

On 9 May, by appointment, the General Deputation from provincial manufacturing towns and outports held a conference with the Duke of Wellington at Downing Street, which the Chancellor of the Exchequer (Henry Goulburn) and the President of the Board of Control (the Earl of Ellensborough) also attended.[99] The deputies were supported by their Parliamentary friends, Whitmore and William Huskisson, who helped greatly in securing access to these key figures of national politics. In particular, the latter, who represented Liverpool in Parliament and held the office of the President of the Board of Trade, had a strong influence on the course of British economic policy, which began to adopt free trade gradually in the 1820s.[100]

---

95 Committee Minute Book 1829–47, 16 July 1829, p. 14 and 17 September 1829, p. 17.

96 Ibid., 17 March 1831, p. 56.

97 Ibid., 22 April 1829, p. 2 and 28 April 1829, p. 4.

98 Incoming Correspondence 1829–30, 4 and 5 May 1829, letter no. 2.

99 Ibid., 1829–30, 9 May 1829, letter no. 5.

100 J.B. Williams, *British Commercial Policy and Trade Expansion 1750–1850*, 1972, pp. 451–3.

Prior to the conference, on 6 May, seven gentlemen from Glasgow, Liverpool, and other places held a meeting to agree upon the following points for the agenda of the conference: (1) the abolition of restrictions on the residence of British subjects, and the employment of British capital for products in India, (2) the opening of the China trade to British subjects, and (3) the anticipation of benefit derived from the abolition of the monopoly in the China trade by the reduction in the price of tea.[101] Moreover, they aimed to urge Ministers to agree with their opinion that an enquiry should be made into the East India trade and that a committee should be appointed for this purpose.[102] In the conference between the joint-deputation and the Ministry, the Provost of Glasgow and other deputies from Birmingham, Liverpool, Manchester, and Bristol described the distressing condition of each provincial manufacturing town and outport in detail and urged the necessity of entering new markets in Asia. Then John Gladstone from Liverpool explained the events of 1813 and the positive impact of the partial opening of the East India trade after 1814. The statements of the deputies concluded with James Cropper's argument on the negative effect of the tea monopoly on prices and supplies. Although at the meeting the Duke of Wellington initially avoided giving an immediate answer, the Ministry later decided to establish a Select Committee to consider the renewal of the EIC's Charter.

The provincial lobbyists regarded this decision as a triumph of their lobbying activities. On 15 May, the deputies from the places listed above plus Calcutta gathered at Fenton's Hotel in London.[103] In this meeting, they issued a statement that the strong claims of manufacturing towns and outports essentially contributed to the government's pledge to appoint a Select Committee to investigate the issues related to the East India and China trade at a very early stage in the next Parliamentary session. If one takes into consideration the fact that the Ministry's decision came only a few days after that meeting, the provincial lobbyists' view seems to be right. They also recommended the following points: (1) all provincial cities and towns interested in this subject should send their petitions to both Houses of Parliament at the beginning of the next session; (2) all major places should send deputations to London again during the examination of the Select Committee; and (3) a Central Committee should be set up in London during the time of the examination, and, in the meanwhile, the Liverpool

101 Incoming Correspondence 1829–30, 6 May 1829, letter no. 4.
102 Ibid., 9 May 1829, letter no. 5.
103 Ibid., 15 May 1829, letter no. 9.

EIA should act as the Central Committee for communication with those who were concerned with the subject of the renewal of the EIC's Charter. In Glasgow, the General Deputation's initial achievement and the efforts of Alexander Garden, James Ewing, and Charles Stirling—who had acted as its deputation in London—were applauded by other members of the association upon their return.[104]

However, after the return of the deputation, the Glasgow EIA was not very active for the rest of 1829. On the contrary, it seems that the public expectation of the association in the free trade movement immediately after its foundation was so high that its first-year achievement could not meet the members' expectations. At the first annual general meeting, Finlay expressed dissatisfaction, as he found that some members were criticising the association for its failure to engage in as many activities as might have been expected in 1829, although, at the same time, he positively regarded it as proof of the growth of public interest in the debates over the renewal of the EIC's Charter in the city.[105]

After the interval, the lobbying activities organised by Glasgow and other provincial manufacturing towns and outports followed the recommendations of 15 May 1829. In January 1830, according to communication with the Liverpool Central Committee, the members of the Glasgow EIA agreed to take measures to obtain petitions from the authorities and citizens to Parliament against the renewal of the Charter, and for this purpose, a Sub-Committee "to draw up the petition to Parliament to be submitted to the Public Meeting and to make the necessary arrangement as to that meeting" was appointed.[106] Between February 1830 and 23 July 1830, local authorities and other organisations submitted nearly 190 petitions against the renewal of the Company's Charter to the House of Commons.[107]

On 9 February 1830, following Robert Peel's proposal, the Select Committee was appointed to investigate "the affairs of the Company and the trade between Great Britain and China" in the House of Commons.[108] Its members were selected from several quarters, including the state, the EIC, and provincial mercantile and manufacturing interests. More than 40 witnesses were called to testify before the Select Committee from the Company's side and its opposition. On 11 February, the inhabitants of Glasgow appointed

---

104 Committee Minute Book 1829–47, 16 July 1829, pp. 12–4.

105 *Glasgow Courier*, 27 March 1830.

106 Committee Minute Book 1829–47, 21 and 27 January 1830, pp. 18–20.

107 The number includes petitions from British colonies such as Cape of Good Hope. *Journal of the House of Commons*, Vol. 83, Sess. 1830.

108 *Hansard's Parliamentary Debates*, New Series, Vol. XII, pp. 271–305.

at a public meeting the Lord Provost (Alexander Garden), Kirkman Finlay, and James Oswald to the second deputation to London from the city to provide the Select Committee with the necessary evidence and to arrange the witnesses for them.[109]

One of the main points for the Select Committee was whether or not the present mode of the Company's monopoly in the China trade was advantageous for other British merchants. In the Select Committee, some of the witnesses—mainly British private traders and American merchants who engaged in the trade with China and other parts of the East Indies—insisted that the present system of the China trade based on the EIC's monopoly provided them with no advantage for their trading activities there; rather, they complained about it.[110] In contrast, other witnesses, most of whom were from the Company, insisted that the presence of the Company in the local trade protected British private traders. For example, the influence of the Company prevented the Chinese government from making an attempt to seek to obtain ships itself.[111]

However, the most significant part of the Select Committee's investigation was on the purchase of tea by the EIC in China and the system of importation and sales of tea in Britain. On the one hand, in the Select Committee, many witnesses, including both those who were connected with the Company and some British private and American traders, stated that due to the large and regular purchases in its system of contract the EIC could buy tea, particularly black tea, at a comparative advantage.[112] On the other hand, a group of other British private and American merchants gave evidence that the Company's monopoly in the tea trade led to a very heavy tax upon the public amounting to between around £1 million and £2.6 million per annum.[113] The high prices of tea in Britain were also highlighted in comparison with prices in other European countries and in the United States.[114]

In terms of British exports to China, many witnesses, mainly private traders and Americans, expressed their belief that the opening of the China trade would lead to a large increase in the export of British manufactured

109 Outgoing Correspondence 1829–36, 16 February 1830, letter no. 13.

110 Parliamentary Papers, *Report of the Select Committee on the Affairs of the East India Company and the Trade between Great Britain, the East Indies and China*, 1830 (644), p. viii.

111 Ibid.

112 Ibid., p. xii.

113 Ibid., p. xvii. For example, Joshua Bates estimated that the extra financial burden on the public per annum in the case of monopoly was around £1.5 million; Thomas Thornely, £1.73 million; Robert Rickards, £2.59 million; and John Crawfurd, £0.98 million.

114 Ibid., p. xviii.

products. However, in the Select Committee, James Cosmo Melvill, an auditor of the Company, expressed the view that a large increase in British exports would be restricted by the Company's obligation regarding the significant size of remittance from India to Britain, which, in his opinion, was made advantageously through purchasing Chinese merchandise.[115] Furthermore, Melvill and another Company official argued that the large increase in British exports to India was achieved through fiscal regulations. For example, while the British textile manufacturers' lobbying led the British government to prohibit or to set high rates of restrictive duties on imported cotton and silk manufactured products from India to protect their British counterparts until the 1820s, the system of free trade allowed British manufactured goods to flow into the Indian market. The British held political power in India, but the situation was different in China, where the Chinese governed. Those who had an interest in the EIC insisted that, under the conditions in which British manufacturers did not have an economic advantage deriving from Britain's political dominance of India, exports of British products could not increase significantly after the opening of the China trade.

The Select Committee took a significant amount of time to investigate the question of the opening of the tea trade with China. Kirkman Finlay reported daily on its progress to his home town, and a large amount of the members' early communication was focused on the need to procure adequate witnesses for the provision of evidence related to the China trade. The association also received from the Liverpool EIA a copy of John Crawfurd's letter to ask them to send any witnesses to London prior to the examination of the China trade.[116] The communications between the Glasgow EIA, their deputation in London, and other associations show that the Glasgow EIA had difficulty obtaining witnesses in Scotland because the number of Scottish merchants who had personal experience in Asia, especially in China, was small in spite of the partial opening of the East India trade in 1814. Even when the members of the association found such men, the information that they could provide was sometimes too old. Nevertheless, from Glasgow and other parts of Scotland, in response to the requests from the association, two gentlemen, John Deans of Ayrshire, who had previously resided in the Eastern Archipelago as a merchant and agent for about 20 years, and Mr. Maxwell, living near the city, who had also been engaged in the East India trade as a merchant and commission agent and

[115] Ibid., pp. xx–xxi.
[116] Incoming Correspondence 1829–30, 15 February 1830, letter no. 33.

had experience visiting Singapore, Java, and China, were asked to proceed to London.[117] In the Select Committee, for instance, in response to the question, "Do you believe that tea could be supplied for consumption in this country at two-thirds the price it now bears, if the Company's monopoly no longer existed?", John Deans replied that the price would be lower, particularly if the British could pay with manufactured goods through free trade.[118] He supported the advantages of the abolition of the tea monopoly. Furthermore, Deans supported the possible increase in the Chinese imports of British manufactured goods after the abolition of the EIC's monopoly. He believed that the British manufacturers would imitate the tastes of the Chinese and increase the consumption of their products, although it would take time.[119]

To compensate for having only these two witnesses from Glasgow and neighbouring areas, the directors of the Glasgow EIA suggested to Finlay in London some merchants who resided there as potential witnesses.[120] Among the witnesses called to the Select Committee during this period, Joshua Bates of the house of Baring, Brothers & Co. and Charles Everett, both American commission merchants engaged in the China trade, were on the list of possible witnesses that Finlay received from the association. Bates was probably a familiar face among the cotton manufacturing interests in the provincial towns because Baring, Brothers & Co. supplied American raw cotton to them as a part of their engagement in the North Atlantic trade.[121] The words of Bates, who established a very respectable status in the British mercantile community, had more weight than those of many others.[122] After his two examinations by the House of Commons on 15 and 30 March, Finlay sent a letter to Bates to try to persuade him to refute remarks made by James Cosmo Melvill before the Select Committee.[123] Initially, Bates could not decide whether or not to do so. He stated in his letter to Alexander Baring, "I fear to be mixed up in the affair with the

[117] Ibid., 24 February 1830, letter no. 18; *Report of Select Committee*, 1830, pp. 233–44 and pp. 245–53.

[118] Ibid., p. 240.

[119] Ibid., p. 244.

[120] Committee Minute Book 1829–47, 22 February 1830, p. 26.

[121] J. Orbell, Baring *Brothers & Co., Limited. A History to 1939*, 1985, Chap. 5.

[122] Outgoing Correspondence 1829–36, 19 March 1830, letter no. 29.

[123] Parliamentary Papers, *First Report from the Select Committee of the House of Commons on the Affairs of the East-India Company, China Trade*, 1830 (644), pp. 218–33 and pp. 329–32; Baring Archive 209803, 17 March 1830, Letter from Joshua Bates to Alexander Barings, giving details of evidence requested by the Committee.

friends of free trade, most of whom differ from me".[124] Nevertheless, eventually he ended up reappearing before the Select Committee on 3 June.[125] Furthermore, the Glasgow EIA's correspondence indicates that the provincial mercantile and manufacturing interests communicated with the partner of the famous house throughout the campaign, although the details of their meetings were not recorded.[126]

Regarding the previous free trade campaigns, I have found few connections between the provincial manufacturing towns and outports and the London East India houses, although some provincial manufacturing interest groups that traditionally provided the EIC with commodities for export supported the renewal of the Company's Charter. As Webster argued, after the opening of the India trade, some London East India houses developed closer relationships with the provincial interests by consigning their products to the East Indies and providing them with financial advances.[127] As a consequence, these two metropolitan and provincial groups could share more interests and collaborate more easily in lobbying for free access to the Asian markets than previously. Eyles very briefly pointed out the collaboration between the London interests and the provincial lobbyists in his thesis. He described the establishment of a free trade committee called the "Association for Colonization to India, and Free Trade to China" in London in 1828 and F. Ferguson's visit to Liverpool in October of the same year on behalf of the committee to give information on the renewal of the Charter to the free trade interests of the city.[128] Detailed information on this association is not available, but based on his reference to his petitioning the Treasury for the importation of tea from Holland, this committee was surely connected to the private trading interests of London.[129] Communication between the provincial lobbyists and Joshua Bates gives further evidence of the connection between the province and the metropolis.

In addition, Abel Coffin, whom the Secretary of the association recommended as a witness to Crawfurd because of his experience commanding a ship in the China trade three times, gave evidence.[130] The Report of the

---

124 Ibid.

125 Parliamentary Papers, *First Report from the Select Committee*, pp. 497–500.

126 Records of the Glasgow East India Association, Correspondence Incoming 1833–1834 (MS 891001/6, Glasgow Mitchell Library), 22 April 1833, letter no. 37 and 27 April 1833, letter no. 38.

127 Webster, "The Strategies and Limits of Gentlemanly Capitalism", pp. 747–8.

128 Eyles, "The Abolition of the East India Company's Monopoly 1833", pp. 171–2; *Liverpool Mercury*, 10 October and 12 December 1828.

129 Ibid.

130 Outgoing Correspondence 1829–36, 19 February 1830; *Report of Select Committee*, 1830, pp. 115–31.

Select Committee revealed that many of the witnesses expected that the consumption of British goods would increase as a result of the opening of the China trade. This was based upon the experience of the export of British goods to China by American merchants, as well as the large increase in British exports to India after the opening of the India trade.[131]

As one of the deputies from Glasgow and the Chairman of the General Deputation in London, Kirkman Finlay's effort to negotiate with other deputies, parliamentary members, and other individuals concerned with this subject, to look for witnesses and to provide the necessary evidence to the Select Committee during the period were considerable. After his return to Glasgow, the members of the association showed their gratitude.[132] Finlay's efforts in this free trade campaign can perhaps be compared with Charlton's account of James Cropper's leadership of the Liverpool EIA at that time. His leading position in the General Deputation symbolised the significant role of the Glasgow EIA in the national movement.

Although the investigation of the China question by the Select Committee had ended, the Glasgow EIA continued its efforts in support of the complete opening of the East India trade. During John Crawfurd's visit to Glasgow in September, he insisted that Glasgow should continue to petition Parliament from session to session until it achieved its ultimate objective.[133] In November, when Grey's government replaced Wellington's, the association began to prepare new petitions to Parliament and further lobbying activities in London, although Charles Grant, who became the new President of the Board of Control, told the Chairs of the EIC that the China monopoly was to cease.[134] As a result of its communication with the Liverpool EIA and following the example set by Liverpool, in a monthly meeting held on 20 January, the directors of the Glasgow EIA set up a subcommittee to prepare a draft of resolutions as the foundation of the petitions. They also agreed to send Oswald, Garden, and Henry Dunlop as their deputies as soon as they could to "bring prominently to the notice of the Ministry the importance of a Free Trade to India & China" in conjunction with the representatives from Merseyside.[135] The deputation left Glasgow to arrive in London in time for the joint-deputation's interview with Earl Grey on 5 February, but because of a snowstorm, their arrival was delayed

[131] *Report from the Select Committee of the House of Commons on the Affairs of the East-India Company. China Trade*, 1830, p. 47.

[132] Committee Minute Book 1829–47, 21 July 1830, p. 46.

[133] Ibid., 10 September 1830, p. 48.

[134] Philips, *The East India Company*, p. 289.

[135] Committee Minute Book 1829–47, 20 and 25 January 1831, pp. 51–2.

and they missed Grey's personal invitation.[136] However, the House of Commons had appointed a Select Committee to examine the Indian branch of the question on the previous day. In this examination, J. Crawfurd and some of those who engaged in the East India trade, such as Mr. Bracken of the house of Alexander & Co., one of the seven major agency houses in Calcutta before the financial crisis of the early 1830s, gave evidence.[137] The association expected most of these witnesses' evidence to support free trade with India.[138]

However, the question of the renewal of the EIC's Charter failed to attract wider attention in the country because the debates on the Reform Bills dominated national politics. According to Philips, the Select Committee's reports could not give a clear guide on the India Bill to the government, which could also not afford time to consider the question of the administration of British India.[139] During the time of the heated debates on the Reform Bills in early 1832, the Glasgow EIA communicated with Liverpool and Crawfurd with respect to the propriety of their opposition to the Charter's renewal.[140] The members of the association insisted that they should continue to make public demonstrations until the Reform question was settled. Nevertheless, after their communications, the Glasgow EIA decided to suspend its appeals to the Ministry for a while and not to send a deputation to London that year.[141]

Apart from the Charter renewal, other subjects related to free trade were debated during this period. These included the heavy duties incurred on British goods in Java, the Netherlands' India, and the objection against the exclusion of the American traders from Singapore. This confirms Webster's explanation that the British manufacturing interests related to Southeast Asia found their political voice through the EIAs.[142] The Glasgow EIA's lobbying activities on these issues emphasised the strong influence of Crawfurd's opinion on these subjects. During the special meeting of the association's directors with Crawfurd, the members agreed to send the

[136] Ibid., 12 February 1831, pp. 53–4.

[137] Ibid., "The Second Annual Report of the Committee of the Glasgow East India Association Submitted to the Minutes", 31 March 1831, p. 60; Philips, *The East India Company*, p. 278.

[138] Committee Minute Book 1829–47, "The Second Annual Report", p. 61.

[139] Ibid.; Philips, *The East India Company*, pp. 289–90.

[140] Outgoing Correspondence 1829–36, 5 February 1832, letter no. 62 and 9 February 1832, letter no. 63; Committee Minute Book 1829–47, 16 February 1832, p. 68.

[141] Outgoing Correspondence 1829–36, letter no. 62; Committee Minute Book 1829–47, 16 February 1832 and 29 March 1832.

[142] Webster, *Gentlemen Capitalists*, p. 117.

Secretary of State for Foreign Affairs memorials on the heavy duties on British goods in Java and on their desire to open the port of Singapore to the Americans.[143] Regarding the question of Singapore, the association insisted that the restrictions, which excluded Americans from Singapore, prevented the port from playing a role as the hub of commercial intercourse in this region; instead, the American ships were using the Dutch small free port of Rhio nearby.[144] Moreover, the Glasgow EIA's standpoint with respect to Britain's general foreign trade policies was clearly shown in these subjects. The association's memorial to Earl Grey in regard to Singapore best shows the preference of the merchants and manufacturers in Glasgow and its neighbouring areas for the liberalisation of Britain's economic policies and the application of free trade to international trade.[145] In February 1832, the Board of Control sent its letters regarding the trade and finance of India to the parties concerned with the East India question and requested their opinions on this subject.[146] The Chamber of Commerce of Glasgow was one of them, and its sub-committee drafted the replies to the queries.[147]

In the summer of 1832, when the general election of members to the reformed Parliament was approaching, the EIAs of manufacturing towns and outports discussed an appropriate measure to increase the number of parliamentary opponents of the EIC's monopoly. In July, in the special meeting, the subject came up for discussion.[148] After a long debate, the directors of the Glasgow EIA rejected the suggestion of some members of the Liverpool EIA that they should ask the candidates for a declaration of opinions or their pledges to clarify their attitudes towards the East India question. Instead, their decision was more moderate: they agreed "to address the public at present on the India & China Trade with reference to the expected Election for Members to Parliament" and to print and circulate their resolutions in which they appealed to the electors to consider this question.[149] In the election, although the association was not very active, the East India question was one of the issues. As a result of the Parliamentary Reform, two seats were allocated to Glasgow. James Oswald, John Crawfurd,

---

143 Committee Minute Book 1829–47, 10 June 1831, p. 65.

144 Outgoing Correspondence 1829–36, "The Memorial of the East India Association of the City of Glasgow", 21 June 1831, letter no. 57.

145 Ibid.

146 Committee Minute Book 1829–47, 16 February 1832, p. 68.

147 Ibid., 18 and 24 February 1832, pp. 69–76; Parliamentary Paper, *Reports from Committees: 1831–2. East India Company's Affairs. II. – Finance and Accounts – Trade*. Vol. III-Part II. Appendix No. 4, pp. 504–90.

148 Committee Minute Book 1829–47, 10 July 1832, pp. 82–4.

149 Ibid.

and James Ewing, who were affiliated with the association, stood with other candidates for the election. Oswald and Crawfurd were politically liberal, whilst Ewing's stance was that of a 'liberal' Tory. Apart from these three candidates, Daniel K. Sanford also made a long speech to support the abolition of the EIC's monopoly at the meeting of electors.[150]

While all of these candidates supported the complete abolition of the Company's monopoly, Ewing's attitude towards the equalisation of duties on East Indian and West Indian sugar and the general principles of free trade was more ambiguous than that of the others, as he held the main commercial interests in the West India trade. For this reason, during the election campaign, his views on free trade were criticised by his opponents.[151] Like John Gladstone in Liverpool, whose case will be explained in the next chapter, this criticism shows Ewing's contradictory position as a member of both the WIA and the EIA. Although he supported the opening of the East India and China trade, he also needed to defend the West Indian interests as one of the city's leading West Indian traders. Eventually, in December 1832, James Ewing and James Oswald, members of the association, were returned as MPs for Glasgow. Crawfurd's defeat indicates that the abolition of the restrictions imposed on the East India and China trade was not a decisive influence in the results of the election in Glasgow. Moreover, Ewing and Oswald had stronger local connections than Crawfurd. Nevertheless, these two MPs were members of the association. As in the case of 1812–13, the Glasgow EIA had its own representatives in Parliament again.

In January 1833, on the eve of Parliament's assembling, merchants and manufacturers of Glasgow started to prepare for their final battle for the abolition of the EIC's monopoly and the establishment of free commercial intercourse with the East Indies. In January and February, the Glasgow EIA discussed with Liverpool the propriety of sending their deputations to London but concluded at the beginning of March that it was too soon to proceed.[152] Prior to the arrival of the deputation, the situation in London relative to the question of the renewal of the East India Charter was regularly relayed to Glasgow by the two MPs, as well as by Crawfurd.

---

[150] Anon., *Speech of Sir Daniel K. Sanford at a Meeting of Electors and Inhabitants of Glasgow, in the Traders' Hall, Wednesday, September the 19th, 1832*, 1832.

[151] Anon., *Letter to James Ewing, Esq. L.L.D. of Dunoon Castle*, c. 1832.

[152] Committee Minute Book 1829–47, 22 January 1833, pp. 86–7, 21 February 1833, pp. 88–9, and 2 March 1833, pp. 90–1.

Although the association was confident that the China trade would be opened, it thought that the other points were still uncertain.[153] Even the government did not make final decisions on some points. For instance, in the middle of February, Charles Grant, the President of the Board of Control, sent an inquiry to W.W. Whitmore about the opinion of provincial commercial and manufacturing interests in regard to the "rules, restrictions and conditions under which they [the British subjects] should be allowed to settle in the interior of India".[154] Then, copies of Grant's letter were sent to the parties concerned with this subject, including the associations of Liverpool and Glasgow. In Glasgow, the directors agreed that it was more proper for them to send Grant a joint answer than a separate reply.[155] However, the members of the Glasgow EIA felt that "it was rather beyond our province to become Indian law makers".[156] Its members were unable to prepare their own draft for this matter by themselves because of their lack of knowledge of India's legal system. Therefore, while they awaited John Crawfurd's notes on the inquiry from the Board of Control, they also asked the Liverpool EIA to write the draft and to send it to Glasgow for its consideration.[157]

In the middle of March, Robert Gordon of the Board of Control also asked Ewing, lobbying in London, about Glasgow's ability to act as a bonding port to secure duties on tea.[158] To answer this question, the Glasgow EIA sent an inquiry to Greenock and Port Glasgow on the conditions of the bonded warehouses there.[159] Moreover, Oswald and Whitmore agreed that Glasgow should send a deputation to London immediately since the President of the Board of Control would be willing to hear from them on the bonded warehouses of outports before the Easter recess.[160] After observing the proceedings of the debates over the new India Bills in Parliament and the opinions of the Ministry, on 22 March, the Glasgow EIA appointed Kirkman Finlay, J.G. Hamilton, Henry Dunlop, Walter Buchanan, and W.P. Paton as its deputation to London, who would act in conjunction with the deputation from Liverpool. Then, acting on advice from Oswald and Whitmore, the association sent a deputation to London.[161] The Board

153 Ibid., 21 February 1833, p. 89.
154 Ibid., 12 March 1833, p. 91.
155 Ibid., pp. 91–2; Outgoing Correspondence 1829–36, 12 March 1833, letter no. 78.
156 Ibid.
157 Ibid.; Committee Minute Book 1829–47, pp. 91–2.
158 Committee Minute Book 1829–47, 26 March 1833, p. 95.
159 Outgoing Correspondence 1829–36, 25 March 1833, letter no. 84 and 85.
160 Incoming Correspondence 1833–34, 25 March 1833, letter no. 23.
161 Ibid.; Committee Minute Book 1829–47, 22 March 1833, pp. 93–5.

of Control's inquiries into the provincial mercantile and manufacturing interests imply that, for the Ministry, not only the London mercantile interests and their alliance but also the provincial interests' views were significant criteria in the formation of Britain's imperial policies in Asia.

In London, the deputation from Glasgow continued lobbying with other deputations before the introduction of the Bill. Finlay, one of the deputies, held discussions with the Board of Control daily, and he also privately submitted to the government his opinions on the necessary arrangements for the opening of the China trade and the duties that should be levied on tea.[162] The government estimated that the consumption of tea would be 30 million lbs., while, in Finlay's personal view, it would amount to 40 million lbs.[163] He insisted that the government's calculations on the consumption of tea after the opening of the China trade were underestimated in order to persuade it to open the China trade immediately and to levy moderate duties on the Chinese products. The directors of the association supported his argument and left the matter to Finlay's discretion.[164]

Although the Glasgow EIA's lobbying activities against the discriminating duties on East and West Indian products continued, its activities in opposition to the renewal of the EIC's Charter almost ended by the time Grant introduced the India bill into Parliament on 13 June 1833. In terms of the clauses of the new Charter Acts with which the Glasgow EIA was concerned, they were favourable to the free trade supporters. The Company's monopoly in the China trade was to be abolished, including the tea trade. On 22 April 1834, the Company was to abandon all of its commercial privileges, close its commercial business, and sell its unnecessary commercial properties both in the homeland and abroad to settle its financial obligations. The restrictions on British inhabitants' purchasing and holding lands in India were also abolished.

Conclusion

This chapter has analysed the lobbying activities of the Glasgow EIA from 1829 to 1833. After the opening of the India trade in 1814, the East Indian

162 Incoming Correspondence 1833–34., 22 April 1833, letter no. 37 and 30 April 1833, letter no. 39; Committee Minute Book 1829–47, 10 March 1833, p. 99.

163 Outgoing Correspondence 1829–36, 10 May 1833.

164 Ibid.; Committee Minute Book 1829–47, 10 May 1833.

interests of Glasgow organised few lobbying activities until the end of the 1820s because they did not have a proper institution that could represent their interests. Nevertheless, they eventually re-established the Glasgow EIA to organise their lobbying efforts against the renewal of the Company's Charter and to address other subjects connected to their interests.

In studies conducted by Greenberg and by Eyles regarding the renewal of the EIC's Charter during this period, both scholars emphasised the roles of the Lancashire merchants and manufacturers. Nevertheless, it is clear that, under the initiative of Kirkman Finlay, this Scottish organisation played a major role in the national campaign, although its policies often followed the opinions of Liverpool. The records of the Glasgow EIA indicate the significant influence of John Crawfurd, who connected with British private merchants in the East Indies, not only in the case of Glasgow but also over the theoretical arguments and general lobbying tactics adopted by free trade supporters of the provincial manufacturing towns and outports as a whole. Nevertheless, this Scottish Orientalist's importance in the campaign attracted little attention from historians compared with Buckingham. In fact, Crawfurd was a man who linked provincial mercantile and manufacturing interests with private traders in the East who had close connections with the London gentlemanly capitalists in the 1829–33 campaign.

The means and general tactics of the Glasgow EIA's lobbying activities followed its previous attempts in 1812 and 1813. The provincial mercantile and manufacturing interests decided upon their lobbying strategies through close communication among the different provincial lobbying groups and their supporters. The Glasgow EIA's deputies could access Ministers through Parliamentary supporters such as Huskisson and Whitmore. The state's decision regarding the appointment of the Select Committee just after the meeting between the General Deputation and the Ministers implies the effective lobbying of the provincial interest groups. The records also indicate that the provincial lobbyists made significant efforts to find witnesses who could give favourable evidence for free trade, and their search extended to the London mercantile community. Moreover, inquiries from the Board of Control to the provincial lobbyist groups indicated that the provincial interest groups were significant enough for the state to consider their opinions.

The analysis of the association's subscribers has revealed that their economic interests were varied, just as those of the previous association's subscribers had been. However, whilst the West Indian interests were no longer one of the largest economic interest groups, those who were involved in the cotton industry maintained their significant position within the re-established association. As Webster argued, their consigning manufactured goods to the East Indies through London agency houses, which developed after the opening of the India trade, created their connection with the London interests. During this free trade campaign, the development of the connection between them served as a background for the collaboration between the provincial mercantile and manufacturing interests and some of the gentlemanly capitalists in the metropolis and their nexus in Asia.

CHAPTER FOUR

AIMING FOR THE PREMIER PORT OF THE EMPIRE: THE LIVERPOOL EAST INDIA ASSOCIATION, 1812–1813 AND 1829–1833

Introduction

Through the examination of the Glasgow EIA's lobbying activities, the previous two chapters have argued that the provincial merchants and manufacturers exercised a strong influence on the formation of British imperial policies in the East Indies. The main aim of this chapter is to reinforce the previous chapters' evaluation of the effective campaigns of provincial lobbying groups from 1812 to 1813 and from 1829 to 1833 through an analysis of Liverpool's lobbying activities.

> The port of Liverpool has been raised to its present proud pre-eminence..., and, within my own time, has been elevated from the rank of a third or fourth-rate town to that of a second. Though Liverpool has a leg tied up, she is now running a race with the metropolis; they are neck and neck, and let but that leg be untied which now restricts the motion of one of the competitors, and we may venture to anticipate that the same enterprise which has carried Liverpool so far, will soon lead her beyond the port of London itself.[1]

The above speech, made by Samuel Hope, a banker in Liverpool, clearly described the position of the city in the first half of the nineteenth century. During this period, Liverpool participated in the general trend of the growth in Britain's overseas trade.[2] The port gradually established its significant position and overwhelmed the port of London in some branches of British overseas trade, notably the slave trade during the second half of the eighteenth century and then the importation of raw cotton from the United

[1] The Liverpool East India Association, *Report of the Public Meeting at Liverpool on Wednesday, January 28, 1829, for the Purpose of Taking into Consideration of the Best Means of Removing the Restrictions Imposed upon Commerce by the Present Charter of the East India Company*, 1829, p. 24.

[2] According to Davis' calculation, the annual average of total exports (excluding re-exports) from Britain increased from £12,690,000 in 1784–86 to £44,474,000 in 1814–16, whilst that of total imports rose from £20,386,000 to 64,741,000, respectively. See R. Davis, *The Industrial Revolution and British Overseas Trade*, 1979, pp. 88–9 and 92–3. The Irish trade is excluded from these values.

States and other places during the nineteenth century. Nineteenth-century Liverpool had a different economic structure from Glasgow. As described, Glasgow's economy was based on both foreign trade and manufacturing; in Liverpool, foreign trade and related sectors held a dominant position. The growth of the city's economy increased its political influence and put it at the centre of the nationwide free trade campaign.

This chapter shows that, in spite of its varied political and economic interests, the Liverpool EIA took the leadership in the two campaigns of 1812–13 and 1829–33 obtaining support from powerful local MPs, and that it communicated with other towns closely to organise their lobbying effectively. The internal divisions within the Liverpool mercantile community, notably the antagonism between the West Indian and American traders, did not affect its strong challenge to the dominance of the London mercantile elite over the East India and China trade.

The main archival sources for this chapter are articles from such contemporary newspapers as the *Liverpool Courier* and the *Liverpool Mercury*, in addition to other local archival sources, including Liverpool Town Books and John Gladstone's correspondence.[3] Apart from these sources, the analysis of this chapter draws on the Glasgow EIA's records, which contain correspondence between Glasgow, Liverpool, and other towns. To examine how provincial merchants and manufacturers, with their varied economic interests and different political views, formed their overall lobbying strategies, this source is very useful.

Development as the Second Port of the British Empire

Like other provincial manufacturing and commercial centres in England and Scotland, Liverpool experienced rapid economic social and demographic changes in the late eighteenth and early nineteenth centuries. The population of the city increased dramatically from approximately 7,000 in 1708, to 77,653 by 1800, and 116,000 by 1811. That is its population rose more than fifteen times.[4] The economy of the city depended on its port. By 1760, Liverpool merchants overwhelmed their London and Bristol counterparts

---

[3] Liverpool Town Books (352 MIN/COU I 2/8, Liverpool Record Office); Glynne-Gladstone MSS 288 (Flintshire Record Office).

[4] R. Lawton, "The Genesis of Population", in W. Smith and others (eds.), *A Scientific Survey of Merseyside*, 1953, pp. 121–2; N. Collins, *Politics and Elections in Nineteenth-Century Liverpool*, 1994, p. 2.

in the slave trade.[5] The triangular trade that connected Britain, the West African coasts, and the West Indies was highly speculative and hazardous and required a highly organised trading system, which contributed to the rise of banks in the city. The multilateral character of the South Atlantic trade also helped in the development of a trading settlement system based on bills of exchange. To remit their profits to the home country from the West Indies, Liverpool slave traders could access the financial facilities of London's West Indian interests, which dominated the West Indian economy.[6] At the same time, the port facilities and the networks of roads and canals that connected Liverpool with local manufacturing towns were significantly improved by the early nineteenth century.

Although Liverpool was famous for the slave trade before its abolition in 1807, its economic contribution to the growth of the city was significant but partial.[7] At the end of the eighteenth century, Liverpool emerged as the leading British port in the trade with the United States. The city became the hub of exports of manufactured products from the North and the Midlands and of imports of raw materials. The port attracted the cotton textiles of Lancashire, the woollen goods of the West Riding, the iron of South Yorkshire, the pottery of Staffordshire, and the hardware of Birmingham for export to the United States and the West Indies. In return raw materials, especially raw cotton, were imported to meet increasing demand from English manufacturing towns.[8] Between 1820 and 1850, over 80 percent of Britain's importation of raw cotton arrived in Liverpool every year.[9] Although the West Indian and American traders were dominant elements of Liverpool's overseas trade during this period, the city represented not only its own mercantile and shipping interests but was firmly connected with many manufacturing interests of the North and the Midlands. The rapid growth of Liverpool was the most successful part of the British economy during this period.

---

5 B.L. Anderson, "The Lancashire Bill System and its Liverpool Practitioners: The Case of a Slave Merchant", in W.H. Chaloner and B.M. Ratcliffe, *Trade and Transport: Essay in Economic History in Honour of T.S. William*, 1977, p. 62.

6 R.B. Sheridan, "The Commercial and Financial Organization of the British Slave Trade, 1750–1807", in *The Economic History Review*, New Series, Vol. XI, No. 2, 1958, pp. 249–63.

7 E.F. Hyde, *Liverpool and the Mersey: An Economic History of Port 1700–1970*, 1971, Chapter 3.

8 B.H. Tolley, "The Liverpool Campaign against the Orders in Council and the War of 1812", in J.R. Harris (ed.), *Liverpool and Merseyside*, 1969, Chapter. 5.

9 D.M. William, "Liverpool Merchants and the Cotton Trade 1820–1850", in J.R. Harris (ed.), *Liverpool and Merseyside*, Table 1.

The city's political and social characteristics also help us to understand Liverpool's participation in the free trade campaign. In terms of the local politics of nineteenth-century Liverpool, the Tory Party dominated the Corporation members.[10] The conservative part of the city was best represented by the West Indian and the West African traders, who were the old part of the city's economic interests and deeply connected with the colonial trade. On the one hand, they were inclined to believe that their trade benefited from England's traditional mercantile policy of the seventeenth and eighteenth centuries; on the other hand, they were critical of policies that restricted their trading activities.[11] In spite of the abolition of the slave trade and the relative decline of the West India trade in the early nineteenth century, the West Indian traders still maintained a strong influence in Liverpool's political life.

Meanwhile, such non-conformists in the city as the Unitarians, the Quakers, and the Presbyterians were excluded from local politics. The descendants of Scottish immigrants, many of whom were Presbyterians, were also outside the mainstream of local politics. Such groups included some highly successful and respected merchants who conducted trade with the United States and the West Indies, notably William Rathbone, James Cropper, and William Ewart.[12] Along with the group of professionals, such as William Roscoe and James Currie, in the Philosophical and Literary Society these non-conformists were related to the Whig elements and to the radicals of the city, and they were critical of the privileged group of old mercantile and shipping interests and the Tory Corporation.[13]

Problems before the Campaign of 1812–13

While Liverpool experienced a general trend of rapid economic growth, its merchants felt uncertainty regarding the future of their trading activities. The outbreak of the Napoleonic Wars caused confusion in its foreign trade with the European continent, the United States, and the West Indies. For instance, Napoleon's economic blockade of Britain after the Berlin-Milan

---

[10] S.G. Checkland, "American versus West Indian Traders in Liverpool, 1793–1815", in *The Journal of Economic History*, Vol. XVIII, No. 2, 1958, pp. 141–2; Collins, *Politics and Elections in Nineteenth-Century Liverpool*, Chap. 1.

[11] Ibid.; S.G. Checkland, "Economic Attitude in Liverpool 1793–1807", in *The Economic History Review*, New Series, Vol. V, No. 1, 1952, pp. 58–9.

[12] S.G. Checkland, *The Gladstones: A Family Biography 1764–1851*, 1971, pp. 30–1.

[13] Ibid.; Checkland, "Economic Attitude", pp. 66–74.

Decrees of 1806 and 1807, followed by the annexation of Holland, Westphalia, and the northern German territories and Britain's counter-blockade by the Orders in Council, directly caused a serious disruption to Liverpool's economy. Nevertheless, such external political events were not the single cause of this uncertainty. Domestically, in 1793, Liverpool suffered from London's financial crisis.[14] In the event, the failure of Charles Caldwell & Co., one of the leading banking houses in Liverpool, damaged confidence and led to a ruinous contraction of circulating medium.[15] The crisis forced the Corporation to step in to rebuild confidence by obtaining an Act of Parliament to issue its own notes. In addition, the city's West Indian traders were under pressure from the anti-slavery movement.

The deterioration of Britain's relationship with the United States worsened this situation. The British government issued the Orders in Council, which restricted Americans' neutral trade, and the latter retaliated with counteractions. As the leading British port of the American trade, the disruption of this trade was particularly serious for Liverpool merchants. According to William Rathbone's estimation, the US trade amounted to about 30 per cent of Liverpool's commerce in 1808.[16] During the disputes between the two countries trading operations were very high-risk. When the embargo was imposed by the US government, merchants had to keep a large stock of goods in anticipation of its removal in the near future. When the United States temporarily lifted the embargo in May 1810, after raw cotton had hit their highest prices from 1808 to 1809, the flood of American commodities to Liverpool and the huge accumulation of stocks as well as the lack of demand from the manufacturing areas of Lancashire, caused a collapse in prices.[17] In the city, those concerned with trade with the United States were represented by the American Chamber of Commerce (ACC). Among its members, the Rathbones, Croppers, Bensons, Hodgesons, Thornelys, Martins, Richardsons, and Binns, who operated their trade primarily with the United States, opposed the Orders in Council.[18]

The West India trade gradually lost its commercial importance after the prosperity it experienced in the late eighteenth century. The trade depended upon tropical commodities and, unlike the United States, the small islands and their heavily indebted plantation economy could not offer a large

14 F.E. Hyde and B.B. Parkinson, "The Port of Liverpool and the Crisis of 1793", in *Economica*, New Series, Vol. 18, No. 72, 1951, pp. 366–7.

15 Ibid., pp. 367–8.

16 Tolley, "The Liverpool Campaign", p. 102.

17 Ibid.; Checkland, "American versus West Indian Traders in Liverpool", p. 156.

18 Ibid., p. 150.

market to British goods or meet the increasing demand for corn and raw cotton from Britain's rapidly growing manufacturing centres. Moreover, the slave trade, which was under pressure from abolitionists all over the country, declined at the turn of the century. The number of Liverpool ships engaged in the slave trade went down from one out of every 12 ships in 1792 to one out of every 24 by the time of its abolition.[19] Devine has argued that in Glasgow the relative decline of the West Indian merchants led to the establishment of the Glasgow WIA in 1807 to maintain and promote their interests. The foundation of a similar association by Liverpool merchants in 1799, when the liquidity crisis occurred, may indicate a similar position for them at the turn of the century.[20] The abolition of the slave trade in 1807 did not lead directly to the city's economic crisis, but certainly this political event damaged the West Indian merchants' prospects.

The wars with France also impacted Liverpool's West Indian traders. Checkland has pointed out the vulnerability of the West India trade in wartime conditions due to its more speculative nature than the American trade.[21] The main markets for the West Indian commodities were on the European continent. Although the Napoleonic Wars gave the West Indian interests an opportunity to exclude European rivals from this traffic, they needed continental markets, in which they could sell only small quantities at high prices under the French economic blockade. In such a commercial environment, they could not expect stability or large profits. Under these circumstances, it was essential for the West Indian interests to exclude the Americans from their trade. Therefore, while many of the prestigious Liverpool merchants engaging in the American trade were hostile to the Orders, the West Indian merchants and planters were the main supporters of the Ministry and the Orders in Council. For example, the political stance of John Gladstone, father of the Prime Minister, William Ewart Gladstone, had been that of a Whig at first. However, his economic interest in the West India trade and plantations increased during the 1800s and combined with his patriotic attitude and his Episcopal beliefs, this led him to become a supporter of the Conservative government and the Orders.[22]

---

[19] E. Williams, *Capitalism and Slavery*, 1994, p. 162.

[20] T.M. Devine, "An Eighteenth-Century Business Elite: Glasgow-West India Merchants, c. 1750–1815", in *Scottish Historical Review*, Vol. 57, 1978; Checkland, "American versus West Indian Traders in Liverpool", p. 145.

[21] Ibid., p. 150.

[22] S.G. Checkland, *The Gladstones*, Chapter 8 and 9.

Table 5. Trade and dock duties collected in Liverpool (1810–16).

	Number of Ships	Tonnage	Duties (£)
1808	5,225	516,836	40,638
1809	6,023	594,601	47,580
1810	6,729	734,391	65,782
1811	5,616	611,190	54,752
1812	4,599	446,788	44,403
1813	5,341	547,426	50,177
1814	5,706	548,957	59,741
1815	6,440	709,849	76,915
1816	6,888	774,243	92,646

Note: In 1812, a new mode of levying rates on goods and tonnage was introduced.
Source: T. Baines, *History of the Commerce and Town of Liverpool, and the Rise of Manufacturing Industry in the Adjoining Countries*, 1852, pp. 6–7.

The difficulty of Liverpool's merchants before the renewal of the EIC's Charter is indicated in Table 5, which lists the trade and dock duties collected in the port of Liverpool from 1808 to 1816. Between 1810 and 1812, both the number of ships and the total amount of tonnage declined significantly. In addition, although in 1812, the port changed the mode of levying dock duties with the expectation of annual revenues of around £60,000, it failed to achieve this figure until 1815 due to the uncertain trading conditions.[23]

Napoleon's economic blockade and the disputes between Britain and the United States over the Orders in Council were having a profound impact on Liverpool's economy before the beginning of its lobbying for the opening of the East India trade, as was the case in Glasgow. According to Moss, in the case of Birmingham its manufacturers that dominated the local economy exported their goods to the United States and also opposed the Orders together.[24] In the case of Liverpool, the situation was more complicated because the strong West Indian interests existed along with the American trade interests. The Liverpool mercantile community exhibited serious divisions in the debates over the Orders in Council.

---

23 T. Baines, *History of the Commerce and Town of Liverpool, and the Rise of Manufacturing Industry in the Adjoining Countries*, 1852, p. 557.

24 D.J. Moss, "Birmingham and the Campaigns against the Orders-in Council and East India Company Charter, 1812–13", in *Canadian Journal of History*, Vol. XI, Issue 1, 1976, pp. 181–2.

The Beginning of Liverpool's Campaign

By the beginning of 1812, some merchants in Liverpool had started lobbying for the opening of the East India and China trade on an individual basis. In February, General Gascoyne, one of two MPs for Liverpool, stated in the House of Commons that the merchants of Liverpool expected the state to create a Select Committee to examine the issue of changing the current arrangement of the East India trade.[25] In the next month, following requests from several inhabitants of Liverpool and other British towns, such as Birmingham, from where Thomas Attwood had written a letter to urge them to petition Parliament, the Mayor of Liverpool called a meeting to discuss the subject of the opening of the East India trade.[26] On 16 March, the Mayor and other council members held a Special Council and Meeting of the Trustees of the Dock in the Town Hall of Liverpool to discuss petitioning Parliament in opposition to the renewal of the EIC's Charter.[27] This was the first official meeting of the Corporation about petitions to Parliament in opposition to the East India Charter during this period. In this meeting, the Corporation and the Trustees prepared two petitions and then nominated a committee to undertake their lobbying.[28] The petition of the Trustees of the Dock was one of the characteristics of Liverpool's campaign. The Trustees insisted in their petition that after the Liverpool Dock Act had been passed in the previous session they had started several projects to expand and to improve the dock facilities to meet not only the current needs but also to provide for the future requirements of the East India trade.[29] The next day, at a meeting led by the committees appointed in the previous day's meeting, the merchants, ship-owners, tradesmen and other inhabitants of the city approved the sending of another petition.[30] In this petition they argued that free trade with the East Indies and China was "the common birth right of all his Majesty's subjects" and attacked the monopoly of the EIC as "highly injurious to the general interests of this at large as greatly discouraging the commercial spirit which from the nature and local

---

25 *The Parliamentary Debates*, Vol. XXI, 6 February 1812, p. 676.

26 Records of Glasgow East India Association Correspondence Incoming 1812–1813 (MS891001/3, Glasgow Mitchell Library), letter no. 1.

27 Liverpool Town Books, 16 March 1812.

28 The members of the committee were Aldermen, Thomas Earle, Henry Blundell Hollinshead, John Bridge Aspinall, Peter Whitfield Brancker, Thomas Molyneux, James Drinkwater, Thomas Hinde, Samuel Staniforth, Thomas Case, William Nicholson, and William Rigg.

29 Liverpool Town Books, 16 March 1812.

30 *Liverpool Courier*, 18 March 1812, p. 3.

situation of these Islands, is indispensable to their prosperity, and upon which their security at this moment essentially depends".[31]

An event during this meeting indicated the desperation of Liverpool's American traders. That is to say, William Roscoe, whose radical views were shared by some of the major American traders of the city, interrupted the proceedings.[32] He and his supporters went to the meeting to express to the public their argument against the Ministry's foreign trade policy. This clearly reveals the debates within Liverpool itself. He rejected the view that the opening of the East India trade would increase Britain's resources for war with France. He argued that although such a hope seemed possible, there were still two years left before the expiration of the EIC's Charter, and the trade would take several more years to be established and eventually to become fruitful. From his and his followers' viewpoint the East India trade would not be able to provide Britain with enough resources to execute the war; only their trade with the United States could do so.

Furthermore, Roscoe was sceptical of the argument that the abolition of the EIC's monopoly would be a remedy for the county's depressed economy. He argued that:

> It was not the East India Company that had brought our ruin. War was the foundation of the distress: and it was completed by the Orders in Council ... it was ridiculous to suppose that the opening of the East India trade would remove the present calamities of the nation. These had no connexion with present subject.[33]

His speech was interrupted by the Mayor, who insisted that the purpose of the meeting was not to discuss the Orders in Council but the East India trade. The Corporation members were firm supporters of the government's policy on the Napoleonic Wars and resented Roscoe's criticism of the Ministry at the public meeting. In spite of the Mayor's interposition, Roscoe received praise from some sections of the audience at the meeting. It was true that the depressed trading conditions of Liverpool led its merchants to their movement against the renewal of the EIC's Charter. However, for some of the American merchants and other inhabitants of the city, their prior political issue was not the East India trade but the removal of the Orders, as they did not think that the East Indies and China would be able to replace the United States immediately as a supplier of raw materials and

---

31 Ibid.
32 Ibid.
33 Ibid.

market for British manufacturing goods. Nevertheless, regarding their free trade campaign against the renewal of the Charter, in spite of their different views, there was no actual split between those who were in conflict with each other over the issue of the Orders in Council. In the long view, the East India and China trade, which London merchants had exclusively enjoyed under the EIC's monopoly, would also be attractive to them.

At the same meeting, another committee was appointed to lead the free trade campaign. Table 6 shows the names of the members of the committee, their designations, and their economic interests. Compared with the previous committee, this new committee reflected the broader economic interests of Liverpool's free trade campaigners more clearly because the members were elected from among the merchants, ship-owners, and tradesmen of the city. Due to the city's commercial orientation, most members were merchants, and no person whose main economic interest was manufacturing was included. Although the table is incomplete, it shows that many of the members or the companies in which they held stakes were featured on the list of members of either the Liverpool WIA or the ACC. For example, John Gladstone and William Rathbone were prominent figures in the West India trade and the American trade, respectively, and both of them held the office of chairman of each organisation during their lifetimes. Although historians such as Checkland and Tolley have explained the collaboration between the West Indian traders and the American traders, it is clear that, among 21 members, 12 were West Indian merchants and only 4 were American merchants. In number, the West Indian interests clearly overwhelmed the American merchants. As the debates over the Orders in Council showed, the West Indian interests held a mercantilist view; they supported the state's intervention into trading activities for the national interest. Their involvement in the campaign for the abolition of the EIC was exactly characteristic of "the typical Liverpool merchant of the last quarter of the eighteenth century [who was represented by the West Indian merchant]", as highlighted by Checkland.[34] In spite of their mercantilist view, they supported free trade in the East Indies for practical reasons rather than for their free trade beliefs based on Adam Smith's ideology. This also indicated the diversity of economic and political interests among the provincial lobbyists. Considering the number of the West Indian interests and the American traders' attitude towards the opening of the East India trade in the public meeting of 17 March 1812, the core of the Liverpool lobbyists was the West Indian merchants and planters.

34 Checkland, "Economic Attitudes in Liverpool", p. 58.

Table 6. Membership of the committee appointed at the General Meeting held in Liverpool on 17 March 1812.

Name	Designation (1811 Directory)	West Indian/American Trader
William Roscoe	Banker	
John Gladstone	Merchant (John & Robert Gladstone)	WI (GD 1807)
Cyrus Morrall	Merchant	A (Morrall & Boarland) (ACC)
William Barton	Merchant	WI (GD 1807)
John Richardson		A (John Richardson & Co.) (ACC)
George Irlam	Merchant	WI (GD 1807)
Richard Pilford	Merchant	WI (GD 1807)
Thomas Bourne	Swedish Consul	
Joseph Leigh	Merchant	WI (GD 1807)
John Tobin	Merchant	
Thomas Fletcher	Merchant	WI (GD 1810)
Adam Lodge	Merchant	A (Lodge & Tooth) (ACC)
Anthony Littledale	Merchant	
Charles Lawrence	Merchant	WI (GD 1807)
Moses Benson	Merchant	WI *1
Charles Turner	Merchant	WI (GD 1807)
Joseph Brooks Yates	Merchant	WI *2
Jacob Fletcher	Merchant	WI (GD 1807)
Robert Bagott	Merchant	
William Ewart	Merchant	WI (GD 1807)
William Rathbone	Merchant	A (W. & R. Rathbone) (ACC)

Note. 'WI' =a merchant listed as a member of the Liverpool WIA. 'A' =a merchant listed as a member of the American Chamber of Commerce. '(GD)'=in *Gore's Directories*. '(AAC)'=in "The American Chamber of Commerce for the Port of Liverpool".

Source: *Liverpool Courier*, 18 March 1812, p. 3; *Gore's Directories*, 1807 and 1810; W.O. Henderson, "The American Chamber of Commerce for the Port of Liverpool, 1801–1908", in *Transactions of the Historic Society of Lancashire and Cheshire*, Vol. 85, 1985, Appendix A and B. *Gore's Directories* of 1807 and 1810 contain the lists of the members of the West India Committees and those of the American Chambers of Commerce.

*1 Checkland, "American versus West Indian Traders in Liverpool", pp. 141–2.

*2 Parliamentary Papers, *Minutes of Evidence before the Committee of the Whole House of Commons Relating to Orders in Council* 1812, Vol. III, p. 375.

Thus, the Committee of the Common Council and that of the Merchants, Ship-Owners, and Tradesmen were founded in Liverpool. These two committees together formed the United Committee, which represented Liverpool's interests in the opening of the East India and China trade. Thomas

Earle and William Ewart were selected as its chairman and deputy-chairman, and J.M. Brackenbury was recruited to fill the post of secretary. It is unfeasible to identify the total sum of the group's campaign funds. However, according to Liverpool Town Books, the Corporation decided to pay the necessary expenses for the purpose of free trade, up to £500, from the Corporation Treasurer's account.[35] The rest of the expenses were paid for by subscriptions from the public collected at several banks and public coffee-rooms throughout the city.[36] As Glasgow's case study in the previous chapters shows, in Liverpool, the local authority also strongly supported its free trade campaign.

The Proceedings of Liverpool's Campaign, 1812–14

In the first week of April, following a call from the Committee of Birmingham, John Gladstone, a member of the Liverpool WIA, travelled to London as a deputation from Liverpool. John Bourne, who was then Mayor, joined him to form the General Deputation with deputies from other outports and manufacturing towns.[37] The deputies from Liverpool attended several meetings with other deputies and the Ministry. Moreover, on 23 March, General Tarleton, MP for the city, presented the House of Commons with three petitions from the Liverpool Corporation, the Trustees of the Dock, and its merchants, ship-owners, and other inhabitants.[38] During the presentation of these petitions he had a heated discussion with Thomas Creevey, a Liverpool-born radical Whig, and other members regarding the economic conditions of Liverpool. Tarleton claimed that Creevey had overstated the number of people who were receiving charitable aid; the Whig man had previously stated that the number of such people increased from 8,000 to 15,000.[39] The *Liverpool Mercury* also previously claimed a similar number, near 16,000 people.[40] Creevey blamed Liverpool's economic conditions on the standstill of the American trade. General Tarleton put forth a counter-argument by quoting the report that the Corporation of the city had issued. He insisted that, although a number of Irish and Welsh workers who had worked for the construction of the dock were out of employment,

35 Liverpool Town Books, 16 March 1812.
36 *Liverpool Courier*, 1 April 1812.
37 Ibid.
38 *The Parliamentary Debates*, Vol. XXII, 23 March 1813, pp. 111–8.
39 Ibid.
40 *Liverpool Mercury*, 14 February 1812.

no more than 3,000 to 4,000 people received aid from a soup committee for their relief.[41] After their argument, General Gascoyne, another Tory MP for Liverpool, stated that he would take a middle position. He took it for granted that the diminution of the trade with the United States led to the downturn of Liverpool's economy, but he believed that it would be temporary.[42] He argued that the depression of the colonial trade was the real problem afflicting Liverpool.[43] Alexander Baring, who represented the London interests and opposed the Orders in Council, thought that the Liverpool Corporation members, who were firm advocates of the Ministry's policy, distorted the actual state of the city's distress.[44] Their exchange of hot words over Liverpool's economic conditions in the presentation of the petition for the abolition of the EIC's monopoly was another example of the division of the Liverpool community over the issue on the Orders in Council.

Nevertheless, in spite of the disagreement among Liverpool merchants over the government's policy related to Britain's counter-blockade against France, the campaign of Liverpool merchants against the renewal of the Charter was very active. London merchants, traders, and others held a meeting at the City of London on 23 April and passed their resolutions for the confinement of the East India trade to the port of London. The United Committee of Liverpool immediately held a meeting on 27 April, expressed the members' "extreme surprise" at the London movement, and published their resolutions in all local newspapers.[45] The merchants, ship-owners, and manufacturers of London had two main arguments. The first point was that the opening of the East India and China trade to the outports would damage a number of London merchants, ship-owners, manufacturers, and others who were currently engaged in the East India trade through the privileged position of the port of London. Second, the extension of the East India trade to the outports would not be able to secure the revenues because of the lack of suitable facilities at these ports. The Liverpool Committee refuted these claims. First, as argued in its petitions, the Committee's demand for free access to the East Indies was grounded on the birthright of all British subjects, and the state should impose all restrictions on them on equal terms. The Committee claimed that:

---

41 *The Parliamentary Debates*, Vol. XXII, 23 March 1813, pp. 111–8.
42 Ibid.
43 Ibid.
44 Ibid., 23 March 1812, pp. 114–5.
45 *Liverpool Courier*, 29 April 1812.

> ... to debar any portion of them from carrying on trade with the same facilities and advantages as their fellow subjects, or deprive certain places of the right of trade, in order to confer it on other places, would be a new and dangerous innovation on the Constitution and Law of the Land.[46]

Then, regarding the customs revenues, the Committee members insisted that

> ... it has, without monopolies or partial advantages, established a commerce which returns a very large proportion of the general revenues of the Majesty ... such revenues are as faithfully paid as duly collected and accounted for in the port of Liverpool as in that of the Metropolis.[47]

They thought that Liverpool, as one of the major ports of the country, had long-term experience in overseas trade with English colonies and foreign countries, and that their experience in overseas trade and the advanced facilities of Liverpool's port could guarantee customs revenues after the opening of the trade with the East. Although, as described in Chapter 2, some London merchants comprising a part of the gentlemanly capitalists supported a partial relaxation of the East India trade, the London mercantile community had a general consensus about maintaining its dominant position in the East India trade. The Liverpool lobbyists' immediate response to the claim of the London interests indicated their strong rivalry against them in the competition for the position of Britain's leading port and their serious engagement in the debates over the renewal of the Charter.

As the General Deputation in London received information that the Ministry had no intention of bringing the subject of the renewal of the Company's Charter before Parliament in that session, the deputation was dissolved after their meeting on 11 May. The General Deputation requested that the United Committee of Liverpool take over their roles until their reassembly during the next session of Parliament.[48] The resolution referred to a geographical advantage that Liverpool was a "town from its central situation being best adapted" for the purpose of correspondence with the parties of London and provincial manufacturing towns and outports, which were concerned with the renewal of the Charter.[49] However, there were other reasons. The first reason was that, as described above, Liverpool was deeply connected with the major industrial areas of Britain. To say nothing

---

46 Ibid.
47 Ibid.
48 Ibid., 24 June 1812.
49 Ibid.

of such neighbours as Manchester and other Lancashire manufacturing towns, even Birmingham's economy was deeply connected with the city. With its own merchants and ship-owners' desire to share the East India trade with their London rivals, it was expected that the Liverpool Committee would be able to execute their duties in the wider aspects of the renewal of the Charter. Second, the city had strong political and economic connections with London. In fact, according to Checkland, Liverpool's overcoming of a series of liquidity crises in the 1790s was attributed partly to its close connection with the Bank of England and the Treasury.[50] In addition, the meeting requested that J.M. Brackenbury, an agent to the ACC of Liverpool and others, who had acted as the Secretary General to the General Deputation, continue his role.[51] In consequence, Liverpool held the best position to know the opinions of all parties involved in this question. Indeed, the Liverpool Committee was granted the power to request that all provincial manufacturing towns and outports obtain consent from it before translating their ideas into action, whilst the Liverpool lobbyists could communicate with the Ministry whenever they thought it was proper.[52] Accordingly, the Liverpool Committee obtained leadership in the free trade movement, despite the clear split in the Liverpool membership.

Before lobbying for free trade resumed, another important event happened in Liverpool. When Parliament was dissolved in September, John Gladstone and other West Indian interests brought George Canning to the city as a candidate. Canning was a very able politician with excellent oratorical skills and became the Prime Minister later in life. He had been the Foreign Secretary in the Ministry of the Duke of Portland until he resigned over a duel with Lord Castlereagh in 1809. He also had a long-term personal relationship with Lord Liverpool, the Prime Minister at that time, since they had studied together at Oxford.[53] In the general election, he and General Gascoyne, both Tory candidates, defeated Brougham and Creevey, the Whig opposition. Due to their total defeat, the Whig supporters in the city became more determined in their opposition. For instance, for the purpose of lobbying Parliament more effectively for the Liverpool merchants' commercial interests, in the same year, they set up the Liverpool office in

50 Checkland, "American versus West Indian Traders in Liverpool", pp. 147–8. In 1793, Liverpool merchants succeeded in petitioning Parliament for the Act to entitle the Liverpool Corporation to issue its own notes, whilst in the crises of 1795 and 1799, loans of Exchequer bills were made to Liverpool's West India interests.

51 *Liverpool Courier*, 24 June 1812.

52 Ibid.

53 W. Hide, *George Canning*, 1973, p. 17.

London.[54] To maintain the office, such commercial interest groups of Liverpool as the WIA, the ship-owners, and the Baltic Association decided to subscribe. The American traders refused to do so for political reasons. Nevertheless, in terms of the debates on the renewal of the EIC's Charter the city acquired Canning as a powerful and able spokesman in Parliament for its campaign.

Little information exists about the activities of the United Committee of Liverpool until November 1812. The correspondence between Liverpool and other towns suggests that the Committee took few actions during the period. The Records of the Glasgow EIA do not contain any correspondence from this period between Glasgow and Liverpool except one letter regarding the General Deputation's records on West Indian products.[55] This is probably because of the Ministry's decision to postpone the debates on the renewal of the Charter in Parliament until the next session and the subsequent dissolution of Parliament and the general election in autumn. Moreover, the Bristol Committee criticised the Liverpool Committee for its inactivity, and John Gladstone and George Canning were personally condemned by their political rivals in the city. John Loudon MacAdam of Bristol told Gladstone that:

> All our efforts however are paralyzed by the inactivity of the central Committee of Liverpool from whom we have had no communication since the separation of the Deputies and whose silence has occasioned some speculation here – This has been increased by the reports most industriously propagated by your political opponents at Liverpool and eagerly disseminated here by their partisans, that you and Mr. Canning had made the oppositions to the E. I. monopoly stalking horse of your ambition and that, having succeeded in carrying Mr. Canning's election, you and he have left the best interests of the Country to be made a property of by ministers and the East India Directors who they say are busily employed in the discussion of Patronage and the other valuable spoil.[56]

This indicated the continuity of political division in the city after the general election. However, the United Committee of Liverpool became more active in December 1812. Immediately after the receipt of the above criticism, the Liverpool Committee exercised its leadership in preparing for the provincial lobbyists' new campaign. The committee circulated letters to

[54] Checkland, *The Gladstones*, p. 73.

[55] Records of the Glasgow East India Association Correspondence Outgoing, 1812–1814 (MS891001/12, Glasgow Mitchell Library), 24 November 1812, letter no. 29.

[56] Checkland, *The Gladstones*, pp. 71–2; A letter from John Loudon MacAdam to John Gladstone, 4 December 1812,Glynne-Gladstone MSS 288 (Flintshire Record Office).

other towns and outports to instruct them to prepare new petitions to Parliament, as they regarded it as proper to do so after the general election. The letter reminded these activists of the necessity of sending a deputation to London.[57]

After the general election, George Canning influenced the measures that the Liverpool Committee adopted during its renewed campaign. In late December, Canning suggested to the committee the necessity of sending a memorial to Lord Liverpool.[58] Prior to the General Court of the EIC held on 5 January 1813, where Liverpool's lobbyists expected some communication from the Ministry would be submitted, they accepted Canning's advice and asked him to transmit their letter and his personal observations to Lord Liverpool.[59] In this letter, they expressed their desire for the opening of the trade with both India and China and insisted that, with respect to the China trade, if they had an opportunity, they could prove the secure collection of customs revenues.[60]

In the General Court of the EIC, it became clear that the Ministry desired to open the India trade to the major ports of the country: London, Liverpool, Bristol, Hull, Glasgow, Dublin, and Cork. Meanwhile, the China trade would remain in the hands of the Company.[61] As described in Chapter 2, the priority of the provincial lobbyist groups was to gain the opening of the import trade to the outports, and their success in lobbying for this purpose became obvious. As he knew the Ministry's intention, Canning started thinking that the free-trade-supporters would need to compromise on the part regarding the China trade. John Foster secretly communicated his intention to John Gladstone. He stated that:

> There are three great parties in Parliament upon this question, viz. the Majesty, the East India Company, and the friends to the Outports and an open trade, and it was clear to him that any two of these parties uniting would beat the other. That it was pretty certain Ministers were not prepared at present to concede on open Trade to China, and it was quite certain the East India Company would join the Ministers on this question, and according to his decided opinion these two parties would carry that point. It therefore become a matter of prudence to consider whether it was expedient for the Outports to contend for the China Trade but to rest satisfied at present with accepting what was proposed by Ministers rather than take any hostile line of conduct which might possibly produce the effect of being serviceable to those who

57 Liverpool Papers (British Library, Add. MSS. 38410), ff. 183–4, dated 1 January 1812.
58 Incoming Correspondence 1812–13, 1 January 1813, letter no. 20.
59 Ibid.
60 Ibid., 2 January 1813, letter no. 21.
61 *Liverpool Mercury*, 5 January 1813.

> under any circumstances wished to confine the Trade exclusively to the Port of London.[62]

In fact, he personally thought that the Company should not abandon its monopoly over the China trade:

> As to the China trade, it had been said that it was necessary to the support of the government of India, but it remained to be proved, even if pecuniary aid were necessary, that it should be derived from this branch of trade, and not from some other source ... He [Canning] did not wish that the trade should open at present...[63]

Checkland explained that the provincial lobbyists accepted this advice and gave up the China trade to concentrate all their efforts upon India.[64] Taking the results of the debates surrounding the East India Charter during this period into consideration, Canning gave sensible advice to the provincial lobbyists. However, on this issue, they rejected his view. It is correct that the provincial lobbyists focused on the opening of the India trade more than on the China trade in their lobbying campaign. However, they did not give up their lobby for the China trade at this point. Although the Ministry showed its clear intention regarding the renewal of the Company's monopoly in the China trade, public opinion in Liverpool and other manufacturing towns and outports continued to insist on the abolition of the monopoly in this branch of trade. In the middle of February, the Corporation, the Trustees of the Dock, the merchants, and others prepared new petitions and submitted them to Parliament. The London correspondents of the *Liverpool Courier* also emphasised the disadvantages of the EIC's monopoly under pseudonyms, MERCATOR and AMICUS, referring to the common arguments of free trade supporters.[65]

In spite of these attempts to rouse public opinion and to lobby for the opening of the China trade, they failed to persuade the Ministry to change its mind, which became much clearer when the General Deputation in

---

[62] Checkland, *The Gladstones*, p. 72; A letter from John Fletcher to John Gladstone, 6 January 1813, Glynne-Gladstone MSS 330 (Flintshire Record Office).

[63] *The Parliamentary Debates*, Vol. XXVI, 1813, p. 637.

[64] Checkland, *The Gladstones*, p. 72.

[65] *Liverpool Courier*, 18 January and 3 February 1813. MERCATOR criticised the following points: (1) the monopoly prices of goods imported by the Company, (2) unfair competition under the confinement of the import trade to the port of London, (3) the Company's insistence on the increase in smuggling and decrease in customs revenues under free trade, (4) the admission of foreign traders to trade from which British subjects were excluded, and (5) the Company's argument on the possible troubles between private traders and the Chinese government. AMICUS mainly promoted the increase in the India trade after the abolition of the Company's monopoly.

London held a meeting with the Ministry on 8 February.[66] Although Canning personally did not agree with the opening of the China trade, he supported the provincial lobbyists' efforts for the opening of this trade. In Parliament, after the introduction to the bill for the renewal of the EIC's Charter, Canning and Ponsonby made attempts to win some last concessions with respect to the China trade. On 14 June, Ponsonby moved an amendment of the bill for reducing the term of the Charter from 20 years to 10 years.[67] After the rejection of his amendment, the House was divided again on Canning's motion to limit the monopoly of the China trade to 10 years. When their attempt failed, the free trade supporters of outports and manufacturing towns needed to be satisfied with the partial abolition of the Company's monopoly.

In spite of the settlement of the China trade issue, Canning continued to defend Liverpool and other provincial interests in Parliament. At the end of the debates on the renewal of the Charter in Parliament, on 14 June, in the House of Commons, Alexander Baring, who represented the London mercantile interests, made an attempt to limit the import trade to the port of London. In the debates, he argued:

> He thought it much better that the proposed alteration in the trade as it present existed, should be effected gradually, and to this end he conceived the best course to pursue, in the first instance, would be, at the same time that vessels were allowed every port of the empire to India, that in their return they should be confined to the port of London.[68]

On the one hand, some members connected to the Company and the London mercantile society—such as Pascoe Grenfell and Charles Grant, Sr.—supported the amendment.[69] On the other hand, Canning strongly objected to the amendment together with Finlay and other members. He argued that:

> If the amendment were adopted, its direct operation would be to pronounce trade to be synonymous with the prosperity of London only. The out-ports would be doomed to wait like hand-maids upon the metropolis, and to receive, if he might use the expression, her cast off cloths as the gift of her bounty ... It was not right that London should be allowed to prosper at the expense of the other ports of the kingdom...[70]

---

66 Incoming Correspondence 1812–13, letter no. 24.
67 *The Parliamentary Debates*, Vol. XXVI, pp. 622–59.
68 Ibid., p. 681.
69 Ibid., pp. 682 and 687.
70 Ibid., pp. 695–6.

Canning showed his ability as a very able orator in the debates. Regarding Canning's speech, Robert Bargen commented in his rhetorical analysis that:

> His use of sarcasm as a mode of persuasion was most effective. He demonstrated an ability to cut through the various rationalizations presented on behalf of the Company, praising its patriotism and solicitude. Canning's speech was an outstanding example of nineteenth century parliament debating.[71]

Furthermore, as other members supported the original bill, eventually, Baring's amendment was rejected.

Regarding Canning's role in the provincial lobbying campaign, he had neither the personal influence to reverse the Ministry's decisions in Parliament nor a decisive influence on the provincial interest group's lobbying strategies, as Checkland described. Nevertheless, through Canning the provincial lobbyists were able to obtain precise information on the course of negotiations between the Ministry and the EIC, as well as debates on the EIC's Charter in Parliament. After the introduction of the East India Bill, he acted as an effective orator and defended the provincial lobbyists' interests from MPs who represented the Company and other London mercantile interests, although his personal view about the China trade was different from those of his constituents. His significant role in the provincial free trade campaign was symbolised by the name of the ship, the 'George Canning', that Kirkman Finlay sent to Calcutta after the first ship, the 'Earl of Buckinghamshire', for direct trade from the Clyde to India, as described in Chapter 2.

The Liverpool EIA and the Debates over Sugar Duties before 1829

After the partial opening of the East India trade in 1814, merchants in Liverpool lost no time in entering this trade. Table 7 shows the number and the total tonnage of the vessels that cleared from Liverpool for the East Indies between 21 July 1813 and 9 June 1818. The figures indicate the initial expansion of Liverpool's trade with the East Indies. It is a well-known fact in the city's local history that the first ship sent from the port of Liverpool

[71] R.B. Bargen, "An Historical Analysis of the Critical Parliamentary Debates on the Renewal of the Charter of the British East India Company in 1793 and 1813", unpublished PhD thesis, the University of Nebraska, Lincoln, 1974, p. 281.

to the East was the 'Kingsmill', owned by J. Gladstone & Grant, in 1814. However, this was the only vessel sent from Liverpool to the East Indies in that year. In 1815, Cropper, Benson & Co. and Rathbone, Hodgeson & Co. jointly sent another ship. The following years saw the real expansion of the trade; the number of vessels increased from 2 in 1815 to 34 in 1817 and the total tonnage from 808 tons to 13,925 tons. Although the table shows only the first half year of 1818, the tonnage for this year already exceeded the level of the previous year. In spite of the exclusion of private traders from the China and tea trade, the Liverpool merchants' involvement in the East India trade showed their initial success after the abolition of the slave trade in 1807, which had created uncertainty about the future of the West India trade, in which many Liverpool merchants held large stakes.

The East Indian interests in Liverpool were represented by the Liverpool EIA, whose name was changed to the Liverpool East India and China Association after the opening of the China trade. The records of the Glasgow EIA noted that the Liverpool EIA had existed for many years.[72] However, it is not clear whether this association had continued since the last free trade movement against the renewal of the EIC's Charter or had been re-established after a short interval. Webster's study mentioned that the

Table 7. The number and the total tonnage of vessels that left Liverpool for the East Indies between 21 July 1813 and 9 June 1818.

	No. of vessels	Total tonnage
1814	1 (0)	512 (0)
1815	2 (0)	808 (0)
1816	17 (1)	7,410 (376)
1817	34 (5)	13,925 (1,827)
1818	33 (1)	14,100 (453)
Total	87 (7)	36,755 (2,656)

Note: The figures include American vessels that cleared out from Liverpool, and their number and total tonnage are shown in brackets. Most of these American ships were owned by Liverpool merchants, such as Humberstone & Co., W. & J. Brown, and Rathbone & Co. The 33 vessels in 1818 include 7 vessels that entered for loading but had not cleared out at the time of the data's publication.

Source: *Gore's Directory* 1818, pp. 140–1.

[72] Records of the Glasgow East India Association Committee Minute Book 1829–1847 (MS 891001/2, Glasgow Mitchell Library), Special Meeting 23 March 1830, p. 37.

Liverpool EIA had existed continuously since 1813, but Charlton's earlier study stated that the association was established in 1818.[73] Both scholars failed to specify the source of the evidence. Major Liverpool associations and institutions during this period were recorded in the series of *Gore's Directory*. According to this source, other major associations of the city's commercial interests, including the Liverpool WIA and the ACC, appeared in the directories of the earlier years, but the Liverpool EIA was recorded only after 1818.[74] There is no evidence of the existence of this association between 1813 and 1817. Therefore, it is probable that the Liverpool Committee was organised in 1812, discontinued after the renewal of the Company's Charter in 1813 and, after a short interval, the Liverpool EIA was established in 1818 with John Gladstone as the chairman.

The early 1820s was a period when the Liverpool EIA was very active before the real debates of the renewal of the Company's Charter began in 1829. The association pointed out that the following problems persisted after the partial opening of the East India trade in 1814:

(1) The restriction as to tonnage.
(2) The restriction of British ships to certain ports.
(3) The system of licensing, both as to ships and persons.
(4) The restriction that prevents British merchants from trading between China and the European continent.
(5) The restrictions imposed upon the importation of sugar into this country from the East Indies.[75]

These points became agenda items in Parliamentary debates, and a Select Committee was set up to examine the means of extending and securing foreign trade during the sessions in 1820 and 1821.[76] A major gain for the free trade supporters during this period was the removal of the restriction on the tonnage of ships trading to the East Indies in 1823. The EIC's Charter of 1813 had restricted the tonnage of British ships engaged in the trade between

---

[73] A. Webster, "Liverpool and the Eastern Trade 1800–1850: A Paper for the CLAMS Conference on Liverpool and Empire", 2006, p. 9; K. Charlton, "Liverpool and the East India Trade", in *Northern History*, Vol. VII, 1972, p. 56.

[74] *Gore's Directory*, 1818.

[75] *Report of a Committee of the Liverpool East India Association, Appointed to Take into Consideration the Restrictions on the East India Trade*, 1822, pp. 3–4.

[76] Parliamentary Papers, *Report* [*Relative to the Trade with the East Indies and China*] *from the Select Committee Appointed to Inquire into the Means of Extending and Securing the Foreign Trade of the Country, and to Report to the House*, 1821.

Europe and India to over 350 tons, but the size of the ships owned in Liverpool did not normally exceed 200 tons. To enter the East India trade after 1814, the provincial merchants needed to spend time to establish their new trading networks. Nevertheless, the size of the ships was also one reason that only a few ships could go to the East Indies in the couple of years immediately after the relaxation of restrictions on the East India trade in 1814. However, the British trade with the western coast of South America and the success of the American merchants in the East Indies and China showed the capability of smaller ships for long-distance overseas trade.[77] Moreover, they insisted that the smaller vessels availed themselves of more trading opportunities and that, although they tended to incur comparatively greater expenses, they had the advantage of quicker and more flexible operations than larger vessels.[78] An argument that smaller vessels "might be exposed to frequent depredation from pirates" was refuted by the experience of the American merchants and by the fact that there was no difference in insurance rates between large and small vessels.[79] As a result, the Select Committee admitted the inexpediency of the restriction upon the tonnage of vessels engaged in the East India trade with its recommendation for direct and circuitous trade "between any Ports within the limits of the EIC's Charter (except the dominion of the Emperor of China) and any Port or Ports beyond the limits of the said Charter, belonging to any State or Countries in amity with His Majesty".[80]

While Liverpool's East Indian interests achieved the removal of the restriction on the tonnage of vessels, their campaign—in collaboration with other provincial towns such as Manchester—in opposition to the discriminating duties on East Indian sugar in favour of West Indian goods encountered greater difficulties because they needed to overcome the very influential lobbying of the West Indian interests in London and other places in the United Kingdom, including Liverpool itself. The debates within Liverpool's business community over the equalisation of the sugar duties were far more active than in Glasgow. Apparently, this difference derived from the fact that, in Liverpool, both the West Indian and the East Indian traders had their own associations that could represent their own interests.

---

[77] Ibid., pp. 4–5; *Report of a Committee of the Liverpool EIA*, 1822, pp. 6–7.

[78] Ibid.

[79] *Report from the Select Committee on the Foreign Trade*, 1821, p. 4.

[80] Parliamentary Papers, *Second Report from the Select Committee Appointed to Consider of the Means of the Improving and Maintaining the Foreign Trade of the Country*, 1821, p. 4; *Third Report from the Select Committee Appointed to Consider of the Means of Improving and Maintaining the Foreign Trade of the Country*, 1821, p. 208.

In contrast, in Glasgow, while the West Indian interests organised a strong lobbying group, the East Indian interests did not have a means to express their views until the end of the 1820s.

Although the Report of the Liverpool EIA of 1822 explained the five points addressed above, the argument about the restrictions imposed on imports of East Indian sugar occupied the largest part of the pamphlet. When the India trade was opened in 1814, the protecting duty of 10s per cwt. on East Indian sugar was established in favour of West Indian sugar.[81] Moreover, the sales of the former were restricted to the United Kingdom market, whilst the latter was free to be sold in any part of the world. In 1821, the West Indian interests tried to increase the protective duty by an additional 5s on clayed sugar and its equivalents.[82] From the viewpoint of West Indian interests, it was appropriate to protect West Indian sugar from the competition of East Indian sugar due to the lower production costs of the latter compared to the former. They claimed that the equalisation of the duties would 'ruin' the West Indian planters, who had been suffering from a depression for some time past.[83] For instance, William Huskisson, one of the MPs for Liverpool who represented the interests of the West Indian merchants and planters, although he was a principal advocate of the policy of free trade during the 1820s, insisted that:

> ... if it was true that the production of slavery was more costly than that of free labour, that would be additional reason for not depriving him of the advantage of his protecting duty.[84]

The report of the Liverpool EIA condemned the protection of West Indian sugar because this arrangement forced the public to pay higher prices than they would under free competition, while the West Indian interests obtained the tax concessions.[85] In fact, the association's arguments were largely put forward by James Cropper, one of the most successful merchants in Liverpool and an advocate of the anti-slavery movement. He linked the question of West and East Indian sugar with that of slavery, although the Liverpool EIA tended to avoid entering debates on slavery.[86] During the

---

[81] *Report of a Committee of the Liverpool EIA*, 1822, pp. 17–8.

[82] Ibid.; Charlton, "Liverpool and the East India Trade", pp. 56–7.

[83] *The Parliamentary Debates*, New Series, Vol. IX, 1824, pp. 444–67.

[84] Ibid., pp. 464–5.

[85] *Report of a Committee of the Liverpool EIA*, 1822, pp. 17–58; Charlton, "Liverpool and the East India Trade", p. 58.

[86] Ibid., pp. 56–8; K. Charlton, "James Cropper and Liverpool's Contribution to the Anti-Slavery Movement", in *Transaction of the Historic Society of Lancashire and Cheshire*, 1971, Vol. 123, p. 59.

1820s and 1830s, he published several pamphlets in which he criticised the preferential treatment of West Indian planters and refiners, arguing that it actually encouraged unhealthy and inefficient management.[87] In his view, without the preferential treatment, the West Indian sugar—produced under the inefficient slavery system—could not compete with the East Indian sugar produced by "free men".[88] Moreover, as the reduction of duties on the East Indian sugar would increase production in the East Indies and the consumption of sugar at home, it would not affect the King's revenue.[89] On the other hand, Thomas Fletcher, a member and former chairman of the Liverpool WIA, justified the advantages given to West Indian sugar on the basis that the development of the plantation systems and the sugar trade had relied on the trade restrictions. He insisted that the West Indian planters had a right to supply sugar to the British Dominions exclusively and urged the state to relieve the planters experiencing financial difficulty.[90]

In this debate, John Gladstone, who held stakes in both the West and East Indies, failed to reconcile these competing interests. In a comparison between Gladstone and Cropper, Charlton summarised their arguments on the equalisation of sugar duties and the abolition of slavery that:

> Cropper's [arguments] maintain throughout a cool style of argument, insisting always on the need for a public debate to be based on information and enquiry. Gladstone's, on the other hand, are full of minor debating points...[91]

Gladstone supported the equalisation of sugar duties on behalf of the East Indian interests, while he also defended the plantation system and slavery for the West Indian interests.[92]

The equalisation of duties between West Indian sugar and East Indian sugar was not directly related to the renewal of the EIC's Charter. Nevertheless, a bottleneck in the East India trade was the shortage of product for return cargoes to the United Kingdom. While the tea trade was still restricted to the Company, sugar was one of the most promising agricultural products from the East that could solve this problem, along with indigo and raw cotton. The removal of restrictions on East Indian sugar was

[87] J. Cropper, *Relief for West Indian Distress Shewing the Inefficiency of Protecting Duties on East-India Sugar*, 1823.

[88] Charlton, "Liverpool and the East India Trade", p. 56.

[89] Ibid., p. 58.

[90] Ibid., pp. 58–9.

[91] Ibid., p. 61.

[92] Ibid., pp. 61–2.

significant for private merchants, as they needed products to fill the holds of their inward-bound vessels. At the same time, although provincial manufacturers were not directly connected to sugar imports, they also had interests in this commodity because they needed the goods payable in exchange for their manufactured products exported to the East. However, during the 1820s, facing the strong West Indian interests, the Liverpool EIA and other East Indian interests around the country failed to achieve the equalisation of duties between West and East Indian sugar.

Consequently, before the debates over the renewal of the Company's Charter started in the late 1820s, Liverpool's East Indian interests had already led the free trade movement against some restrictions imposed on the East India trade because their lobbying association had existed since the 1810s, and Liverpool's East Indian interests were able to organise their lobbying activities under it, although there was a short interval after the opening of the India trade until 1818. Liverpool's active lobbying during the 1820s was quite a contrast to the inactivity of Glasgow's East Indian interests. Such liberalisation of the East India trade as the removal of the tonnage limitation on British vessels in this trade and the legalisation of the direct and circuitous trade were achieved successfully, whilst facing the strong West Indian interests, the campaign led by James Cropper in support of the equalisation of sugar duties failed. Nevertheless, as will be described below, their long experience in lobbying activities allowed them to lead the free trade movement against the renewal of the EIC's Charter from 1829 to 1833.

The Liverpool EIA and the Beginning of the Charter Debates

As early as August 1827, Liverpool's East Indian interests started to point out the disadvantages of the renewal of the Company's Charter in the city's local newspaper, and the Liverpool EIA published a new report in 1828.[93] It was the Liverpool EIA's first report since 1822, as the organisation thought it was a proper time to warn the public of the approaching renewal of the Charter. However, its campaign truly started in early 1829 with the arrival of James Silk Buckingham and a series of his lectures as a part of his national tour, as well as a public meeting organised by the Liverpool

[93] The Liverpool East India Association, *Report of the Committee of the Liverpool East India Association, on the Subject of the Trade with India: Presented to the Association at a General Meeting, 21 March 1828*, 1828.

EIA.[94] Philips and Eyles stressed that the public of Liverpool warmly welcomed him, as in many other provincial towns.[95] His relationship with the Liverpool EIA seems to have been better than that with the association of Glasgow. The Glasgow EIA did not support him, although individual merchants and manufacturers did, and his lectures were very popular in the city. Moreover, there were differences of opinion over the administrative system in India, and some members, notably Kirkman Finlay, did not regard him highly. By contrast in Liverpool the prominent figures of the free trade movement, including Nicholas Robinson, the Mayor, and James Cropper, attended his lectures, and the *Liverpool Mercury* reported the details of his lectures and views exclusively.[96] In addition, the Liverpool EIA in 1830 subscribed to a fund to support Buckingham's plan to travel around the globe by way of the East Indies.[97] He showed his appreciation for this support from Liverpool's merchants by donating £100 raised from his lectures to James Cropper, John Ewart, and William Rathbone, leading Liverpool merchants, for the purpose of promoting free trade.[98]

A series of Buckingham's lectures inspired the enthusiasm of people in Liverpool for the opening of the East India trade. His lectures were an ideal prologue for the public meeting on 28 January called by the Mayor, who responded to the request from "one hundred sixty of the most influential persons connected with the trade of the port" for "the purpose of taking into consideration of the best means of removing the restrictions imposed upon commerce by the present charter of the East India Company".[99] The members of the Liverpool EIA played a major role in organising this meeting, which was led by the two most influential figures in Liverpool's mercantile society, John Gladstone and James Cropper. The resolutions claiming the total abolition of the Company's monopoly were introduced to the public by these two and other major merchants of Liverpool, including William Rathbone, William Ewart, Henry Booth, William W. Currie, J.T. Alston, Robert Benson, Thomas Brocklebank, and Samuel Hope.

---

94 *Liverpool Mercury*, 3 August 1827.

95 C.H. Philips, *The East India Company 1784–1834*, 1940, p. 289; D. Eyles, "The Abolition of the East India Company's Monopoly 1833", unpublished PhD thesis, University of Edinburgh, 1955, pp. 198–9.

96 *Liverpool Mercury*, 2, 16 and 23 January 1829.

97 J.S. Buckingham, *Subscribers to a Public Fund for Effecting a Voyage round the Globe, by the Route of India, China, Japan, and the Pacific Isles*, p. 7.

98 *Liverpool Mercury*, 6 January 1829.

99 The Liverpool EIA, *Report of the Public Meeting at Liverpool on Wednesday, January 28, 1829*, 1829.

Apart from the aspect of the natives' moral improvement by the free residence of British subjects, Liverpool merchants confined their arguments to the commercial aspects of the renewal of the Company's Charter and did not intervene in the debates on the administrative mode in India. Their ultimate aims in this campaign were the opening of free trade to China and the abolition of unnecessary restrictions imposed on the commercial activities of British merchants in the India trade. Liverpool merchants believed that the opening of the China trade would lead to a great extension of markets for British manufactured products. However, the restrictions imposed on British subjects by the Charter prevented British manufactured goods from being exported to the East. During the public meeting, Cropper pointed out that imports of raw cotton to Liverpool had increased by 100 per cent in ten years, while exports of plain calicoes to the East had increased by 93 per cent in thirty years.[100] They believed that there was a large demand for cotton manufactured pieces from the huge populations of both India and China. The opening of the China trade would give a new opportunity to provincial manufacturers to increase exports of their products from England, which could increase employment in the manufacturing industry and, consequently, increase tea consumption in Britain. In addition, Henry Booth introduced Cropper's view that the further relaxation of the East India and China trade would improve employment and income in Ireland's poor economic condition.[101]

Nevertheless, in terms of the China trade, the most significant point for the merchants of Liverpool was the opening of the tea trade. In the 1828

Table 8. Comparative prices of English and Dutch tea in 1772 and 1827.

	London prices, 1772	Dutch prices, 1772	London Prices, 1827	Dutch prices, 1827
Bohea	1s. 10 1/4d.	2s. 0 8/15d.	1s. 7d.	0s. 5 2/5d.
Congou	3s. 0 1/4d.	3s. 7 7/8d.	2s. 5 8/10d.	1s. 0 9/10d.
Hyson	7s. 0 3/4d.	6s. 8 11/16d.	4s.11d.	2s. 7 1/8d.
Average	4s. 0 3/4d.	4s. 1 11/16d.	2s.11 9/16d.	1s. 4 47/100d.

Source: The Liverpool East India Association, *Report of the Committee of the Liverpool East India Association, on the Subject of the Trade with India: Presented to the Association at a General Meeting, 21st March, 1828*, 1828.

[100] *Liverpool Mercury*, 30 January 1829.

[101] Ibid.; K. Charlton, "The Present State of Ireland in the Eighteen-twenties: James Cropper's Plan", in *Irish Historical Studies*, Vol. XVII, No. 67, 1971, pp. 320–39.

report of the Liverpool EIA, the subject was exclusively argued, and then it was quoted at the public meeting again.[102] Entering the most profitable branch of the East India and China trade was a long-term desire of Liverpool traders. In 1828, the private traders made an attempt to enter the tea trade by pointing out the difference in the prices of tea in the United Kingdom and the European continent. The Parliamentary Act of 1745 obliged the Company "to keep the price of tea in this kingdom, upon an equality with the price thereof in other neighbouring countries of Europe", and if the EIC "shall, at any time, neglect to keep this market supplied with a sufficient quantity of tea, at reasonable prices, to answer to the consumption thereof in Great Britain", the Lord Commissioner of the Treasury had the power to issue licences to individual merchants to import tea from the European continent.[103] In the 1770s, there was little difference between the London prices of tea and the Dutch prices, as Table 8 shows. However, by 1827, the price difference was noticeable. In spite of the Commutation Act of 1784, the Company's tea prices fell by only 25 per cent, whilst Dutch tea prices fell by approximately 66 per cent. According to those provisions, in 1824, the merchants of Liverpool applied to the Treasury to import tea from the European continent.[104] However, E. Walpole rejected their request, claiming that the Customs Consolidation Act of 1825 had repealed the provisions and that other acts expressly banned the tea trade except the Company's direct importation from tea-producing areas to the port of London.[105] At the public meeting, Robert Benson expressed his wish that the government restore the inadequately repealed statutes. At the end of the meeting, the Liverpool Committee was appointed for the purpose of obtaining support from the Mayor and the Common Council, gathering evidence, corresponding with similar institutions in other towns, and preparing petitions to the legislature. On the same occasion, they resolved that a subscription would be opened for these purposes.

Consequently, as Philips explained in his classic work, at the beginning of the campaign, both the Liverpool EIA and the citizens of the city largely welcomed a series of lectures conducted by Buckingham, in contrast to the case in Glasgow.[106] Immediately after his lectures, the city held its first public meeting for the purpose of opposing the renewal of the Company's

102 The Liverpool EIA, *Report of the Committee of the EIA, 1828*.

103 Ibid., pp. 5–6. 18th Geo. II. cap. 26, sec. 10 and 11.

104 *Liverpool Mercury*, 30 January 1829.

105 Huskisson Papers (British Library, Add. MSS. 38765), f. 143. 4th Geo. IV. cap. 80, sec. 9th and 6th Geo. IV. cap. 105, sec. 1.

106 Philips, *The East India Company*, p. 289.

Charter, in which the members of the Liverpool EIA took the initiative and showed strong interest in the opening of the China trade, especially the tea trade.

The Economic and Political Interests of the Members of the Liverpool Committee

During the previous campaign of 1812–13, the Liverpool Committee had consisted mainly of West Indian and American traders, although the former had held the majority. They sought new overseas markets because they had been suffering from the disruption of overseas trade caused by the Napoleonic Wars and the deterioration of Britain's relationship with the United States. This section will analyse the economic interests of the members of the Liverpool Committee and their political stances from 1829 to 1833 to explore the economic and social background of this campaign.

Appendix V, created based on *Gore's Liverpool Directory* and Liverpool's local newspapers of 1829, shows the names and economic interests of the Liverpool Committee members appointed at the public meeting. In this directory, as was the case in other contemporary business directories, many Liverpool businessmen described themselves only as 'merchants' and did not specify the type of merchant, and manufacturers also often called themselves 'merchants'. In addition, 'gentleman' and the title 'Esq.' are not occupational descriptions. Therefore, to complement the information, shipping information recorded in the local newspapers has been used. The information about imports to Liverpool in the *Liverpool Mercury* contains the names of countries and regions from which the ships returned and the owners of consignments. The lists of senior members of Liverpool's associations related to overseas trade have also been examined to identify their economic interests. Nevertheless, this table does not show all the economic interests of the committee members. For instance, according to his testimony in the Select Committee of 1830, although Thomas Thornely engaged in the East India trade and was "drawing bills from China upon houses of good credit in England", he does not appear.[107] Another problem is that the table does not show the economic interests of those who were not involved in trading and shipping activities directly, such as bankers and maritime

[107] Parliamentary Papers, *First Report from the Select Committee on the Affairs of the East India Company and the Trade between Great Britain, the East Indies and China*, 1830, pp. 267–9.

insurance brokers. Nevertheless, in spite of these limitations, the table still shows some characteristics of the Liverpool Committee.

First, although almost two decades had passed since the campaign of 1812–13, 4 of the 21 members of the Liverpool Committee of 1812–13 remained members of the newly appointed committee: John Gladstone, John Leagh, William Rathbone V, and Joseph Brooks Yates. In particular, Gladstone had played a central role in the previous movement as a deputy from the city. Their experience and know-how from the previous campaign were valuable to the Committee, which adopted a similar strategy for lobbying Parliament and the government and for rousing public opinion.

Second, although the table is not perfect, it indicates that the Liverpool Committee consisted of not only the East Indian interests but also several other different trading interests. They actually engaged in different branches of overseas trade, i.e., trade with the West Indies, North and South America, the European continent, Africa, and other regions. On the one hand, John Gladstone and James Cropper, who had held large stakes in the West India trade and the American trade, respectively, entered the East India trade after 1814, and they were also regarded as East Indian traders thereafter. Alston, Finlay & Co., one of the five biggest 'American Houses' in Liverpool in 1829, along with Cropper, Benson & Co. (of James Cropper), was a Liverpool branch of James Finlay & Co. of Glasgow, which was also engaged in the East India trade.[108] T. & J. Brocklebank, a shipping company, entered the trade after 1814, and soon it became one of the main branches of the company's commercial activities.[109] On the other hand, for example, J.B. Yates was a West Indian merchant, and merchants such as John Bolton's Bolton, Ogden & Co. and Charles Tayleur, Son & Co. had their main stakes in the Anglo-American trade rather than trade with the East Indies.[110] Liverpool's lobbyists had varied commercial interests.

Furthermore, Table 9 shows that many of the committee members were the senior members (chairs, secretaries, treasurers, or committee members) of merchants' associations in Liverpool or had experience occupying these posts. In addition, many of them belonged to two or more different associations. Apart from eight members who belonged to the Liverpool EIA, at least seven members were senior members of the ACC, two were

---

108 S. Chapman, *Merchant Enterprise in Britain: From the Industrial Revolution to World War I*, 1992, pp. 86 and 106.

109 See J.F. Gibson, *Brocklebanks, 1770–1950*, 1953.

110 Chapman, *Merchant Enterprise in Britain*, pp. 104–6; J. Killick, "Bolton, Ogden & Co.: A Case Study in Anglo-American Trade, 1790–1850", in *Business History Review*, Vol. 48, No. 4, 1974, pp. 501–19.

Table 9. The Liverpool Committee members who held senior posts in Liverpool merchants' associations.

East India Association (East India and China Association)	J.T. Alston R. Benson J. Ewart	J. Garnett J. Gladstone T. Leathom	W. Potter D. Willink
West India Association	G. Grant C. Horsfall		
American Chamber of Commerce	E. Barclay R. Benson T. Leathom	R. Radcliffe T. Thornely D. Willink	J.A. Yates
Liverpool, Brazil, South American & Mexican Association	D. Willink		
Portugal and Brazil Association	G. Grant D. Heyworth		
Baltic Association	J. Gladstone		
Mediterranean and Levant Association	J. Garnett T. Leathom R. Radcliffe		
Ship Owners Association	J. Gladstone G. Grant C. Horsfall	J.B. Yates	

Source: created from Appendix V.

from the WIA, three members were from the Mediterranean and Levant Association, another three were from associations related to the South American trade, i.e., the Portugal and Brazil Association and the Liverpool, Brazil, South American and Mexican Association, and four members were from the Shipping Owners Association. There is a possibility that further research would reveal additional such committee members. This also confirms that a group consisting of several different commercial interests organised Liverpool's lobbying campaign.

In terms of politics, the committee included men who had different political views. The members who held office in the Liverpool Corporation, i.e., J. Bourne, W.W. Currie, William Earle, C. Horsfall, N. Robinson, and J. Ewart, were all Tories except for Ewart.[111] Gladstone and John Bolton were also Tories and had been great supporters of George Canning, who had pursued moderate Tory policies, whilst the merchants, Cropper, Rathbone, and T. Thornely stood on the Whig-radical line. Edward Baines, Jr., who

[111] *Liverpool Mercury*, 22 November 1833.

supported liberal policies (except notably in factory legislation), was a son of Edward Baines, who was returned as a Whig MP for Leeds after the Parliamentary Reform.[112]

The *Liverpool Mercury* best described the free trade interests in Liverpool in its article on the public meeting as follows:

> The requisition, in compliance with which the Mayor has called this meeting at the Town-hall, was most numerously and respectably subscribed, by Tories, Whigs, Radicals, and middle-course men, whose motto is "Medio tutissimus ibis". So unusual an amalgamation of parties reminds us of Swift's observation, that "Money is neither Whig nor Tory."[113]

Like Liverpool's committee of the previous campaign and the Glasgow EIA, respecting both commercial and political interests, the Liverpool Committee was heterogeneous. During the 1820s, debates over British economic policies stirred up divisions in Liverpool's mercantile society as the question on the Orders in Council had done during the Napoleonic Wars of the 1800s and 1810s. The East Indian interests and the anti-slavery lobbying group, and the West Indian interests in the city were not reconciled in their debates over the equalisation of the duties between West Indian and East Indian sugar and the abolition of slavery. However, Liverpool merchants were again able to unite in the campaign against the renewal of the EIC's Charter. Disregarding the different commercial sections and political views, a large part of Liverpool's commercial society supported the campaign in the wider context of the course of economic and political liberalisation during the 1820s.

The Proceedings of Liverpool's Campaign for the Total Abolition of the Monopoly

On 4 February 1829, in Liverpool, the Common Council decided to deal with the subject of the East India trade in a special committee when it received the memorial from the committee appointed at the public meeting, and it unanimously agreed to contribute up to £500 to the subscription.[114] Ten days later, the members of the committee held a meeting with

---

112 A.G. Crosby, "Baines, Edward (1774–1848)", in *Oxford Dictionary of National Biography*, 2004 [http://www.oxforddnb.com/view/article/1089, accessed 29 May 2006].

113 *Liverpool Mercury*, 23 January 1829.

114 Liverpool Town Books, 4 February 1829; *Liverpool Mercury*, 6 February 1829.

James Cropper and Samuel Hope, the representatives from the committee appointed at the public meeting, and after discussion, the Common Council decided to create a separate committee, which acted closely with the Liverpool Committee.[115]

In April, the Liverpool Committee decided to send a deputation to London. To urge other outports and provincial manufacturing towns to cooperate with a deputation from Liverpool in their interview with some Ministers regarding the East India and China trade, they sent circulars to them. The Liverpool Committee's communication with Manchester was particularly close because of their geographical proximity and economic connection.

Liverpool's free trade movement against the renewal of the Company's Charter was largely driven by William Huskisson, MP for the city. He had served as the President of the Board of Control under Lord Liverpool's Ministry and was a key person in the economic reforms of the 1820s. Under his (and George Canning's) directions, Britain adopted such liberal economic policies as the relaxation of the Navigation Acts and tariffs and reciprocal treaties with other European countries. Liverpool businessmen succeeded in recruiting such an able man as their own representative in Parliament after Canning, and they were able to exploit his strong influence on national politics. On 12 May, Huskisson and the Marquis of Lansdowne presented petitions from Liverpool and Manchester, respectively, to the House of Commons.[116] Huskisson also made arrangements for the interview of the deputations from several outports and manufacturing towns by the Ministry. When the Liverpool Committee wrote to him to arrange the interview, he replied that the government had no intention of objecting to W.W. Whitmore's motion for a Select Committee of inquiry and that he personally agreed with the Liverpool Committee that it was the proper time to start its lobbying activities.[117] Furthermore, he insisted that the Liverpool Committee should stir up public opinion across the whole of British society. He advised them that:

> They are not the interests alone of the commerce and industry of the country but those of the whole community which are involved in the considerations connected with the Charter of the East India Company, and it is therefore material that all classes should be made sensible that they have an interest in

[115] Liverpool Town Books, 14 February 1829.

[116] *Liverpool Mercury*, 15 May 1829.

[117] Records of the Glasgow East India Association Correspondence Incoming 1829–1830 (MS 891001/4, Glasgow Mitchell Library), 4 May 1829, letter no. 2.

> obtaining their relaxations which are more immediately called for by the commercial and manufacturing towns.[118]

This advice persuaded the Liverpool Committee to urge free traders in other outports and manufacturing towns to attend the interview. During the free trade movement, assembling the deputies from the main commercial and manufacturing towns of the United Kingdom and petitioning Parliament (as well as the publication of several pamphlets, but on a smaller scale than in 1812–13) were adopted as the main strategies by the free trade interests. At the interview, Huskisson assisted the General Deputation with Whitmore.[119] Later, James Cropper acknowledged his contribution to the lobbying activities for "promoting an extension of trade with East India and the opening of that with China".[120] The Liverpool lobbyists were able to exploit Huskisson's connection with the Ministry in their lobbying efforts.

A few days after the interview, just before the dissolution of their meeting in London, the deputies held a meeting at Fenton's Hotel, and as they had done during the previous campaign of 1812–13, they requested the Liverpool Committee to act as the Central Committee for the purpose of communicating with all other associations.[121] In early 1830, the Liverpool Committee decided to petition Parliament as a part of its lobbying activities and to instruct other outports and manufacturing towns to petition Parliament. The free trade interests needed to urge the Ministry to set up the Select Committee to investigate the East India questions for Parliament to give notice to the Company at the earliest possible time in 1831.[122] The provincial manufacturing towns and outports adopted the method of petitioning Parliament more widely than in the previous campaign. According to Philips, 255 petitions were laid before Parliament from 1829 to 1830, whilst there had been only 135 petitions from 1812 to 1813.[123]

When the Select Committee for "the affair of the Company and the trade between Great Britain and China" was established in February, the Liverpool Committee expressed dissatisfaction with the selection of its members since the Select Committee did not adequately represent the interests of all the parties involved in this question.[124] The members criticised the fact that the chairs of the Select Committee had strong views in favour of the

118 M. Greenberg, *British Trade and the Opening of China 1800–42*, 1969, p. 182.
119 Incoming Correspondence 1829–30, 9 May 1829, letter no. 5.
120 Huskisson Papers, f. 210.
121 Incoming Correspondence 1829–30, 15 May 1829, letter no. 9.
122 Ibid., 21 January 1830, letter no. 26.
123 Philips, *The East India Company*, p. 289.
124 *Liverpool Courier*, 3 March 1830.

Company. At the same time, the committee organised direct lobbying in London under their leadership. Liverpool urged other towns and outports to send deputations to London again to lobby Parliament and the Ministry. Glasgow, Calcutta, Manchester, Bristol, Leeds, Birmingham, Edinburgh, Hull, the Staffordshire Iron Trade, Plymouth, and Darlington responded to it.[125] Although the purpose of the General Deputation in London of the provincial commercial and manufacturing interests was to lobby Parliament and the government, as Eyles argues, the significant point of this assembly was that they succeeded in demonstrating in the political centre of the country that all major commercial and manufacturing places of the country were in favour of the complete opening of the trade and that the abolition of the monopoly was the general wish of the British nation.[126]

In January 1831, a public meeting called by Thomas Brancker, the Mayor, was held in the Session House on Chapel-street in Liverpool "to take into consideration the propriety of petitioning Parliament" against the EIC's Charter and the China monopoly.[127] In this meeting, the report prepared by the Liverpool Committee on the proceedings of the debates over the Company's Charter since the beginning of their campaign in January 1829 was read. In spite of the unfavourable selection of the Select Committee and the report produced by its members, Liverpool's merchants had an optimistic view of the opening of the China trade after the investigation. In December 1830, Kirkman Finlay had expressed his opinion in Manchester that the debates on the China trade were already settled in favour of the opening, and by January, it became clear that the China trade would be opened.[128] Nonetheless, they still thought it was necessary to push their opinions. Cropper expressed his belief in the meeting that:

> ... after the full and conclusive evidence there adduced on that subject, he could hardly have supposed it necessary for the people of Liverpool again to assemble to assert their rights, for they might naturally have expected that after such conclusive evidence of the injurious effects of the monopoly of the China trade, and the advantage which would attend its abolition, the question would at once have been given up to the country; but though the people of Liverpool knew so much of the advantage of free trade that they required no further evidence to convince them that free trade was better than monopoly, this was not the case with the inhabitants of other towns and places in the

---

[125] Minutebook of the Manchester Chamber of Commerce and Manufacture (MCCM) 1827–1833 (M8/2/2, Manchester Archives and Local History), 31 March 1830, p. 202.

[126] Eyles, "The Abolition of the East India Company's Monopoly 1833", pp. 177–8.

[127] *Liverpool Mercury*, 21 January 1831.

[128] Minutebook of the MCCM 1827–33, 17 December 1830, p. 241.

> empire; and therefore it was the duty of the people of Liverpool to exert themselves, and to impress upon the minds of the country at large the necessity of a strenuous and unanimous opposition to the renewal of the charter of the East India Company.[129]

There was nothing particularly new in their statements and resolutions at this meeting, but as Cropper addressed it, this was the last public meeting in Liverpool for the purpose of opposing the renewal of the EIC's Charter.

After the public meeting, few articles on the renewal of the Charter were published in local newspapers before 1833, but the Liverpool Committee continued its efforts. On 21 January, after considering John Crawfurd's opinion, they took the initiative to send a deputation to London and called on other provincial towns to do so as well to influence the new nomination of the Select Committee for the East India question by demonstrating their strong representation to the Ministry.[130] On 5 February, the deputations from Liverpool, Calcutta, Manchester, Bristol, and Birmingham held an interview with Earl Grey, Lord Althorp, the Chancellor of Exchequer, and Charles Grant, the President of the India Board.[131] At this meeting, Cropper explained the advantages of the opening of the China trade based on the positive consequences derived from the opening of the India Trade and then insisted on the "necessity of considering the China trade as quite distinct from the Government of India and their claim for the opening of the trade on the ground of their natural rights" and criticised the Company's monopoly for the higher prices of tea imposed on consumers to make up the huge expenses of its management.[132] Although the Minister avoided making a pledge to them, as the Select Committee had just been reappointed the previous night, Crawfurd, who accompanied the deputies, expressed his gratitude with respect to their selection in his letter that:

> The contrast between this audience [Earl Grey] and that granted by the Duke of Wellington and his associates was certainly great. The Committee is formed and consists of 40—13 of them being new performers of whom are Liberals… I have tried to exert heads—But of the 40 members 24 are I think with us and perhaps 16 against us—Majority 8.[133]

In 1832, as the Parliamentary Reform question attracted the attention of the whole nation, Liverpool and other towns' committees agreed not to raise

129 *Liverpool Mercury*, 21 January 1831.
130 Minutebook of the MCCM 1827–33, 26 January 1831, p. 247.
131 Ibid., Letter from Mr. Braidley dated 5 February 1831, p. 252.
132 Ibid.
133 Records of the Glasgow East India Association Correspondence Incoming 1831–1832 (MS 891001/5, Glasgow Mitchell Library), February 1831, letter no. 5b.

the East India and China questions before the settlement of the Reform question. Therefore, the free trade movement at the national level fell relatively silent. Nevertheless, in February, the Board of Control contacted the Committees of Liverpool and some other provincial towns, including Manchester, Glasgow, Hull, Birmingham, and Bristol, for their opinions relative to India affairs.[134] Although the Board of Control addressed eleven queries to them, they responded with similar answers because they communicated with each other to draw up the answers. On several different occasions, many free traders debated such questions as the positive and negative impacts on their businesses after the opening of the India trade in 1814 and the effects of "the Union of Government with trade in India", but probably the most significant point of their answers was related to the Company's commercial operations and the system of remittance from India to Europe. They argued that the Company's large commercial transactions as an importer of Indian goods dislocated commerce. Liverpool and other towns responded to the Board's query that private agents were able to make remittances. For instance, in Liverpool's answers, they argued that:

> We see no reason to doubt the practicability of effecting remittances to the country, bring through private agency and otherwise to the full extent of the Company's wants.'[135]

Then, regarding the methods of remittance after the cessation of the Company's trade, Liverpool, Manchester, and Glasgow all referred to drafts on India, export financing in India, transporting specie and bullion, or their combinations as the means of remittance from India to Britain, to be conducted by natives and European agents.[136]

Mutsuki Matsumoto's study pointed out that, after the abolition of the EIC's monopoly, the Company's sales of drafts on India in the United Kingdom and its export financing for Indian commodities became the main means of remittance from India to the United Kingdom, as the free

---

[134] Incoming Correspondence 1831–32, April 1832, Answers of the Liverpool Committee, located between letter no. 37b and 38a; Parliamentary Paper, *Reports from Committees: 1831–2. East India Company's Affairs. II. – Finance and Accounts – Trade*, Vol. III, 1832, Appendix no. 4, pp. 504–90.

[135] Incoming Correspondence 1831–32, April 1832, Answers of the Liverpool Committee Q. 6th, located between letter no. 37b and 38a.

[136] See each town's answer to Query 8, and Parliamentary Paper, *Reports from Committees: 1831–2. East India Company's Affairs. II. – Finance and Accounts – Trade. Vol. III*, 1832, pp. 542–3.

trade advocates had expected.[137] According to his study, the annual average of the EIC's supply of drafts on India in the United Kingdom from 1834 to 1839 was approximately £1.72 million, rising to £ 3.37 million from 1850 to 1854. In contrast, although the remittance through export financing for Indian commodities initially performed well and its annual average from 1834 to 1839 reached £1.4 million, this means of remittance virtually ended in 1849, mainly as a result of the criticism of the Company's export financing. In addition, the annual average of remittance in the form of specie was only approximately £69,000 from 1834 to 1857. Although, after 1834, remittance in the form of drafts on India became the main means of remittance from India, it could not sufficiently compensate for the Company's deficits in the home account. After the cessation of its commercial functions, its deficits were initially made up by the profits from selling its commercial assets during the 1830s and capital raised by issuing its bonds in the United Kingdom during the 1840s. Moreover, after the 1850s, the Company requested that the Indian railway companies pay capital instalments to its treasury under their respective Deeds of Contracts with the EIC, and although the expenses for construction and management of the railways were paid from the pool of this capital, the Company could divert the surplus of the capital to repay its debts.[138] Therefore, in reality, the remittance system that the free trade supporters of outports and manufacturing towns proposed to the government in the Charter debates could not fully meet the increasing level of remittances from India to the United Kingdom.

In July 1832, Thomas Langton, the secretary of the Liverpool Committee, asked the Glasgow EIA and the Manchester Committee to consider the propriety of asking the candidates their opinions regarding the question of the East India monopoly in the general election for the Reformed Parliament. The Committee Minute Book of the Glasgow EIA describes the heated debates of Liverpool's lobbyists on this subject as follows:

> ... some [members of the Committee] think a pledge should be asked for, others see objections to this; some think an address to the Electors of the United Kingdom, signed with the names of Chairmen of the several towns would be the best form; some that resolutions in the style of the annexed would

[137] M. Matsumoto, *Igirisu no Indo touchi* [*India under the Control of Britain*], 1996, Chapter 3, Section 2. Advances to the exporters of Indian commodities were made by the Company in India, and then repayments were made in the United Kingdom.

[138] Ibid., pp. 83–4; Parliamentary Papers, *Return of Contracts with Any Company for Making Railways Public Roads, Canals, Works for Irrigation, or Other Public Works in India*, 1859, Session 1 (259), Vol. XIX.

> be preferable, whilst some doubt the propriety of taking any steps of the kind.[139]

Although both the Glasgow and Manchester Committees recommended that the electors should take the significance of the East India and China questions into consideration in their votes, they did not take any further measures in this respect.[140] In contrast, the Liverpool Committee thought that it was proper to ask candidates for their opinions before they contacted other associations. Nevertheless, it is not clear whether or not, in Liverpool, they requested that the candidates declare themselves in favour of the complete opening of the East India and China trade. However, in the election, they at least asked the candidates about their attitudes towards the equalisation of the duties on West Indian and East Indian sugar. Thomas Thornely and William Ewart were in favour of the equalisation of duties, but Lord Sandon supported the West Indian interests by insisting on the reduction of duties on their goods, and Sir Harold Douglas avoided replying to the question.[141] This indicated that subjects of communication between the provincial lobbying groups were not confined to the timing of sending petitions and their deputies to London. Although they failed to reach consensus, they tried to exploit the opportunity of the general election for their free trade campaign.

Due to the limitation of available sources, it is more difficult to describe Liverpool merchants' lobbying activities in detail in 1833, especially after April, than for previous years, but these existing records can tell us some stories about this period. After January 1833, the Liverpool Committee, the Glasgow EIA, and their parliamentary members closely communicated with each other to seek the proper time to send deputations to London. While they were waiting for detailed information about the government's plan, they continued their activities regarding some agenda items related to the East India trade. In the middle of March, they knew that the government had decided that the China trade would be opened according to Lord Sandon's letter to the Mayor of Liverpool.[142] At the same time, it was their intention that the tea imported to the outports should be stored in warehouses within the walls of docks before auction sales to reduce the risk of smuggling and to secure customs revenues. The members of the Liverpool

139 Committee Minute Book 1829–47, 10 July 1832, pp. 82–3.

140 Ibid.; Minutebook of the MCCM 1827–33, 11 July 1832, p. 411.

141 *Liverpool Mercury*, 14 December 1832.

142 Records of the Glasgow East India Association Correspondence Incoming 1833–1834 (MS 891001/6, Glasgow Mitchell Library), 15 March 1833, letter no. 18a.

Committee expressed strong objections, as they thought that these conditions were "incompatible with that economical management of the China trade".[143] The committee lobbied against this point through their MPs and Whitmore, although the free trade supporters eventually failed to persuade the government to change these conditions in the new East India Charter.[144]

Moreover, it may be reasonable to refer again to Charles Grant's inquiry in February to Whitmore regarding the opinion of provincial commercial and manufacturing interests in regard to the "rules, restrictions and conditions under which they should be allowed to settle in the interior of India".[145] Thus, as described previously, the Glasgow EIA asked the Liverpool Committee to write a draft for it because the former did not have the latter's knowledge of the legal system in India.[146] The free trade interests of the provincial manufacturing towns and outports tended to focus on the commercial aspects of the East India and China questions. Nevertheless, the Liverpool Committee showed the ability to address the broader aspects of the question than Glasgow could.

Conclusion

This chapter has examined the lobbying activities of Liverpool merchants in opposition to the renewal of the Charters between 1812 and 1813 and between 1829 and 1833. During the first period, Liverpool's free trade campaign was organised by the two major commercial interests of the city of that time, the West Indian traders and the American traders. Although historians such as Checkland and Tolley have previously discussed their collaboration, it has been demonstrated here that the West Indian interests dominated the Liverpool Committee. Like other outports and manufacturing towns of the country, Liverpool merchants struggled in the unstable commercial environment, which was created primarily by the Napoleonic Wars and the deterioration of the Anglo-American relationship as a result of their economic dispute over the Orders in Council. On the one side, the West Indian traders and planters, who held strong influence within the Corporation, were firm supporters of the Orders in Council; and on the other side, many American merchants blamed the Orders for their

143 Ibid., 20th, March 1833, letter no. 16a.
144 Ibid.
145 Committee Minute Book 1829–47, 12 March 1833, p. 91.
146 Ibid.

difficulties and demanded that the state repeal them. Their opposing views surfaced during their lobbying activities, such as the debates over the economic condition of Liverpool in the House of Commons. George Canning's capture of a parliamentary seat for the city was also a result of the conflict between the two groups. Later, this led to the American merchants' refusal to subscribe for the foundation of the Liverpool Office in London. Nevertheless, as far as the renewal of the East India Charter was concerned, in spite of their different views over the Ministry's wartime economic policy, these remained minor obstacles to the Liverpool lobbyists. They were able to maintain their consensus on the opening of the East India trade, as both of them needed to look for new markets under the depressed economic conditions, and Liverpool was able to lead the provincial lobbyists' campaign. This study shows that, except for the interval period of 1812, the Liverpool Committee maintained close communication with other parties to organise an effective campaign, as Glasgow did.

Furthermore, the provincial interests' political connection to London should not be ignored, as the case of Liverpool shows. In addition to the city's traditional political connection with the state, which became clear in such events as the financial crisis of 1793, it was fortunate for Liverpool, which played a role as a Central Committee for the campaign during the interval, to obtain a very able man such as Canning as its representative in Parliament. As one of the best friends of free trade advocates, Canning, who was at the centre of national politics, was able to know the Ministry's intention on the renewal of the Charter well. He played a role as one of the representatives for the provincial lobbyist groups in Parliament. His opinions strongly influenced their lobbying strategies, but not as strongly as Checkland described in his work. In fact, the provincial lobbyists rejected his advice that they should give up their lobbying against the China monopoly in early January 1813. Nevertheless, in spite of his personal opinion against the opening of the China monopoly, he sought the best possible outcomes for the provincial interests in the debates over the renewal of the Company's Charter in Parliament.

In the campaign from 1829 to 1833, Liverpool merchants took the lead again. Within the city, while the West Indian interests and the East Indian interests were opposed to each other in the debates over the equalisation of the sugar duties and the abolition of slavery, Liverpool merchants in different trading branches and with different political views succeeded in uniting again to secure the complete opening of the East India and China trade. In the initial stage of the campaign for the total abolition of the Company's monopoly, the Liverpool merchants largely owed their lobbying activities, such as arranging their meeting with some Ministers in London, to Huskisson before he was killed in the railway accident. Although the main aims of their campaign were the opening of the China trade and the abolition of the licence system in India, Liverpool merchants, in particular, showed a strong desire to enter the tea trade, probably more than any other British city. The city's economic significance as the major British port along with the port of London and its "long-established" EIA gave its merchants strong initiative in the campaign. The records of the Glasgow EIA show that Liverpool merchants maintained close communication with other outports and manufacturing towns, as well as their Parliamentary supporters, not only for organising the General Deputation but also for sending more effective petitions and memorials to Parliament and the Ministry and attempting to exploit the opportunity of the general election for their lobbying efforts.

CHAPTER FIVE

SEARCHING FOR NEW MARKETS: THE MANCHESTER CHAMBER OF COMMERCE AND MANUFACTURERS, 1829–1833

Introduction

While it is much more difficult to reconstruct the lobbying activities of Manchester in the earlier movement in detail because of a lack of historical sources, the minutebooks of the Manchester Chamber of Commerce and Manufacturers (MCCM) provide one of the most comprehensive historical sources, along with those of the Glasgow EIA, for historians interested in the lobbying activities of provincial merchants and manufacturers for free trade in Asia after 1820. The main difference between the records of the MCCM and those of the Glasgow EIA is that, apart from the minutebooks, the latter contains a large collection of corresponding letters between the Glasgow EIA and other associations and individuals, including material from Manchester. Glasgow's materials can provide additional information to that provided in previous studies of Manchester's campaign. Moreover, examining these different cities' records can more clearly show the similarities and differences in the lobbying activities of Manchester and other towns.

Such historians as Eyles, Greenberg, and Redford have already used the MCCM's records widely in their studies of the free trade movements of this period.[1] Through examining the MCCM's lobbying for the abolition of the restrictions imposed on the tonnage of vessels for the India trade, Eyles pointed out that Manchester's prime concern after 1814 was to remove the remaining restrictions imposed on the India trade rather than to open the China trade. Nevertheless, Eyles and the other two historians mentioned above used these records to explore the provincial lobbyists' 1829–33 campaign as a whole rather than focusing specifically on Manchester's lobbying activities. Therefore, emphasising Manchester's campaigners, this chapter will explore their collaboration with other provincial organisations and

[1] M. Greenberg, *British Trade and the Opening of China 1800–42*, 1969; D. Eyles, "The Abolition of the East India Company's Monopoly 1833", unpublished PhD thesis, University of Edinburgh, 1955; A. Redford, *Manchester Merchants and Foreign Trade 1794–1858*, 1934.

their contribution to the free trade movement of 1829–33. The close analysis of the economic interests of those, who were involved in Manchester's campaign, and their lobbying activities will reveal that their prime concern in the movement was different from that of Glasgow and Liverpool.

Growth of the Cotton Capital of the World, 1780–1830

During the first half of the nineteenth century, Manchester became one of the largest provincial cities in Britain, along with Liverpool and Glasgow. Its population grew rapidly from about 24,000 in 1773 to 108,000 in 1821 and reached 142,000 by 1831.[2] Manchester was synonymous with 'cottonopolis' after the Industrial Revolution. The city became the very centre of the cotton industry in Britain after the 1780s. In 1781, Richard Arkwright built the city's first steam-powered mill. After the success of his business, the city and its neighbouring area experienced the rapid growth in the cotton industry, although, in spite of the diffusion of the factory system, this new system did not immediately replace the traditional putting-out system. In the weaving branch of the cotton industry factories were slow to develop, because of the technological limitations of the power-loom, which was not suitable to fine yarns before the 1820s.

Even during the 1830s, the cotton industry consisted of a large number of small firms.[3] Nevertheless, after the 1820s, the Manchester region experienced the rationalisation of the cotton industry—that is to say, the spread of the factory system and the power-loom. Because the competitive condition of the market during the 1820s reduced their profit margins, firms needed to adjust their business structures by increasing the size of their production and turnover.[4] Technological innovations enabled spinning and weaving branches to be integrated within a factory.[5] This concentration of industry resulted in an increase in the size of firms.

Historians such as Roger Lloyd-Jones, Myrddin Lewis, and Michael Fores have focused on the development of Manchester's commercial sector in their studies, conducted during the 1980s.[6] On the one hand, Ronald Smith

---

2 D. Read, *Peterloo: The Massacre and its Background*, 1958, p. 4.

3 R. Smith, "Manchester as a Centre for Manufacturing and Merchanting Cotton Goods, 1820 to 1830", in *University of Birmingham Historical Journal*, Vol. IV, 1953–1954, pp. 50–1.

4 R. Lloyd-Jones and M.J. Lewis, *Manchester and the Age of the Factory*, 1988, pp. 110–1.

5 Ibid., chap. 5.

6 Lloyd-Jones and Lewis, *Manchester*; M. Fores, "The Myth of a British Industrial Revolution", in *History*, Vol. LXVI, 1981.

argued by pointing out the development of the warehouse system during the period that Manchester emerged as an entrepot for the local cotton industry after the end of the Napoleonic Wars.[7] On the other hand, Lloyd-Jones and Lewis contended that the commercial activities played a more significant role in Manchester's economic activities even before the 1820s. In their research, Lloyd-Jones and Lewis used data from the Manchester Poor Rate Assessment Books and reconstructed its business structure in the first half of the nineteenth century. Warehouse businesses showed their much superior economic position in terms of the total value of property assets compared to that of factories in the middle of the 1810s.[8] The city in this period was "a warehouse town" and "Manchester's symbolic role as the centre of the factory may best be understood in terms of labour rather than capital".[9] From these studies on the structure of Manchester's economy it is clear that factory owners and warehousemen held a significant position in Manchester during the 1820s.

With respect to local politics, the cotton merchants (warehousemen) tended to support the Tories, while most cotton manufacturers (spinners) were Whigs during the post-Napoleonic Wars period.[10] In spite of this political difference, Manchester's business community during this period was a firm supporter of the *laizzez-faire* principle. However, their support for free trade and the *laizzez-faire* principle derived from their practical interests rather than blind pursuance of economic ideology, as in the case of Liverpool's merchants. In fact, Lloyd-Jones and Lewis argued that, in Manchester before the mid-1820s, there were hostilities and conflicts between the various economic interest groups over Britain's foreign trade policy.[11] For example, a part of the Manchester business community, mainly a group of warehouse manufacturers, opposed cotton spinners who exported their yarns to foreign countries, and they petitioned Parliament for its prohibition before 1820 because they thought that the exportation of yarns could only benefit foreign cotton manufacturers and was against the interest of the domestic manufacturing industry.[12]

Manchester was also a centre of the radical movement in Britain, and the maintenance of public order was one of the major concerns among its

---

7 Smith, "Manchester as a Centre", p. 63.
8 Lloyd-Jones and Lewis, *Manchester*, p. 30, Table 3.5.
9 Ibid., p. 32 and p. 37.
10 Read, *Peterloo*, p. 7.
11 Lloyd-Jones and Lewis, *Manchester*, chapter 5.
12 Ibid.

middle class. As the Peterloo massacre of 1819 showed economic distress usually caused social disturbance. The cotton industry and its related businesses, which dominated the city's economy, increasingly depended on the international market, and Manchester's economic structure became vulnerable to market fluctuations.[13] Trade depressions often severely damaged the living standards of a large number of cotton weavers and spinners and their families in the city, which resulted in popular riots. A lesson from the Peterloo massacre for Manchester businessmen was the necessity of organising an institution that could overcome conflicts between the different economic interest groups and unite the interests of the city's business community.[14] As a result, the MCCM was established in the following year. This institution represented the interests of the Manchester business community and lobbied the government and Parliament for the liberation of their economic activities from such restrictions as the monopoly of the EIC and the Corn Laws.

The Manchester Business Community and its Lobbying before 1829

Before the nineteenth century, the British textile manufacturers regarded the import to Europe of Indian cotton pieces, with their superior quality and competitive prices, as a serious threat. Therefore, in the initial phase of industrialisation, cotton manufacturers in Lancashire and South-western Scotland demanded that the government protect their infant industry. In 1788, British cotton spinners criticised the EIC's importation of Indian cotton products for damaging the domestic industry, and demanded that the Company reduce the importation of piece goods and increase that of raw materials, instead.[15] Moreover, at the time of the renewal of the Company's Charter in 1793, the cotton manufacturers organised a campaign against the Company's importation of finished products from India.[16] In January 1791, "Muslin and Cotton Manufacturers and Cotton Spinners" of the Manchester district, in their meeting on the EIC's competition, argued:

---

[13] The vulnerability of the industry is indicated by the number of business failures during this period. In fact, between 1815 and 1825, 60 per cent of the factory firms of the cotton industry failed; in the latter year, newcomers comprised 56 per cent of all factory firms. Ibid., p. 107.

[14] Ibid., p. 135.

[15] P.J. Marshall, *Problems of Empire: Britain and India 1757–1813*, 1968, pp. 85–6 and document 35.

[16] Ibid., p. 86.

> That the cotton and muslin manufactures are of the greatest consequence to this kingdom, giving employment to nearly half a million of his Majesty's subjects.
>
> ... That the British manufacturers... are exposed to continual danger and immense losses by the importation of muslins and cotton goods from the East Indies, manufactured by persons—the price of whose labour does not exceed the amount of taxes paid to Government by individual labourers in Great Britain. That such importation of manufactured goods is highly injurious to the nation, by transferring the price of labour from this country to the inhabitants of the East.[17]

Furthermore, according to Marshall, when Lord Hawkesbury, the President of the Board of Control, made his inquiry to manufacturing towns in the same year as to "what goods they expected to be able to sell in the area covered by the Company's monopoly, if they were allowed to trade there on their own account", they failed to answer him.[18] These events indicate that the main interest of the British cotton industry at that time was still the protection of the industry from the import of cotton piece goods from India rather than the export of its own products to the East.

However, in the next two decades, their position changed. Table 10 shows the rapid increase in the productivity of spinning mules during the late eighteenth and the early nineteenth centuries. At the end of the eighteenth century, the productivity of a power-assisted mule was roughly 160 times higher than that of Indian hand spinners of the eighteenth century. Due to the increase in the productivity of machinery and the diffusion of these

Table 10. Labour productivity in cotton spinning (number of operative hours to process 100 lbs. of cotton for 80's cotton yarn).

Indian hand spinners	Over 50,000
Crompton's first mule in 1780	2,000
Mules with around 100 spindles	1,000
A pair of power-assisted mules with 240 spindles driven at 2,250 rpm in 1795	300
The 600-spindle mules in 1825 at 3,000 rpm	135
Most efficient modern machinery in 1970	40

Source: S.D. Chapman, *The Cotton Industry in the Industrial Revolution,* p. 20; H. Catling, *The Spinning Mule*, 1970, p. 54 (Original source).

[17] A. Redford, *Manchester Merchants and Foreign Trade, 1794–1858*, 1934, pp. 108–9.

[18] Marshall, *Problems of Empire: Britain and India*, pp. 96–7.

technological innovations across the country Lancashire's cotton industry became able to compete with its Indian counterpart, especially in the market for coarser goods, by the time of the renewal of the Company's Charter in 1813. The industry's view of India changed from that of a strong competitor to that of a potential market for British manufactured products. At the same time, as explained previously, because of the intensification of the Napoleonic Wars and the outbreak of the Anglo-American War, British cotton manufacturers faced difficulty in exporting their products to their traditional markets in the European continent and North America. Moreover, increasing competition from foreign rival manufacturers under protectionism curtailed demand for British manufactured products. These political and economic factors encouraged British manufacturers to look for new markets for their products and alternative suppliers of raw materials in the East and in Latin American countries.

In the first free trade movement of 1812–13, Manchester joined the campaign of provincial merchants and manufacturers. The business people of Manchester petitioned Parliament and sent a delegation to London to join the General Deputation for the abolition of the Company's monopoly. Manufacturers in Manchester benefited significantly from the partial opening of the East India trade in 1814: exports of cotton cloth increased from about 0.8 million yards to over 43.5 million yards from 1814 to 1828, and exports of cotton twist increased from 121,000 lbs. in 1823 to upwards of 4.5 million lbs. in 1828. The total exports in official values expanded from £1.6 million in 1814 to £5.8 million in 1829.[19] The Asian market also increased its relative importance in the export of British cotton goods. From 1804 to 1806, the Asian market—including China—occupied less than 1 per cent of the total exports.[20] However, two decades later, the share increased to 7.7 per cent, and to 10.8 per cent three decades later.

During the 1820s, the merchants and manufacturers of Manchester, led by the newly established MCCM, organised campaigns against the limitation of the tonnage of vessels from the United Kingdom to the East Indies and in favour of the equalisation of duties on West Indian and East Indian sugar, along with Liverpool and other provincial manufacturing towns and outports.[21] In February 1827, they set up a committee "to enquire into the

---

[19] Huskisson Papers (British Library, MSS 38765), f. 175.

[20] Calculated from R. Davis, *The Industrial Revolution and British Overseas Trade*, 1979, pp. 96, 98 and 99, Table 43, 45 and 46.

[21] Minutebook of the Manchester Chamber of Commerce and Manufacture 1821–1827 (M8/2/1, Manchester Archives and Local History), 17 April 1822, pp. 63–5, Copy of Petition

state of our Trade and the East and to report thereon".[22] In this report, on the one hand, they expressed pleasure at the large increase in the exports of cotton goods, which comprise approximately two-thirds of the total amount of British exports at that time.[23] On the other hand, they expressed concern about increased competition in the traditional foreign markets under protectionism.[24] In particular, competition from the rival manufacturers of the United States was a great concern among British manufacturers. In April, the MCCM drafted a petition to Parliament based on this report. In this petition, the members argued that:

> ... in many of the old markets the demand for our Cotton Goods has been curtailed by the increasing competition of foreign rivals aided in some instances, and especially in the United States of America, therefore necessary to maintain the actual extent of that manufacture.[25]

Moreover, they referred to the equalisation of sugar duties. They insisted that, if the discriminating duty on East Indian products in favour of their West Indian counterparts were abolished, it would bring an increase in demand for British cotton goods from the East and compensate for the reduction in their sales in other regions.[26]

However, although they sent petitions and a deputation to London to deal with the question of the sugar duties, compared to the lobbying activities organised by the Liverpool Committee, it seems that the MCCM's lobbying activities tended to be passive and less enthusiastic. The organisation sent its deputies and petitions only in response to requests from the Liverpool EIA. In addition, according to Manchester's minutebook of this period, the MCCM did not make any significant suggestions about the sugar duties to the Liverpool EIA in response to that group's communications. Many merchants and manufacturers in Manchester recognised that the country needed to import agricultural products and raw materials in exchange for British manufactured products, but unlike the East Indian interests of Liverpool and Glasgow, they were not directly involved in the trade. Therefore, while, in Liverpool, the East Indian interests widely debated the duty on East Indian sugar and published several pamphlets on

against the Limitation of the Tonnage of Vessels from Great Britain to the East Indies, 24 April 1822, pp. 66–7 and 81–2.

22 Minutebook of the Manchester Chamber of Commerce, 1827–1833 (M8/2/2, Manchester Archives and Local History), 28 February 1827, p. 6

23 Ibid., 14 March 1827, Report regarding the East India Trade, p. 20.

24 Ibid.

25 Ibid., 25 April 1827, pp. 38–9.

26 Ibid.

this question, Manchester's response to the question of the sugar trade was slower and weaker than that of its neighbouring port. Moreover, Manchester showed a similar response during the debates on the renewal of the Company's Charter from 1829 to 1833.

The MCCM and the Debates over the Renewal of the EIC's Charter

Although the MCCM supported such free trade measures as the abolition of the restriction on the tonnage of vessels engaged in the East India trade and the equalisation of sugar duties during the early 1820s, it did not engage in significant activities against the renewal of the Company's Charter until 1829. Cotton piece-goods manufacturers in Lancashire during this period were disappointed by the EIC's sales of their products in China. The Company's sales of cotton-pieces in this market could not increase as quickly as that of private traders' sales in the India market. In fact, the Company sold goods in Canton at a loss until 1827, and moreover, the British buying of nankeens reached their highest point in 1828, and only afterward did British exports of cotton goods to China exceed their purchases.[27]

The cotton industry in Lancashire also encountered a problem on the supply side. Mr. Winter, one of Manchester's prominent businessmen, insisted on the necessity of acquiring new markets in the East Indies and China for goods because of technical innovations in the manufacturing industry. He referred to Richard Robert's new invention of a self-acting mule:

> As a reason for finding new sources of employment to the working class, the great progressive improvement of machinery; and, as an illustration, stated that within these few weeks a mode has been invented of superseding manual labour hitherto necessary for Spinning frames, and that one child would now be sufficient for superintending 600 spindles.[28]

Technical innovation in the industry led to an improvement in productivity and increases in output, but at the same time, the factory owners needed to seek new markets to meet their increasing output and to maintain employment. Middle-class manufacturers were seriously concerned about the social unrest caused by unemployment and high food prices.

---

[27] D.A. Farnie, *The English Cotton Industry and the World Market 1815–1896*, 1979, p. 120.
[28] Records of the Glasgow East India Association Correspondence Incoming 1829–1830 (MS 891001/4, Glasgow Mitchell Library), letter no. 4.

In April 1829, the free trade campaign against the renewal of the EIC's Charter began in Manchester as it did in other provincial manufacturing towns and outports. On 15 April, a meeting of the Board of the Directors of the MCCM discussed the necessity of holding a public meeting to consider the expiration of the Charter. Table 11 is a list of firms and individuals who signed a petition, along with the directors of the MCCM, to Manchester's Boroughreeve and Constables for the opening of a public meeting in the city to discuss the subject of the renewal of the Company's Charter. In fact, many of the directors were partners of these firms. Therefore, they best represented Manchester's interests in the East India trade during the period. They were involved in all major branches of the cotton industry and its related mercantile businesses in and around Manchester, i.e., cotton spinning, manufacturing, calico-printing, smallware manufacturing, and warehouse business. Of the 36 petitioners, at least 29 were engaged in these businesses. In terms of the sizes of their firms, the group represented Manchester's local economy. For instance, according to Stanley Chapman's study, the capital of Henry & James Barton was nearly four times as large as that of James Finlay & Co., the leading Scottish cotton manufacturers and their partner company.[29] Another example was Adam & George Murray, which employed over 1,000 workers as one of the largest factory owners in Manchester.[30] Therefore, the core part of Manchester's East Indian interests reflected its local economy, especially the cotton industry.

On 25 April, William Rathbone and John Garnett visited Manchester as a deputation from the Liverpool EIA and met with the Board of Directors of the MCCM to inform them of their intentions and to request that they send a deputation to London.[31] This is one example that indicates the close communication between Manchester and Liverpool during the campaign. Two days later, merchants, manufacturers, and other persons interested in the East India and China trade held a public meeting at the Town Hall under the auspices of the MCCM.[32] At this meeting, as in the cases of Glasgow and Liverpool, they appointed an East India Trade Committee and then prepared petitions to Parliament and selected the members of the deputation to join the free trade campaign in London. The substance of the resolutions passed in the public meeting was almost identical to those of other

---

[29] S.D. Chapman, *Merchant Enterprise in Britain: From the Industrial Revolution to World War I*, 1992, pp. 90 and 95.

[30] Lloyd-Jones and Lewis, *Manchester*, p. 6.

[31] Minutebook of the MCCM 1827–33, p. 135.

[32] Ibid., 27 April 1829, pp. 138–41.

Table 11. List of the firms and individuals who requested the Boroughreeve and Constables of Manchester for the public meeting along with the Directors of the MCCM.

Name	Type of Business A	Type of Business B
Thomas & Robert Barns	fine spinners	cotton spinners
H.J. & R. Barton	merchants	merchants
Bindlosses & Preston	silkmen	
Birley & Kirk	cotton spinners & manufacturers by power	cotton spinners/ manufacturers and/ or dealers in cotton goods
Joseph Clarke & Sons		cotton spinners/ manufacturers and/ or dealers in cotton goods
Crewdson & Worthington	silk & cotton manufacturers	manufacturers of silk & cotton
Isaac Crewdson	gentleman	
Henry Fielding & Brothers	calico printers	calico printers & print warehouses
Gardner, Braidley & Co.		
Robert & William Garnett	merchants	cotton twist & weft dealers/merchants
William Grant & Brothers	manufacturers & calico printers	calico printers & print warehouses
Samuel Greg & Co.	spinners & manufacturers	cotton spinners/ manufacturers and/ or dealers in cotton good
John Hall & Sons	muslin, gingham, & silk manufacturers	manufacturers of muslin, etc.
Hardman, Powell & Hardman	merchants & calico printers	calico printers & print warehouses/ merchants
Hargreaves, Dugdale & Co.	calico printers	calico printers & print warehouses
Hole & Wilkinson	calico printers	calico printers & print warehouses
The Holywell & Douglas & Co.	merchants	cotton spinners/ merchants
H. Houldsworth Junr.	cotton spinners	

Table 11. (*Continued*)

Name	Type of Business A	Type of Business B
Hoyle & Newbery	silk & cotton manufacturers & furrier	manufacturers of silk & cotton/ manufacturers of smallware
Loyd & Price	calico printers	calico printers & print warehouses
McConnel & Co.	cotton spinners	
Millington, Son & Bailey	merchants, manufacturers, & printers	calico print warehouses/ merchants
Adam & George Murray	cotton spinners	cotton spinners
The New Bridge Mills & Twist Co.		cotton spinners
James Oughton & Co.	Manchester & Scotch warehousemen	
J. & N. Philips		
Philips & Lee	cotton spinners & merchants	cotton spinners
N. & F. Phillips & Co.	merchants & smallware manufacturers	manufacturers of smallware/merchants
Joseph Plant & Co.	fine spinners	cotton spinners
Potter, Mande & Co.	calico printers	calico printers & print warehouses
Richard Hole		
Simpson, Haign & Co.	calico printers	calico printers & print warehouses
Robert Smith & Brothers	spinners & manufacturers	cotton spinners/ manufacturers and/ or dealers in cotton goods
Thomson, Chippendall & Co.	calico printers	calico printers & print warehouses
Philips Wood & Co.	hat manufacturers & merchants	hat manufacturers/ merchants
Wright & Lee	manufacturers & spinners	

Note: 'Type of Business A' indicates the businesses of the firms/individuals recorded in the main pages of the Postal Directory, and 'Type of Business B' indicates business in which the firms and individuals were categorised in the 'List of Trades' section of the Postal Directory.
Source: *The Pigot & Son's General Directory, Manchester, Salford, &c.*, 1829.

provincial interests: (1) the partial opening of the East India trade after 1814 proved beneficial to the British merchants and manufacturers; (2) they expected positive results from free intercourse with the interior of India and China; (3) the Company's monopoly in the tea trade was very injurious to the public and did not give any advantage to state revenue; (4) the settlement of British subjects would prompt capital investment and the diffusion of Christianity in India; and (5) Manchester was to set up the committee (Manchester East India Committee) and prepare petitions to Parliament.

However, a close analysis of the public meeting makes it clear that there were a couple of points peculiar to Manchester.[33] First, compared with Liverpool and Glasgow, Manchester's merchants and manufacturers showed relatively minor interest in the China trade, especially the tea trade. This was similar to the case of East Indian sugar. Of course, Manchester's merchants and manufacturers showed a strong interest in the export of their cotton yarns and pieces to China. However, most of their arguments on the tea trade were based on those put forth by Liverpool. For instance, compared with the first public meeting regarding opposition to the renewal of the Charter held in Liverpool on 29 January 1829, many speakers in this meeting referred to the tea trade, whilst only G.W. Wood did so in Manchester.[34] This was reasonable when taking the economic interests of Manchester into consideration. As the primary interests of its merchants and manufacturers were the cotton industry and related commercial activities, few businessmen held a direct interest in the tea trade, and they had little knowledge of this branch of foreign trade. In addition, although Ward's study revealed that the habit of consuming tea among the working class became common during the Industrial Revolution, this product was still a luxury grocery.[35] One anti-monopolist of Oldham mentioned in the *Manchester Guardian* that:

> The plant may or may not, for aught I know, be deleterious in its effects, but it [tea] is certainly an article more of luxury than necessity: and one which the operatives would be quite willing to give up. In fact, I could mention one extensive spinning establishment of this town, the operatives of which have expressed a willingness, and wish to acquiesce in this proposition.[36]

---

[33] *Manchester Guardian*, 2 May 1829, p. 3; *Wheeler's Manchester Chronicles*, 2 May 1829, p. 3.

[34] Ibid.; *Liverpool Mercury*, 30 January 1829.

[35] J.R. Ward, "The Industrial Revolution and British Imperialism, 1750–1850", in *The Economic History Review*, New Series, Vol. XLVII, No. 1, pp. 44–65.

[36] *Manchester Guardian*, 27 February 1830, p. 4, "Tea Monopoly".

Therefore, unlike their hostility to the Corn Laws, Manchester's manufacturers, some of whom supposed that imports of cheap food from abroad would reduce labour costs and increase the competitive power of their manufactured goods, were not particularly concerned about the price of tea.

The second point was the reverse side of the first point—that is to say, Manchester businessmen showed a strong interest in the problems related to India, especially the free settlement of British subjects and the employment of British capital and skills in India. After the opening of the India trade in 1814, the Indian market proved itself as a significant market for British cotton goods, and free access to the interior would lead to further growth. However, for the manufacturing interests of Manchester, the improvement of commercial crops in India was as important as the creation of new markets for their own manufactured goods. In a public meeting, William Garnett, the Vice-President of the Chamber of Commerce, argued that:

> If there was one article of foreign product more interesting and important to Manchester than any other, it was cotton. The improvement that had been effected in the cultivation of indigo was well known; and it was impossible to hold the opinion that the culture of cotton could not be similarly improved. If English capital were transferred to Hindostan, we might obtain such a supply of cotton from that country as would render us independent of any foreign state in the world.[37]

In the first half of the nineteenth century, American raw cotton increasingly dominated the British market. From 1806 to 1810, 53 per cent of raw cotton was imported from the United States, and two decades later, its percentage increased further to nearly three-fourths.[38] Like those of Glasgow and Liverpool, Manchester's merchants and manufacturers regarded the total dependence on imports of raw cotton from the United States as an unfavourable situation when they took into consideration the possible deterioration of their relationship with the nation or the natural failure of the crop. Their preference for a shift in the supply of raw cotton from the United States to India was further encouraged by American protectionism. Garnett suggested that:

> When they saw what America was doing with her tariff, the object of which was to make her a manufacturing country, and by which British

[37] Ibid., 2 May 1829, p. 3.

[38] T. Ellison, *The Cotton Trade of Great Britain*, 1986, p. 86, originally published in 1886.

> manufacturers were excluded and a bounty given to her own manufactures... it was a measure seriously affecting the [British] cotton trade.[39]

They did not think that it was desirable to import most of their raw materials from a country where their manufactured goods were excluded by a protective policy. Their wish for the improvement of the cultivation of Indian cotton materialised later in the form of their petitioning the EIC for "the better Cultivation of Cotton in India" in 1838.[40] In addition, the export of commercial crops from India would provide the means to import British manufactured products.[41]

At the end of April and the beginning of May, at a meeting of the Manchester East India Trade Committee, a deputation was appointed to form a joint deputation with representatives from other towns in London.[42] In the capital, the provincial deputies prepared for their meeting with the Ministers on 9 May. However, social unrest at home hindered Manchester's lobbying activities in the metropolis. The outbreak of riots in Manchester forced the Constables, who formed part of the Manchester deputation, to return from London to deal with the crisis, and they missed the meeting with some Ministers, although other members of the provincial deputation received a positive impression from them in this interview.[43]

The proceedings of Manchester's campaign for the opening of the East India trade were similar to those of Glasgow and Liverpool throughout the period because the EIAs of the manufacturing towns and outports closely communicated with each other to act in concert together, as described in the cases of Glasgow and Liverpool. Manchester sent a relatively large deputation to London to organise the General Deputation whenever the Liverpool Committee thought it was desirable to do so. In fact, the provincial manufacturing towns and outports gathered in the capital four times between 1829 and 1833, and the Manchester Committee attended all these meetings.

However, compared with Glasgow and Liverpool, the free trade movement in Manchester exhibited a relatively lukewarm attitude towards the opening of the East India trade. One such event happened when the Manchester Committee collected subscriptions. In early 1830, when its

---

39 *Manchester Guardian*, 2 May 1829, Garnett's speech.

40 Minutebook of the Manchester Chamber of Commerce and Manufacture 1833–1839 (M8/2/3, Manchester Archives and Local History), 17 December 1838, pp. 613–6.

41 Minutebook of the MCCM 1827–33, 25 April 1829, pp. 139–40.

42 Ibid., 30 April 1829, pp. 146–8, and 2 May 1829, p. 149.

43 Incoming Correspondence 1829–30, 6 May 1829, letter no. 4.

lobbying activities resumed, the East India Trade Committee of Manchester appointed a sub-committee (the Finance Committee) to collect subscriptions from the public to defray the costs of its lobbying activities in London.[44] The funds for lobbying came mainly from two sources: the subscriptions from the Chamber of Commerce and the public. The Manchester Committee needed to raise at least £1,000 from the subscriptions, but the Finance Committee reported that, by 24 February, apart from £170 from the MCCM, it had collected only about £250 from the public.[45] Therefore, the Committee decided to hold an urgent meeting. However, in spite of its very urgency the meeting was postponed twice because, on both occasions sufficient numbers of members failed to attend.[46] As a result, the President of the Chamber of Commerce sent a letter to the members of the Finance Committee to confirm the availability of their assistance as sub-committee members.[47] It seems that, consequently, the Finance Committee managed to collect the target figure, as it was able to afford its part of the financial responsibility for the costs of its deputation in London. Nevertheless, this incident showed the Committee's less enthusiastic participation in the free trade campaign.

In general, Manchester's free trade campaign tended to be relatively passive, especially when lobbying activities were related to the opening of the China trade. The EIAs of Liverpool and Glasgow made strong efforts to identify proper witnesses for the Select Committees investigating the China trade, and their witnesses actually gave evidence before them, whilst, according to the records of the MCCM, they neither sent any witnesses to London nor even held serious discussions regarding the choice of witnesses in their meetings.

In contrast, as the details of the first public meeting of 1829 indicated, the Manchester lobbyists showed a strong interest in freer access to India and undertook more constructive efforts towards this purpose in their campaign. Manchester's merchants and manufacturers usually just followed the instructions from the Central Committee of Liverpool and did not take the initiative. Nevertheless, in 1832, when Charles Grant, the President of the Board of Control, inquired of the provincial manufacturing towns and outports regarding the "rules, restrictions and conditions under which they should be allowed to settle in the interior of India", the Manchester

44 Minutebook of the MCCM, 1827–33, 23 January 1830, p. 171.
45 Ibid., 24 February 1830, p. 187.
46 Ibid., 27 February 1830, pp. 188–9.
47 Ibid.

Committee completed its own answers to Grant's queries.[48] The answers of Manchester and those of Liverpool were similar, except for a couple of notable differences. First, the Liverpool Committee answered more fully in response to the queries than the Manchester Committee. This difference probably derived from the advantage of the Liverpool merchants, many of whom were directly involved in the trade with the East and held a better position to access the information of the East than the merchants and manufacturers of Manchester. Second, in their answers to Query No. 5—"What is the system pursued by the Company in the conduct of their commercial transactions in England and have their proceedings proved prejudicial or advantageous to the general interests of India commerce?"—the Liverpool EIA tended to link its answers to the China trade, more specifically the tea trade. It answered, "The import of tea being the most important part of the Company's commercial transactions in England..."[49] The arguments of the Manchester interests focused on the India trade: "As the Company are large importer of Indian produce to England, the market is very much ruled by their determination to sell or to hold..."[50] This supports the indication that Liverpool and Manchester held different main interests in their lobbying activities in this period.

Similarly, the Manchester interests showed strong initiative when the questions were directly related to the cotton industry. Their lobbying for the repeal of the duty on printed calicoes was one example. This duty, which was set up in the previous century, was "one of the last arrangements of the wool raw material regime", and the object of this duty was the imposition of the duty on the domestic consumption of printed calicoes to protect the traditional woollen industry.[51] On 25 November 1830, a public meeting was held in Manchester "for the purpose of considering the propriety of supporting the application of the printers for the repeal of the Excise on printed calicoes".[52] At this meeting, George W. Wood, the President of

---

48 Ibid., "Queries of the India Board and Joint Answers from the Board of Directors of the Chamber of Commerce and the East India Committee", 23 May 1832, pp. 383–404.

49 Records of the Glasgow East India Association Correspondence Incoming 1831–1832 (MS 891001/5, Glasgow Mitchell Library), April 1832, Answers of the Liverpool Committee Q. 5th, located between letter no. 37b and 38a.

50 Minutebook of the MCCM, 1827–33, "Queries of the India Board and Joint Answers from the Board of Directors", 23 May 1832, pp. 383–404.

51 M.D. Whitaker, "Raw Materials and the Division of Labor: Textile and Consumption in Urbanization from Manchester to Mohenjo-Daro, General Theory and Empirical Specification II" [www.ssc.wisc.edu/~mwhitake/files/rmadol_ARTICLE2_2-23-02.doc]; *Wheeler's Manchester Chronicle*, 27 November 1830, p. 3.

52 Ibid.

the Chamber of Commerce, argued first that the imposition of this duty was unfair because neither other textile industries, including the woollen and silk industries, nor other branches of the cotton industry were subject to this type of duty. In addition, the Irish industry was excluded from the duty.[53] Second, he insisted that the working class suffered the most from this duty. The rate was fixed at 5s. or 5s.6d. per square yard. This meant that the duty comprised a larger part of the retail price in the case of cheap calicoes than for expensive ones, and that the type of cloth used by more people was more heavily taxed. The merchants and manufacturers of Manchester employed this moral argument to attract support from the working class. Mr. Hindley declared in the meeting that "he stood there to assert the claim of seven million of British females ... because they could not speak for themselves."[54] Manchester's mercantile and manufacturing interests emphasised that the removal of the duty would increase the consumption of the cloth, which would consequently give more opportunities for the employment of surplus capital and additional means for labour. Third, although the duty was levied on all printed calicoes, those for overseas consumption would receive drawbacks of three-fourths of the duty at the time of export. However, Wood pointed out that, as this current taxation and drawback system for the exported calicoes was cumbersome and inefficient, the customs house needed more inspectors and ran a greater risk of individual fraud.

After a public meeting, on 4 December, the directors of the Chamber of Commerce held a meeting and discussed the repeal of the duty on printed calicoes.[55] They decided to send a memorial to the Treasury to urge the immediate and complete repeal of this duty. At the same time, they resolved that they would send a letter to the EIA, the Brazil and River Plate Association, the WIA, the ACC, and the Levant Association in Liverpool asking for their assistance. Although the answer from the Liverpool WIA was negative, as it was "not being so interested", they received a positive reply from David Gladstone, the President of the Liverpool EIA.[56] His organisation would also send a similar memorial to London. In February 1831, a member of the Manchester Deputation transferred a petition for the repeal of the duty to London. Its lobbying activities contributed to the repeal of the duty in the same year.

---

53 Ibid.
54 Ibid.
55 Minutebook of the MCCM, 1827–33, 4 December 1830, p. 237.
56 Ibid., 7 December 1830, pp. 239–40.

Finally, although Manchester's merchants and manufacturers showed strong interest in the further relaxation of restrictions imposed on the India trade and economic activities there, they avoided the political aspects of India. Like Glasgow and Liverpool, they accepted the political status quo, as long as their economic activities were not disrupted by the restrictions.

Consequently, the MCCM and the Manchester East India Trade Committee's lobbying activities against the renewal of the EIC's Charter strongly reflected the interests of Manchester's local economy. Although the Manchester lobbying group fully supported the national campaign for free trade with the East Indies and China, their main interests were different from those of the outports. Whilst the Liverpool EIA and the Glasgow EIA showed a strong interest in the opening of the China trade, the Manchester interests were more concerned with matters related to India to promote the country not only as a market for their products but also as a supplier of raw cotton.

Conclusion

Greenberg's *British Trade and the Opening of China 1800–42*, has emphasised the significant contributions of the manufacturing interests of Lancashire to the opening of the China trade. From his viewpoint, the Manchester and other Lancashire manufacturing interests were synonymous with those of the people who lobbied for the opening of the China trade. It is true that Manchester's merchants and manufacturers held large interests in China as a potential market for their cotton goods and organised their lobbying activities to achieve this purpose. Nevertheless, although this short chapter has focused on the Manchester interests' lobbying activities during the 1829–33 campaign only, it has been able to address the diversity of provincial interests in the free trade campaigns. The case study on Manchester's free trade movement revealed the city's prime interest in this campaign, which was not the China trade and obviously not the tea trade but the free settlement of British subjects and the employment of British capital and skills in India to further increase the export of British manufactured goods to the country and the creation of an alternative source of raw cotton for its cotton industry. Compared with the opening of the India trade in 1814, 1834 is often characterised by the opening of the China (or the tea) trade. Eyles noted that, "It is therefore not surprising that they [Manchester's free trade interests] were not so intensely interested in the Charter monopoly as were Liverpool…"; Manchester made fewer contributions to the complete abolition of the Company's monopoly in the China trade than Liverpool and Glasgow, where more merchants or merchant-manufacturers were directly engaged in overseas trade.[57] Nevertheless, in a broad sense, the Manchester interests' contribution to the provincial merchants' and manufacturers' influential campaign for free trade with Asia was undeniable, particularly for the further relaxation of restrictions imposed on the India trade.

57 Eyles, "The Abolition of the East India Company's Monopoly", p. 188.

CONCLUSION

This book has offered a comprehensive picture of the lobbying activities of provincial interests in Glasgow, Liverpool, and Manchester against the renewal of the EIC's Charter from 1812–13 and 1829–33, focusing on their motives, strategies, methods, and networks. While the EIC developed its political functions after the Battle of Plassey in 1757, it failed to adjust with the growth of the East India trade. The Company's import trade could no longer meet the demand for remittances from India to Britain. As a result, foreign rivals, particularly the Americans, undermined Britain's dominance of the East India trade. Since the necessity of relaxing the restrictions imposed on the East India trade became clear in Britain and in the East, the EIC's monopoly in the East India trade was heavily criticised. Nevertheless, in Britain, the London mercantile community sought a way to maintain its dominant position in the East India trade after the relaxation of the East India monopoly, although a group of London merchants demanded the relaxation of the East India trade. From the provincial interests' viewpoint, the campaign against the renewal of the EIC's Charter was their attempt to break not only the Company's monopoly but also the London mercantile interests' dominance over the East India trade.

The provincial mercantile and manufacturing interests organised effective lobbying activities for the opening of the East India and China trade and succeeded in exerting undeniable influence over the state's imperial policies in the 1812–13 and 1829–33 campaigns. During the 1800s and the early 1810s criticisms against the EIC's monopoly intensified under the depressed conditions of the domestic economy caused by Napoleon's economic blockade and Britain's disputes with the United States over the Orders in Council. In early 1812 and while the EIC and the government negotiated the renewal of the Charter, in Glasgow, Liverpool, Birmingham, and other provincial manufacturing towns and outports, merchants and manufacturers looking for new markets and sources of raw materials in the East Indies started lobbying against the renewal of the EIC's Charter. They prepared to petition Parliament and to send deputations to London for direct negotiation with the Ministry.

It is true that the EIC and the Ministry had already agreed on relaxing the restrictions imposed on the East India trade including the opening of the export trade from the United Kingdom before the provincial lobbyists organised the General Deputation in London. Therefore, the main issues during the campaign of 1812–13 were the opening of the import trade to outports and that of the China trade. The Glasgow EIA's records reveal that in the initial negotiation between the General Deputation and the Ministry the provincial lobbyists recognised the possibility of persuading the Ministry to change its opinion on the import trade.[1] Therefore, the provincial interests set this issue as a main target and continued their lobbying. Provincial manufacturers who employed a large number of workers at their factories were seriously concerned about social stability in their towns, and those who suffered from an unstable supply of raw materials, particularly raw cotton, were also provincial interests. They hoped that the opening of the import trade from India to the outports could relieve such economic conditions. To achieve this, the provincial mercantile and manufacturing interests strongly lobbied the Board of Trade to obtain its support. The Glasgow EIA sent a letter and copies of resolutions passed at a General Meeting to the Earl of Bathurst and George Rose, the President and Vice-President of the Board respectively in March 1812. Furthermore, in the following month the General Deputation held a meeting with Rose, who expressed his opinion that both the India trade and the China trade should be opened.

Perceval's verbal confirmation of the opening of the import trade to the outports during his interview with the General Deputation in May 1812 was the outcome of their lobbying activities, although it was 'nullified' by his assassination. But Buckinghamshire addressed the Company in December 1812, stating that:

> The importance attached to these representations [from the provincial interests], induced His Majesty's Government to revise the arrangement which had been in contemplation ... the merchants belonging to the outports had established a claim against the absolute restriction of the import trade to the port of London...[2]

The arguments made by the provincial lobbying groups successfully persuaded the Ministry to reject the EIC's arguments and revise its view on the restriction of the import trade. These events contrasted with the failure of the Company's or London's mercantile interests to have a significant impact on this question. The provincial interests continued lobbying for an

---

1 Glasgow East India Association Correspondence Incoming 1812–1813 (MS891001/3, Glasgow Mitchell Library), 10 April 1812, letter no. 7.

2 An Impartial Reporter, *The Preliminary Debates at the East India House on Tuesday, the 5th January, 1813, on the Negotiation with His Majesty's Ministers Relative to a Renewal of the Charter*, 1813, p. 47, Appendix No. IX.

opening of the China trade during the first half of 1813, but the Ministry did not change its views, and the trade remained in the Company's hands. Despite this intransigence by the government the lobbyists had learned significant lessons in this period, and they were put to good use in the second campaign, when the lobbyists succeeded in abolishing the Company's remaining monopoly.

The provincial merchants and manufacturers' influence on the state's decision regarding the total abolition of the Company's monopoly between 1829 and 1833 resulted in the Ministry's decision to establish the Select Committee to enquire into the state of the India and China trade in 1829 as evidenced by the fact that their decision came just after the meeting between the Duke of Wellington and the provincial deputation. The Report of this Select Committee was an influential factor in the debates over the abolition of the Company's remaining monopoly in the China trade, and in fact it supported those who claimed that the opening of the China trade would have a more positive impact on British overseas trade, such as increasing the consumption of British manufactured goods there. As the records of the Glasgow EIA show, the provincial mercantile and manufacturing interests made strong efforts to find witnesses who could give evidence that would support their arguments before the Select Committee. For instance, the association sent John Deans and John A. Maxwell, who had been engaged in trading activities in Java and Singapore, respectively, to London as witnesses, and before the committee, these men gave evidence related to the tea trade and opinions on the possible benefits of the abolition of the EIC's remaining monopoly. Moreover, the fact that the Board of Control made some inquiries of the provincial manufacturing towns and outports during the time of the debates indicated that the state was taking their opinions seriously.

The economic and political interests of those who joined in these two free trade campaigns varied. In the campaign of 1812–13, the group that supported the lobbying of the Glasgow EIA consisted mainly of West Indian and American merchants, as well as those who were related to the cotton textile industry. In Liverpool's case, these Atlantic traders also collaborated with each other, as Checkland and Tolley highlighted. However, in Liverpool, the West Indian interests clearly outnumbered the American merchants in the committee appointed at the General Meeting.[3] The presence

[3] S.G. Checkland, "Economic Attitude in Liverpool", in *The Economic History Review*, New Series, Vol. V, No. 1, 1952, pp. 58–75; B.H. Tolley, "The Liverpool Campaign against the Orders

of such varied economic interests had some negative effects on the free trade campaign. For instance, the presence of a large number of West Indian merchants in the free trade campaign prevented the provincial lobbyists from maximising the merits of the opening of the East India trade, as they needed to take the West Indian interests into consideration. The necessity of considering the merits of the West Indian interests led to the fixing of different sugar duty rates, by which East Indian sugar was disadvantaged against its West Indian counterpart, after the partial opening of the East India trade in 1814. Furthermore, whilst they demanded protection for their existing economic interests in the West Indies, Glasgow's case showed that in spite of a number of West Indian traders' contribution to the campaign of 1812–13 few West Indian houses actually entered the East India trade. However, during the campaign, this issue did not affect the unity of the provincial lobbyists. The case study of Liverpool also shows that the conflicts between the West Indian and American merchants over the abolition of the Orders in Council resulted in the division of the mercantile community. This division prevented the American traders from supporting the establishment of the city's London Office during the period. Nevertheless, this was a minor incident in the course of their strong challenge to the London merchants' hegemony over the East India trade.

During the 1820s and the 1830s, there was a collision of interests between the West Indian and the East Indian merchants over the questions of the equalisation of the sugar duties and the abolition of slavery. Particularly, in Liverpool, James Cropper linked these two questions and led a campaign by publishing several pamphlets about them. The members of the local WIA defended the advantages given to West Indian production and slavery on their West Indian plantations. The conflict between these two different economic interest groups over the equalisation of sugar duties continued even after the total abolition of the EIC's monopoly. However, although a number of merchants in Glasgow and Liverpool held interests in the West India trade and the West Indian plantations, this division within the mercantile society of these provincial towns did not affect their lobbying for the abolition of the Company's remaining monopoly in general. In fact, some of those who held economic interests in the West India trade—for instance, James Ewing of Glasgow and John Gladstone of Liverpool—were also involved in the 1829–1833 campaign, although they were not in the major economic interest group as they had been in the previous campaign.

in Council and the War of 1812", in J.R. Harris (ed.), *Liverpool and Merseyside: Essays in the Economic and Social History of the Port and Its Hinterland*, 1969, Chapter 5.

Furthermore, as the analysis of provincial lobbyists' economic interests shows, a large part of the provincial commercial societies, including those that had little or no business interest in the East India and China trade, supported their lobbying activities. This indicated that the provincial lobbyists' campaign was organised not only to break the EIC's monopoly and the dominance of the London mercantile community in the East India trade but also as part of a more general movement towards economic and political liberalisation during this period.

In addition, these case studies have shown that the economic structure of each city was reflected in its motives for being involved in the free trade campaigns. The lobbyists of Glasgow and Liverpool reflected the cities' strong interest in entering the China trade, especially the tea trade, but those of Manchester paid more attention to the questions related to India to achieve further increases in the export of manufactured goods and to develop that country as a source of raw materials for the city's textile industry. In spite of such conflicts among the different economic interest groups within the provincial towns and the different motives of those who joined these two free trade campaigns, the provincial lobbying groups succeeded in uniting and organising the two campaigns against the renewal of the Company's Charter.

This book has also analysed the ways in which the provincial campaigners employed different means of lobbying. They sent letters and printed circulars to other British towns and influential politicians to stir up public opinion and to persuade them to support their campaigns; they published pamphlets and distributed them throughout the country; and the substance of their meetings and resolutions were published in different newspapers. Resolutions passed at the General Meeting held in Glasgow were widely published not only in Glasgow and Edinburgh but also in London's several newspapers.[4] Moreover, whilst a number of provincial manufacturing towns and outports sent petitions to Parliament repeatedly, the major provincial lobbying associations such as those of Glasgow, Liverpool, Manchester, Birmingham, and Bristol organised a joint-deputation in London to lobby the Ministry and other influential political figures directly. To fund these lobbying efforts, the provincial lobbyists organised subscription activities.

The two lobbying campaigns were largely dependent on close communication among the provincial manufacturing towns and outports.

---

[4] Glasgow East India Association Committee Minute Book 1812–1813 (MS891001/1, Glasgow Mitchell Library), 25 March 1812, pp. 3-2–4.

Their timing in sending their petitions and deputies to London and the content of their answers to the inquiries of the Board of Control were carefully decided by the provincial lobbying groups and their supporters after discussing their views. The provincial lobbyists received effective support from their towns' Parliamentary members, such as George Canning and William Huskisson, who were at the centre of Britain's national politics during the 1810s and 1820s. In Canning's case, he also had a personal connection with Lord Liverpool through their common educational background, although he was then outside the Ministry. Such a prosperous provincial city as Liverpool, with its wealthy and economically powerful mercantile community, was attractive enough for able politicians with political ambition to represent it in Parliament. They provided the free trade advocates with valuable information on the state's views and its negotiations with the Company. Huskisson also helped the free trade supporters to arrange interviews with the Ministers in London. The provincial lobbyists' direct negotiations with the government were clearly a key factor in their successful lobbying. Glasgow's case studies have shown, some provincial lobbyists such as Kirkman Finlay in 1812 and James Oswald and James Ewing in 1832 were elected as MPs for the city and directly represented the provincial campaigners' interests in Parliament.

During the 1829–33 campaign, the arguments of the provincial lobbying groups were strongly supported by such men as Crawfurd and Buckingham. Both of them had experience living in the East and held deep knowledge of the local conditions. The role of Crawfurd, who originally represented the interests of private merchants in Calcutta and later stood as a candidate in Glasgow for the Reformed Parliament, was particularly significant in the campaign. The arguments of the provincial lobbying groups for the opening of the East India and China trade depended largely on Crawfurd's contributions. His opinions often held decisive influence over the provincial lobbyists' overall strategies. In his pamphlets, he demonstrated the merits of opening of the East India trade and China trade and explained that the abolition of the EIC's monopoly in the China trade (the tea trade) would increase the exports of British manufactured goods and reduce the price of tea.[5] He also criticised the dependence on raw cotton imports from the United States and insisted that the introduction of skills and capital from Britain to India would improve the production of cotton wool and would, consequently, contribute to the stable supply of raw materials to the British

[5] J. Crawfurd, *A View of the Present State and Future Prospects of the Free Trade and Colonization of India*, 1829, pp. 6–8, and *Chinese Monopoly Examined*, 1830, p. 84.

staple industry.[6] His pamphlets were distributed throughout the United Kingdom through the provincial lobbying networks.

Buckingham gained popularity from the public and several provincial lobbyists through his lecturing tour, but he failed to obtain strong support from the Glasgow EIA. Glasgow's lobbyists were not interested in his arguments on the EIC's administrative functions, as their lobbying strategies confined their campaign to the economic aspects of the East India question, and they avoided intervening in Indian politics. More significantly, according to a careful examination of the Glasgow records, Crawfurd had a much stronger influence on the provincial interests' overall lobbying strategies than Buckingham.[7] Like such men as Stamford Raffles, who established the colony of Singapore, Crawfurd's significant role in British imperialism in Southeast Asia during the 1820s is well known. In spite of his significant influence over the provincial free trade supporters' arguments and their lobbying strategies, his presence in the campaign has attracted much less attention from historians than has Buckingham's. He was a key figure who linked the provincial mercantile and manufacturing interests at home with British private mercantile interests in Asia in the campaign.

Since the introduction of the 'gentlemanly capitalist thesis', the devaluation of the roles of British industrialists in the creation of the British Empire has been one of the main debates surrounding Cain and Hopkins' model. On the one hand, they emphasised the failure of provincial industrialists to unify their opinions to exert political influence over national politics. On the other hand, the case studies of Glasgow, Liverpool, and Manchester have shown the effectively organised campaigns of provincial interests against the renewal of the EIC's Charter during the first half of the nineteenth century, in spite of their distinct economic interests. Regarding the renewal of the Charter of 1813, Cain and Hopkins argued that:

> The decision was not taken at the behest of a lobby representing Britain's new manufactures ..., but with one eye on placating provincial outports and the other on the ambitions of London merchants whose commercial interest had outgrown the bounds set by Company control.[8]

Cain and Hopkins' conclusion ignored the provincial interests' well-organised lobbying strategies, effective means of lobbying, and access to the centre of national politics through their influential parliamentary

6 Crawfurd, *A View of the Present State*, pp. 26 and 40.

7 Philips, *The East India Company*, p. 289; Eyles, "The Abolition of the East India Company's Monopoly 1833", pp. 198–9.

8 P.J. Cain and A.G. Hopkins, *British Imperialism, 1688–2000*, 2001, p. 282.

supporters. Similarly, their argument that "The end of the Company's last monopoly was … the result of efforts made by merchants based in London and India…" also undervalued the roles of the provincial lobbying groups in the total abolition of the EIC's monopoly.[9] Regarding the relationship between the gentlemanly capitalists and the provincial interests, the conclusion of this book better supports Webster's more complex model of the relationship between the East Indian interests in London and the provincial mercantile and manufacturing interests during the first half of the nineteenth century, especially after 1814, than that of Cain and Hopkins.[10] There is no evidence that the provincial lobbyists and the mercantile interests of London collaborated in the 1812–13 free trade campaign. Rather, the latter petitioned Parliament to protect the Company's monopoly when the provincial lobbyists intensified their campaign, as they feared that the opening of the trade would harm their dominant position.

From 1829 to 1833, the free trade campaign of the outports and provincial manufacturing towns was joined by John Crawfurd, whom the Calcutta interests asked to represent them in the United Kingdom. In fact, the Calcutta agency houses, which dominated the mercantile community of Calcutta, were the nexus of the gentlemanly capitalists in the Metropole. Moreover, the Glasgow EIA recommended potential witnesses, including men from the London mercantile community, such as Joshua Bates of the house of Baring, Brothers & Co. The records of the association also show that Kirkman Finlay met with Bates during the campaign. Such evidence clearly shows a much more complex relationship than has previously been assumed between the gentlemanly capitalists in London and the provincial interests.

As Webster argued, this change stemmed from the development of a new connection between the manufacturing interests of the provinces and the London mercantile community by establishing a trading pattern in which the provincial manufacturers consigned their goods to London agency houses for export to the East after the opening of the India trade in 1814.[11] The records of the Glasgow EIA and other sources show several examples of the association's manufacturing interests, which actually

---

9 Ibid.

10 A. Webster, "The Strategies and Limits of Gentlemanly Capitalism: The London East India Agency Houses, Provincial Commercial Interests, and the Evolution of British Economic policy in South and South East Asia 1800–1850", in *The Economic History Review*, New Series, Vol. LIX, No. 4, pp. 743–64.

11 A. Webster, *The Twilight of the East India Company: The Evolution of Anglo-Asian Commerce and Politics 1790–1860*, 2009, Chapter 4.

consigned their goods to the East Indies. In addition, Larpent's testimony before the Select Committee in 1833 clearly shows that a large part of Glasgow's manufacturers that consigned their products to the East were provided with advances by the London agency houses. These facts do not fit the model of Cain and Hopkins' thesis, which stressed the separation between the gentlemanly capitalists of the metropolis and the provincial manufacturing interests.

Devine and Fry's comprehensive works on the Scots' experience in the British Empire emphasised the significance of the Scots' immigration, colonial governing, commercial activities, and military service.[12] Devine's older works also focused on Glasgow's merchants' involvement in the tobacco trade and the West India trade during the second half of the eighteenth century and the early nineteenth century.[13] Nevertheless, Cain and Hopkins' Anglo-centred view paid little attention to it. Furthermore, in terms of research on the renewal of the Company's Charter, previous studies conducted by historians such as Moss, Eyles, and Charlton have focused on the political influence of England's mercantile and manufacturing interests.[14]

Part of the role of this book has been to address this imbalance. It has revealed that the Glasgow EIA was one of the most active provincial lobbying groups for the opening of the East India and China trades, along with the Liverpool EIA. As described, because early nineteenth-century Glasgow held an important position in both the British overseas trade and manufacturing industries, especially those related to cotton textiles, its inhabitants' interest in the opening of the East India and China trade was high. Glasgow's merchants and manufacturers largely owed their two free trade campaigns to the leadership of Kirkman Finlay, who most keenly pursued the opening of this branch of overseas trade in the city and became the chairman of the joint deputation of 1829. During the two campaigns, Glasgow was the centre of the free trade movement in Scotland, and the Glasgow EIA made attempts to rouse public opinion not only within Glasgow but also in other Scottish towns, especially in its neighbouring areas.

12 T.M. Devine, *Scotland's Empire*, 2003; M. Fry, *The Scottish Empire*, 2001.

13 T.M. Devine, *The Tobacco Lords: A Study of the Tobacco Merchants of Glasgow and Their Trading Activities*, 1975, and "An Eighteenth-Century Business Elite: Glasgow-West India Merchants, c. 1750–1815", in *Scottish Historical Review*, Vol. 57, 1978, pp. 40–67.

14 See D.J. Moss, "Birmingham and the Campaigns against the Orders in Council and East India Company Charter 1812–1813", in *Canadian Journal of History*, Vol. XI, Issue 1, 1976, pp. 173–88; D. Eyles, "The Abolition of the East India Company's Monopoly 1833", unpublished PhD thesis, University of Edinburgh, 1955, pp. 184–98; K. Charlton, "Liverpool and the East India Trade", in *Northern History*, Vol. VII, 1972, pp. 55–72; S.G. Checkland, *The Gladstones: A Family Biography 1764–1851*, 1975, pp. 59–62 and pp. 71–2.

However, its influence was not confined to north of the border. The Glasgow EIA held frequent communications with other provincial associations, particularly the Liverpool EIA, which acted as the Central Committee for all provincial campaigners, and the opinions of Glasgow's free trade advocates were usually taken into consideration in the formation of lobbying strategies, including the timing of sending petitions and deputations to London and the choice of witnesses for the Select Committees. In addition, before the summer of 1812, among the 55 places that petitioned Parliament for the opening of the East India trade, 22 were Scottish towns. This also indicated the Scots' involvement in the free trade campaign.

After the partial opening of the East India trade in 1814, the East Indian interests of Glasgow did not have an organisation that could represent them. As a result, they failed to join other provincial East Indian interests' campaigns in such debates as the equalisation of the sugar duties during the 1820s. Nevertheless, as a result of the revival of the association in 1829, Glasgow's merchants and manufacturers were able to again play a major role in the free trade movement of the outports and provincial manufacturing towns. As its records show, the Glasgow EIA continued its lobbying activities to promote its trade with the East even after the opening of the China trade.[15] As soon as the EIC's monopoly was abolished, Kirkman Finlay sent the first ship from the Clyde to Canton in 1834.[16] During the nineteenth century, his firm gradually increased its stakes in the trade with Asia and tea and other plantation business.

Finally, the abolition of the EIC's monopoly in the China trade was not the end of the provincial mercantile and manufacturing interests' lobby for free access to Asia. In spite of the opening of the China trade in 1834, the trade was still under the strict control of the Chinese government, known as the Canton system. The British merchants and manufacturers in the United Kingdom and Asia challenged this restricted trading system and created disputes with China, which culminated in the First Opium War, which lasted from 1839 to 1842. During this period, the provincial pressure groups, including those of Glasgow, Liverpool, Manchester, Leeds, Blackburn, and Bristol, urged the government to protect the British interests there along with the East Indian interests of London and Asia.[17] In their

[15] C. Brogan, *James Finlay & Company Limited: Manufacturers and East India Merchants 1750–1950*, p. 11.

[16] Ibid.

[17] See A. Le Pichon (ed.), *China Trade and Empire: Jardine, Matheson & Co. and the Origins of British Rule in Hong Kong 1827–1843*, 2006, pp. 564–9; Parliamentary Papers, *Memorials Addressed to Her Majesty's Government, by British Merchants Interested in Trade with China*, 1840.

lobbying, not only the East Indian interests of London but also those of Liverpool showed an ability to create separate strategic plans for aggression against China and suggested these to the Ministry by exploiting their accumulated information on the East Indies and China and their connection with British private traders in China, such as William Jardine.[18] As in the debates on the abolition of the EIC's monopoly that took place in 1812 to 1813 and in 1829 to 1833, the lobbying activities of provincial commercial and manufacturing centres again made a significant impact on the government's decision to 'open' China by force.

[18] K. Yokoi, *Ajia no umi no daiei teikoku* [*The British Empire in the Asian Sea*], 2004, pp. 84–90.

APPENDICES

Appendix I. The General Committee of the Glasgow EIA (1812–13) and their economic interests.

Name	Company 1	Interest 1	Company 2	Interest 2	Company 3	Interests 3
Dugald Bannatyne	Johnstone, Bannatine & Co.	Clothing Manufacturing				
James Black		West India Trade				
Robert Bogle	R. Bogle Jun. & Co.	West India Trade	Shotts Iron Co.	Iron Manufacturing		
John Brown						
James Buchanan	Dennistoun, Buchanan & Co.	West India Trade				
Archibald Buchanan	James Finlay & Co.	Foreign Trade & Cotton-spinning				
Alexander Campbell	John Campbell Sen. & Co.	West India Trade	Newark Sugar Refinery	Sugar	New Lanark Cotton & Co.	Cotton Manufacturing
Colin Campbell	John Campbell Sen. & Co.	West India Trade	New Lanark Cotton Co.	Cotton Manufacturing		
Robert Carrick	Carrick Brown & Co.	Commercial Financing	Henry Hardie & Co.	Linen Draper	Brown, Carrick & Co.	Muslin Manufacturing, Bleaching, etc.
David Connell	David & James Connell	West India Trade				
Cunninghame Corbett	Hastie, Corbett & Co.	West India Trade				
Adam Crooks	Leitch & Smith	West India Trade				
James Crum	Alexander & James Crum	Yarn Warehouse				
William Dalgleish	William & James Dalgleish	Manufacturing				
Robert Dalgleish	Dalgleish, Falconer & Co.	Calico-printer				
Robert Dennistoun	G. & R. Dennistoun & Co.	West India Trade	Newark Sugar Refinery	Sugar	New Lanark Cotton Co., Robert Hamphreys & Co	Cotton-Spinning

(*Continued*)

Appendix I. (*Continued*)

Name	Company 1	Interest 1	Company 2	Interest 2	Company 3	Interests 3
James Dennistoun [two possibilities]	Buchanan, Steven & Co., Dennistoun, Buchanan & Co;.	West India Trade	Sandyhills Coals Co., etc.	Coal Mining	Reynolds, Monteath & Co., etc.	Cotton-Spinning
	possibly James & Alexander Dennistoun	Banking				
Thomas Edington	Clyde Ironworks	Pig Iron Industry	Thomas Edington & Sons	Iron Warehouse		Coal Mining
James Ewing	James Ewing & Co.	West India Trade				
Kirkman Finlay	James Finlay & Co.	Foreign Trade & Cotton Manufacturing				
Francis Garden	Francis Garden & Co., Garden, King & Co., etc.	West India Trade				
John Gordon	Stirling, Gordon & Co., John McCall & Sons.	West India Trade	Sugar House Co.	Sugar	James Finlay & Co.	Foreign Trade & Cotton Manufacturing
Robert Hagard		West India Trade				
John Hamilton	John Hamilton & Co., Hamilton, Garden & Co.	West India Trade				
James Hopkirk	Findlay, Hopkirk & Co.	Tobacco Trade	Hopkirk, Cunning-hame & Co., Hamilton, Hopkirk & Co	West India Trade		
Peter McAdam						
John McCall	John McCall & Co.	West India Trade				
John McCaul	John McCaul & Sons	West India Trade				
John McIlwham	James & John Meikleham	Muslin Trade				
Daniel Mackenzie		Commerce				
Henry Monteith	Henry Monteith, Bogle & Co.	Yarn Warehouse				
John More	Cashier of the Royal Bank of Scotland	Commercial Financing	Cotton Mill at Hutcheson town	Cotton Manufacturing		

Appendix I. (*Continued*)

Name	Company 1	Interest 1	Company 2	Interest 2	Company 3	Interests 3
Alexander Newbigging	A. & J. Newbigging	Tobacco Trade, Linen Industry	Archibald Newbigging & Co.	Calico-printer		
James Oswald	Alexander Oswald & Sons	Commerce	Linwood Mill & Co.	Cotton Manufacturing	South Sugar House Co.	
Alexander Oswald	Alexander Oswald & Sons	Commerce	Oswald, Dennistoun & Co.	Tobacco Trade	Linwood Mill & Co.	Cotton Manufacturing
Robert Owen	New Lanark Co.	Cotton-Spinning				
William Penny		Manufacturing				
James Pollock						
Andrew Reid		Manufacturing				
Ebenzer Richardson		Manufacturing				
Basil Ronald		Clothing Manufacturing (Glover and Breeches Maker)				
William Stirling	William Stirling & Sons	Calico & Linen Printing				
Charles Stirling	Stirling, Gordon & Co.	West India Trade				
Robert Thomson	Robert Thomson & Sons	Cotton Manufacturing				
David Todd	Todd, Shortridge & Co., Todd & Stevenson	West India Trade, Linen Printing, Cotton Spinning				
John Wardrope		American Trade, Tobacco Trade				
Alexander Wighton	Watson & Wighton	West India Trade				

Source: The Glasgow East India Association Committee Minute Book 1812–1813, pp. 1–3–f2; *Glasgow Postal Directories*, 1812, 1813, and 1815; Minute Book of Dennistoun, Buchanan & Co. Glasgow 1796–1842; *Glasgow Herald*, 11 October 1811, 16 October 1812, 15 October 1813, "List of the Magistrates & Towns Council of Glasgow"; G. Stewart, *Curiosities of Glasgow Citizenship*, 1881; The Rambling Reporter, *Reprint of Jones's Directory; or, Useful Pocket Companion for the Year 1787. With an Introduction, and Notes of Old Glasgow Celebrities*, 1868; J. MacLehose, *Memoirs and Portraits of One Hundred Glasgow Men*, 1886; C. D. Donald (ed.), *Minute Book of the Board of Breen Cloth 1809–1820*, 1891; Scottish Record Office, *Court of Session Productions c.1760–1840*, 1987; J. R. Anderson, *The Burgesses & The Guild Brethren of Glasgow 1751–1846*, 1935; T. M. Devine, "An Eighteenth-Century Business Elite: Glasgow-West India Merchants, c. 1750–1815" in *Scottish Historical Review* 57, 1978, Appendix I and II; Devine, *The Tobacco Trade*, Appendix I and II.

Appendix II. List of names of subscribers to the Glasgow EIA, the sums of their subscriptions in 1812 and 1813, and the descriptions of their main businesses (£-s.-d.).

Name of Subscriber	1st sub	2nd sub	Total	Description of business from Directory	Description of business from other sources
Chamber of Commerce	105-00-00	210-00-00	315-00-00		
James Finlay & Co.	052-10-00	103-00-00	155-10-00	merchants	CM, foreign trade
Henry Monteith, Bogle & Co.	021-00-00	025-00-00	046-00-00	yarn warehouse	
New Lanark Co.	021-00-00	021-00-00	042-00-00		CM
John Campbell, Sen. & Co.	021-00-00	010-10-00	031-10-00	merchants	WI
Dennistoun, Buchanan & Co.	021-00-00	010-10-00	031-10-00	merchants	WI
Stirling, Gordon & Co.	021-00-00	010-10-00	031-10-00	merchants	WI
William Stirling & Sons	021-00-00	010-10-00	031-10-00	calico-printers	calico & linen printing
Leitch & Smith	021-00-00	010-10-00	031-00-00	merchants	WI
John McIlwham	021-00-00	010-10-00	031-00-00	manufacturer	muslin trade
Findlay, Duff & Co.	021-00-00	005-05-00	026-05-00	brokers and commission merchants	WI
William Scott, Jun.	021-00-00		021-00-00		
G. & R. Dennistoun & Co.	021-00-00		021-00-00	merchants	WI
Corbett, Buchanan & Co.	021-00-00		021-00-00	merchants	
Stiven, Blair & Co.	021-00-00		021-00-00		
Nielson & Hunter	021-00-00		021-00-00	merchants	WI
Alexander & James Crum	021-00-00		021-00-00	print & muslin warehouse	
D. & J. Connell	010-10-00	005-05-00	015-15-00	merchants	WI
Douglass, Brown & Co.	010-10-00	005-05-00	015-15-00	merchants	
James Ewing	010-10-00	005-05-00	015-15-00	merchant	WI
Thomas & James Edgar	010-10-00	005-05-00	015-15-00	merchants	WI
J. & G. Buchanan	010-10-00	005-05-00	015-15-00	cotton-brokers	
John McCaull	010-10-00	005-05-00	015-15-00	merchant	WI
John McCall & Co.	010-10-00	005-05-00	015-15-00	merchants	WI
M. & J. Perston	010-10-00	005-05-00	015-15-00	manufacturers	
Hopkirk & Cunningham	010-10-00	005-05-00	015-15-00	*	WI
Thomas Shield & Co.	010-10-00	003-03-00	013-13-00	calico-printers	
William Harley & Co.	010-10-00	003-03-00	013-13-00	manufacturers	
Watson, Weighton & Co.	010-10-00	003-03-00	013-13-00	merchants	WI
Todd, Shortridge & Co.	010-10-00	002-02-00	012-12-00	calico-printers	linen-printing
R. Eccles & Co.	010-10-00		010-10-00	merchants	WI
Ebenzer Richardson	010-10-00		010-10-00	manufacturer	
James Martin & Co.	010-10-00		010-10-00	merchants or iron mongers	WI (if they were merchants)

Appendix II. (*Continued*)

Name of Subscriber	1st sub	2nd sub	Total	Description of business from Directory	Description of business from other sources
Muir, Brown	010-10-00		010-10-00	manufacturers	
Hunter & Wilkie	010-10-00		010-10-00	manufacturers	
John Bartholomew	005-05-00	005-05-00	010-10-00	manufacturer	
Smith & Wardlaw	010-10-00		010-10-00	agents	
William & James Dalgleish	010-10-00		010-10-00	manufacturers	
Robert Thomson & Son	010-10-00		010-10-00	cotton works	
Robert McGovern	010-10-00		010-10-00		
Francis Garden & Sons	010-10-00		010-10-00	*	WI
P. Playfair & Co.	010-10-00		010-10-00	merchants	WI
William Leckie	010-10-00		010-10-00		W. Leckie & Co., merchants
R. Bogle & Co.	010-10-00		010-10-00	merchants	WI
Alexander Oswald & Sons	010-10-00		010-10-00		Alexander Oswald, merchant
Dalgleish, Falconer & Co.	005-05-00	005-05-00	010-10-00	calico-printers	
Colin Gillespie	005-05-00	005-05-00	010-10-00	merchant	
Archibald Newbigging	010-10-00		010-10-00	*	AT, linen, calico-printer
James Black & Co.	010-10-00		010-10-00	merchants	
Culcreuch Cotton Company	010-10-00		010-10-00	cotton-yarn-warehouse	
Campbell, Rivers & Co.	010-10-00		010-10-00	*	WI
J. Hamilton & Co.	005-05-00	005-05-00	010-10-00	merchants	WI
McCulloch, Penny & Co.	010-10-00		010-10-00	manufacturers	
John Wardrop	005-05-00	003-03-00	008-08-00	merchant	AT
James Leisslie	005-05-00	002-02-00	007-07-00	*	
Andrew Reid	005-05-00	002-02-00	007-07-00	manufacturer	
Peter McGrigor & Sons	005-05-00	001-01-00	006-06-00	calico-printers	
D. McHaffie	005-05-00	001-01-00	006-06-00		
Eason, Alston & Co.		005-05-00	005-05-00	*	WI
George Brown		005-05-00	005-05-00	*	
George Rutherford & Co.	005-05-00		005-05-00		
A. Smith	005-05-00		005-05-00		WI
James Hamilton & Co.	005-05-00		005-05-00	tobacconists	
Crombie & Carnegie	005-05-00		005-05-00	cotton-printers	
Middleton & Tenent		005-05-00	005-05-00	manufacturers	
R. H. Muir	005-05-00		005-05-00		
John More		005-05-00	005-05-00	cashier, Royal Bank	
J. & A. Dennistoun		005-05-00	005-05-00	merchants	foreign commerce
William Russell		005-05-00	005-05-00		
John Hall	005-05-00		005-05-00	wine & rum merchant or merchant	

(*Continued*)

Appendix II. (*Continued*)

Name of Subscriber	1st sub	2nd sub	Total	Description of business from Directory	Description of business from other sources
John Duncan	005-05-00		005-05-00		
Thomson, Baily & Co.	005-05-00		005-05-00		
John Knox	005-05-00		005-05-00	yarn-warehouse or writer	
William Knox & Co.		005-05-00	005-05-00		
John Stewart	005-05-00		005-05-00		
Mathew Urie	005-05-00		005-05-00		
Forster & Corbett	005-05-00		005-05-00	manufacturers	
John Ure	005-05-00		005-05-00		
Henry Houldsworth	005-05-00		005-05-00	cotton-spinner	
William Kelly	005-05-00		005-05-00	Manchester warehouse or cotton-yarn warehouse	
J. Sharp	005-05-00		005-05-00	dry-salter (James S.) or merchant (John F. S. & Co)	
W. Kippen	005-05-00		005-05-00	manufacturer	
Thomas Edington & Sons	010-10-00	005-05-00	005-05-00	Phoenix iron warehouse	coal mining
P. McAdam	005-05-00		005-05-00	merchant	
T. & R. Graham, Stevenson	005-05-00		005-05-00	manufacturers	
James Paterson, Jun.	005-05-00		005-05-00		
A. Grant	005-05-00		005-05-00		
Colin Campbell	005-05-00		005-05-00	merchant (J. Campbell, Sen. & Co. or Campbells, Fraser & Co.)	
James Graham, Jun.	005-05-00		005-05-00	yarn-warehouse	
C. Parker	005-05-00		005-05-00	merchant	
James Croil	005-05-00		005-05-00	merchant	
James Wingate	005-05-00		005-05-00		J. Wingate & Son, manufacturers
Hugh Cross & Co.	005-05-00		005-05-00	manufacturers	
William Graham & Bros.	005-05-00		005-05-00	*	
Lillie & Johnston	005-05-00		005-05-00	insurance brokers	
James Scott, Jun.	005-05-00		005-05-00		
Walter Tassie	005-05-00		005-05-00	*	
James Laird	005-05-00		005-05-00	merchant	
Archibald Wallace	005-05-00		005-05-00	merchant	

Appendix II. (*Continued*)

Name of Subscriber	1st sub	2nd sub	Total	Description of business from Directory	Description of business from other sources
J. Ellis	005-05-00		005-05-00		
Frederic Adamson	005-05-00		005-05-00	manufacturer	
John Stupart		003-03-00	003-03-00		John Stupart & Co., merchants
Robertson Hastie		003-03-00	003-03-00	hosiers	
White Kerr		003-03-00	003-03-00	yarn-merchants	
Patt McMillan		003-03-00	003-03-00		
Robertson, Buchanan & Co.		003-03-00	003-03-00	merchants	
Spiers, Brown & Co.		003-03-00	003-03-00	stocking warehouse	
Joshua Senior		003-03-00	003-03-00	wholesale Manchester warehouse	
Robert Graham		003-03-00	003-03-00		
Forrester, Willis & Co.		003-03-00	003-03-00	hardware-men	
James Croil		003-03-00	003-03-00	merchant	
Dickson & Stewart		002-02-00	002-02-00	wine and spirit-cellars	
James McNair		002-02-00	002-02-00	sugar-refiner or manufacturer	
McNab, McMillan & Co.		002-02-00	002-02-00		
D. Pennie		002-02-00	002-02-00		
William Croil		002-02-00	002-02-00	merchant	
A. Hamilton, Jun.		002-02-00	002-02-00	Bank of Scotland office	
W. & A. Shand		002-02-00	002-02-00	manufacturers	
Brash & Reid		002-02-00	002-02-00	booksellers and stationers	
Lewis Dawson, Jr.		002-02-00	002-02-00	manufacturer	
Anderson & Campbell		002-02-00	002-02-00	manufacturers	
A. Monteith		002-02-00	002-02-00	grocer	
Andrew Duncan		002-02-00	002-02-00		
Thomas Alston & Son		002-02-00	002-02-00	manufacturers	
James Robertson		002-02-00	002-02-00	merchant	
Adam Ferrie	002-02-00		002-02-00	merchant	
Thomas J. Smith		002-02-00	002-02-00	saddler (Thomas S. & Co.) or spirit-cellar (Thomas S.)	
Sorley & McCallum		001-01-00	001-01-00	iron-monger	
Robert Struthers		001-01-00	001-01-00		Robert Struthers & Co., brewers
John Brown		001-01-00	001-01-00		
R. M. Lowry		001-01-00	001-01-00	merchant	

(*Continued*)

Appendix II. (*Continued*)

Name of Subscriber	1st sub	2nd sub	Total	Description of business from Directory	Description of business from other sources
Ronald McNicol		001-01-00	001-01-00	merchant	
J. & J. Robertson		001-01-00	001-01-00	iron and nail merchants	
McLaren & Stwalker		001-01-00	001-01-00	agents	
Gilmore, Morris & Co.		001-01-00	001-01-00	merchants	
Walter Urea		001-01-00	001-01-00	calenderer	
Samuel Kirkland		001-01-00	001-01-00		
A. & J. Brown		001-01-00	001-01-00	grain-merchants	
George Pinkerton		001-01-00	001-01-00	spirit-cellar	
McCulloch, Davidson & Co.		001-01-00	001-01-00	manufacturers	
Samuel Rutherford		001-01-00	001-01-00	manufacturer	
Mitchell & Russell		001-01-00	001-01-00	watch-makers	
John King		001-01-00	001-01-00	manufacturer or cotton-spinner	
A. McCulloch & Sons		001-01-00	001-01-00		
J. & M. Pollock	001-00-00		001-00-00	manufacturers	

Notes: WI=West India merchant, AT=American Tobacco merchant, and CM=Cotton manufacturer. Asterisk marks (*) indicate names listed in the directories but without descriptions of their businesses

Source: Glasgow East India Association Committee Minute Book 1812–13; *Glasgow Postal Directories*, 1812, 1813, and 1815; List of Company and Individual subscriptions in Abstract of the Minute Book of the Glasgow West India Association.

Appendix III. List of members of the Glasgow EIA and the descriptions of their designations and main businesses (1829–33).

Name and other information (title, address, etc.)	Postal Directories (designation/ firm and year of directory)	Merchants' House Matriculation Book (designation and year of registration)	Burgess and Guild Brethren of Glasgow (designation and year of registration)	Advertise-ments of shipping in Glasgow Courier 1829	100 Glasgow men (description of business and Chapter number)	Records of the Glasgow WIA, Dennistoun, Buchanan & Co., and James Finlay & Co.
James Graham Adam	calico printer (1829)	calico printer (1838)	merchant (1844)			
John Agnew	John Agnew & Co., merchants (1829)	merchant (1832)		John Agnew & Co. (EI, SA)		
Robert Allan	Robert Allan & Co., manufacturers (1829)	home trader (1830)	merchant, manufacturer, Commercial Court (1828)			
James Allan					The Allan Line (shipping business) (Chap. 2)	
George Alston	merchant (1829)	home trader (1813)	merchant (1801)			
Robert Douglas Alston	insurance broker (1829)	insurance broker (1813)	merchant (1808)			
John Anderson	merchant (1829)	X		John Anderson & Co. (SA)		
James A. Anderson	merchant (1829) manager, Glasgow Union Bank (1833)	banker (1822)	weaver and then readmitted as merchant (1821)		The Glasgow Union Banking Company (Chap. 3)	
Robert Bartholomew (Rothsay 1843)	J. Bartholomew & Co., merchants, spinning works, & weaving works (1829)	merchant (1832)	merchant (1830)			
John Bartholomew	J. Bartholomew & Co., merchants, spinning works, & weaving works (1829)	home trader (1825)	partner of John Bartholomew & Co., merchants (1818)			

(*Continued*)

Appendix III. (*Continued*)

Name and other information (title, address, etc.)	Postal Directories (designation/ firm and year of directory)	Merchants' House Matriculation Book (designation and year of registration)	Burgess and Guild Brethren of Glasgow (designation and year of registration)	Advertise-ments of shipping in Glasgow Courier 1829	100 Glasgow men (description of business and Chapter number)	Records of the Glasgow WIA, Dennistoun, Buchanan & Co., and James Finlay & Co.
Thomas Bartholomew	J. Bartholomew & Co., merchants, spinning works, & weaving works (1829)	merchant (1832)	merchant (1830)			
David Bell	pullicate manufacturer (1829)	foreign trader (1821)	merchant manufacturer (qualified as merchant) (1818)			
Robert Black		home trader (1825)	merchant (1821)			
James Black (J B & Co.)	at J. Black & Co., manufacturers, ratified as merchant (1832)	home trader (1825)			James Black & Co. (calico printers)	
William Bleaymire	Ellis, Bleaymire & Co., manufacturers (1829)	X	merchant (1810)			
James Bogle, Junior		merchant (1832)	merchant, of Michael Scott (1829)	Robert Bogle & Co. (WI)		WI (the Glasgow WIA)
Francis Brand (Liverpool 1843)	at Archd. McIndoe & Co., calico printers (1829)					
Henry Brock	accountant (1833)	accountant (1834)	merchant (1832)			
Hugh Brown (Linwood 1843)			merchant (1815)			
Alexander Brown, Junior		X				
James Buchanan (DH)	Dennistoun, Buchanan & Co., merchants (1829)					WI, EI (Dennistoun, Buchan & Co.)
James Buchanan, Junior (DH, Liverpool 1841)		X				WI, EI (Dennistoun, Buchan & Co.)

Appendix III. (*Continued*)

Name and other information (title, address, etc.)	Postal Directories (designation/ firm and year of directory)	Merchants' House Matriculation Book (designation and year of registration)	Burgess and Guild Brethren of Glasgow (designation and year of registration)	Advertise-ments of shipping in Glasgow Courier 1829	100 Glasgow men (description of business and Chapter number)	Records of the Glasgow WIA, Dennistoun, Buchanan & Co., and James Finlay & Co.
James Buchanan (J F & Co.)	James Finlay & Co., merchants (1829)	X				cotton manu-facturing, EI, EU, US (James Finlay & Co.)
John Buchanan		X			Possibly King & Buchanan and the Western Bank	
Walter Buchanan	merchant (1832)	foreign trader (1825)	merchant, of Buchanan, Falconer & Co., manufacturers (1813)		Buchanan, Hamilton & Co. (est. 1824, East Indian traders) (Chap. 17)	
William Buchanan		calenderer (1825)	merchant (1813) or merchant, by purchase (1813)			
John Calder	A & J Calder, manufacturers (1829)		weaver (1828)			
Charles Carnie	Thomas Shield & Co., calico printers (1829)		merchant (1808)			
William Church	William Church & Co., manufacturers (1829)	foreign trader (1830)	merchant, of Harper & Church, manufacturers (1810)			
Hugh Cogan	J. Bartholomew & Co., merchants, spinning works, & weaving works (1829)	home trader (1825)	partner in John Bartholomew & Co., merchants (1818)			
Robert Cogan	John & Robert Cogan (1829)	home trader (1825)	merchant, of J. & R. Cogan, manufacturers (1823)			
John Cogan	John & Robert Cogan (1829)	home trader (1825)	merchant (1818)			

(*Continued*)

Appendix III. (*Continued*)

Name and other information (title, address, etc.)	Postal Directories (designation/ firm and year of directory)	Merchants' House Matriculation Book (designation and year of registration)	Burgess and Guild Brethren of Glasgow (designation and year of registration)	Advertise-ments of shipping in Glasgow Courier 1829	100 Glasgow men (description of business and Chapter number)	Records of the Glasgow WIA, Dennistoun, Buchanan & Co., and James Finlay & Co.
Arthur Connell	A. & J. Connell, merchants (1829)	foreign trader (1817)	merchant, of D. & J. Connell, merchants (1817)			WI (the Glasgow WIA)
James Cook	James Cook & Co., engineers & machine makers (1829)	engineer (1825)	merchant, engineer (1829)			
Alexander Couper			weaver, St. Rollox (1825)			
John Cree	merchant and ship agent (1829)	merchant (1832)	merchant (1821)	John Cree (WI, EI, NA, SA, EU)		
John Cross (S C & Co.)	Stewart, Cross & Co., merchants (1829)		merchant (1833)			
John Crum	J. & W. Crum, calico printer & bleachers (1829)	home trader (1817)	merchant (1817)			
Andrew Stephenson Dalglish	Dalglish, Falconer & Co., calico printers (1829)	foreign trader (1825)	merchant (1824)		Dalglish, Falconer & Co. (calico printers) (Chap. 25)	
George Dalglish	Dalglish, Falconer & Co., calico printers (1829)	merchant (1843)	merchant, of Dalglish, Falconer & Co. (1828)		Dalglish, Falconer & Co. (calico printers) (Chap. 25)	
Robert Dalglish	Dalglish, Falconer & Co., calico printers (1829)	foreign trader (1817)	weaver, then readmitted as merchant (1796)		Dalglish, Falconer & Co. (calico printers) (Chap. 25)	

Appendix III. (*Continued*)

Name and other information (title, address, etc.)	Postal Directories (designation/ firm and year of directory)	Merchants' House Matriculation Book (designation and year of registration)	Burgess and Guild Brethren of Glasgow (designation and year of registration)	Advertise-ments of shipping in Glasgow Courier 1829	100 Glasgow men (description of business and Chapter number)	Records of the Glasgow WIA, Dennistoun, Buchanan & Co., and James Finlay & Co.
James Davidson (Ruchill 1843)	James Davidson & Co., manufacturers (1829)	home trader (1817)	merchant (1841) or merchant (1844)			
John Dempster	merchant (1829)	merchant (1832)	merchant (1823)	John Dempster (WI)		
James Dennistoun	banker (1829)	possibly home merchant (1790)	merchant (1817)		James & Alex. Dennistoun (trade in American cotton) (Chap. 26)	
John Dennistoun (MP 1843)	Jas. & Alex. Dennistoun, merchants (1829)	home trader (1825)	merchant (1845)		James & Alex. Dennistoun (trade in American cotton) (Chap. 26)	
John Denny	John Denny & Co., calico printers (1829)					
Alexander Downie	A. & J. Downie, drysalters & merchants (1829)	drysalter (1826)	merchant, of Alex. & John Downie (1831)			
Richard Duncan	cashier of Thistle bank (1829)	possibly home trader (1817)	merchant (1804)			
Charles Dunlop	James Dunlop & Sons, cotton spinners (1833)				James Dunlop & Sons (cotton spinners & weavers) (Chap. 29)	
Henry Dunlop	James Dunlop & Sons, cotton spinners (1829)	foreign trader (1830)	merchant (1829)		James Dunlop & Sons (cotton spinners & weavers) Chap. 29)	

(*Continued*)

Appendix III. (*Continued*)

Name and other information (title, address, etc.)	Postal Directories (designation/ firm and year of directory)	Merchants' House Matriculation Book (designation and year of registration)	Burgess and Guild Brethren of Glasgow (designation and year of registration)	Advertise-ments of shipping in Glasgow Courier 1829	100 Glasgow men (description of business and Chapter number)	Records of the Glasgow WIA, Dennistoun, Buchanan & Co., and James Finlay & Co.
William Dunlop	James Dunlop & Sons, cotton spinners (1829)	merchant (1833)	tailor (1814) or merchant, serving apprentice with Malcolm Dun, weaver (1799)		James Dunlop & Sons (cotton spinners & weavers) (Chap. 29)	
William Dunn		foreign trader (1829)	hammerman in Glasgow, and then readmitted as merchant (1831)			
Septimus Ellis	Ellis, Bleaymire & Co., manufacturers (1829)	home trader (1798)	merchant (1798)			
James Ewing (Levenside 1843)	James Ewing & Co., merchants (1829)	foreign trader (1804)	merchant (1808)	James Ewing & Co. (WI)		WI (the Glasgow WIA)
David Ferguson	Bogle, Ferguson & Co., yarn warehouse (1829)	home trader (1825)	merchant, of Bogle, Ferguson & Co. (1825)			
Thomas G. Ferguson (91 Hutcheson)	Ferguson & Taylor, manufacturers (1829)					
James Finlay	James Finlay & Co., merchants (1829)	foreign trader (1821)	merchant (1821)			cotton manufac-turing, EI, EU US (James Finlay & Co.)
Kirkman Finlay	James Finlay & Co., merchants (1829)	home trader (1798)	merchant (1796)			cotton manufac-turing, EI, EU US (James Finlay & Co.)
John Finlay (Deanston 1843)	James Finlay & Co., merchants (1829)	merchant (1831)	merchant (1824)			cotton manufac-turing, EI, EU US (James Finlay & Co.)

Appendix III. (*Continued*)

Name and other information (title, address, etc.)	Postal Directories (designation/ firm and year of directory)	Merchants' House Matriculation Book (designation and year of registration)	Burgess and Guild Brethren of Glasgow (designation and year of registration)	Advertisements of shipping in Glasgow Courier 1829	100 Glasgow men (description of business and Chapter number)	Records of the Glasgow WIA, Dennistoun, Buchanan & Co., and James Finlay & Co.
Matthew Fleming	Matthew Fleming & Co., manufacturers (1829)	home trader (1808)	merchant (1797)			
John Fleming		foreign trader (1817)		John Fleming (EI)		
Alexander Fletcher	John Todd & Co., calico printers (1829)	foreign trader (1830)	merchant, of John Todd & Co., calico printers (1830)			
Robert Freeland, Junior	manufacturer (1829)	foreign trader (1829)	merchant (1815)			
Alexander Garden	Henry Monteith & Co., bandana & yarn warehouse, dye works (1829)	home trader (1817)	merchant (1810)			
Robert Gilmour			merchant (1824) or weaver, manufacturer (1825)			
William Gilmour	William Gilmour & Co., wholesale woollen drapers (1829)	home trader (1819)	merchant (1798)			
Alexander Glasgow	Frew & Glasgow, manufacturers (1829)	foreign trader (1826)	merchant (1817)			
Alexander Graham	William Graham & Co., merchants (1829)	foreign trader (1829)			Wm. Graham & Co. (manufacturers) (Chap. 41)	

(*Continued*)

Appendix III. (*Continued*)

Name and other information (title, address, etc.)	Postal Directories (designation/ firm and year of directory)	Merchants' House Matriculation Book (designation and year of registration)	Burgess and Guild Brethren of Glasgow (designation and year of registration)	Advertisements of shipping in Glasgow Courier 1829	100 Glasgow men (description of business and Chapter number)	Records of the Glasgow WIA, Dennistoun, Buchanan & Co., and James Finlay & Co.
William Graham, Junior	William Graham & Co., merchants (1829)	foreign trader (1817)	X	William Graham & Co. (EU)	spinner and weaver, Wm. Graham & Co. (manufacturers), The Lancefield Spinning Co. (Chap. 41)	
Robert Gray, Junior		home trader (1817)	merchant (1807)			
John G. Hamilton	Henry Monteith & Co., bandana & yarn warehouse, dye works (1829)	home trader (1825)	merchant and writer (1816)			
James Hamilton		home trader (1817) or foreign trader (1829)				
John Henderson		home trader (1817)				
Robert Henderson	R. & J. Henderson, merchants & drysalters (1829)	home trader (1817)	merchant (1808)			
Laurence Hill	writer (1829)	writer (1814)	writer, qualified as merchant (1814)		Writer (Chap. 44)	
Henry Houldsworth	Henry Houldsworth & Sons, cotton spinners (1829)	foreign trader (1817)			H. Houldsworth & Sons (Chap. 45)	
William Hunter	W. & M. Hunter, merchants (1829)	foreign trader (1825)	merchant (1816) or merchant (1808)	William & George Hunter (EI)		

Appendix III. (*Continued*)

Name and other information (title, address, etc.)	Postal Directories (designation/ firm and year of directory)	Merchants' House Matriculation Book (designation and year of registration)	Burgess and Guild Brethren of Glasgow (designation and year of registration)	Advertisements of shipping in Glasgow Courier 1829	100 Glasgow men (description of business and Chapter number)	Records of the Glasgow WIA, Dennistoun, Buchanan & Co., and James Finlay & Co.
Andrew Hunter	Andrew Hunter & Co., manufacturers (1829)	home trader (1817) or home trader (1804)	X			
Duncan Hunter			merchant (1815)			
William Hussey, Junior	William Hussey & Son (1829)	merchant (1836)	merchant (1838)			
James Hutchison	James Hutcheson & Co., manufacturers (1829) or bookbinder (1829)	manufacturer (1823)	merchant (1813) or merchant (1804)			
Alexander Johnstone MP (1843)	Johnstone, Galbraith & Co., manufacturers & merchants (1829)	foreign trader (1830)	weaver, and then readmitted as merchant, J. G. & Co., merchants (1830)			
John Ker	manufacturer (1829)	merchant (1831)	merchant at Ballantine & Ker (1821)			
Robert Knox	shawl manufacturer (1829) or writer (1829)	home trader (1829)	merchant (1813)			
John London		foreign trader (1829)	merchant (1817)			
James Lumsden	James Lumsden & Son., wholesale stationers (1829)	foreign trader (1830)	merchant (1829)		James Lumsden & Son (stationery business) (Chap. 51)	
John Lumsden (21 Queen st.)	James Lumsden & Son., wholesale stationers (1829)		pocketbook maker, qualified as hammerman (1810)		James Lumsden & Son (stationery business) (Chap. 51)	

(*Continued*)

Appendix III. (*Continued*)

Name and other information (title, address, etc.)	Postal Directories (designation/ firm and year of directory)	Merchants' House Matriculation Book (designation and year of registration)	Burgess and Guild Brethren of Glasgow (designation and year of registration)	Advertisements of shipping in Glasgow Courier 1829	100 Glasgow men (description of business and Chapter number)	Records of the Glasgow WIA, Dennistoun, Buchanan & Co., and James Finlay & Co.
William Mathieson	merchant, at James Ewing & Co. (1829)	foreign trader (1824)	merchant, at James Ewing & Co. (1823)	James Ewing & Co. (WI)		WI (the Glasgow WIA)
John May	Ewing, May & Co., merchants (1829)	foreign trader (1817)	merchant, partner of Messrs. Ewing, May & Co., merchants			
John McDonald		X				
William McDonald						
Dugald McFie (Dunoon 1843)	merchant (1829)	foreign trader (1829)	merchant (1824)	Dugald MacFie (US)		
Archibald McIndoe	Archd. McIndoe & Co., calico printers (1829)	calico printer (1834)	merchant (1817)			
Laurence McKenzie	L. McKenzie & Co., manufacturers (1829)		weaver (1821)			
John Gregory McKirdy	Peter Bogle & Co. (1833)	merchant (1832)	merchant (1829)			
Robert McLellan	Henry Monteith & Co., bandana & yarn warehouse, dye works (1829)	home trader (1817)	merchant, of Messrs. Henry Monteith, Bogle & Co. (1816)		H. Monteith & Co. (Turkey-red, print works at Barrowfield) (Chap. 88)	
John McNair		possibly, home trader (1790)	weaver (1786)	John McNair (EI, SA)		
John McNair, Junior	commission merchant (1829)	foreign trader (1829)	merchant (1808)	John McNair (EI, SA)		
John Miller (131 Ingram st.)	John Miller, Jun. & Co., merchants (1829)		merchant, of John Miller, Junior & Co. (1829)			

Appendix III. (*Continued*)

Name and other information (title, address, etc.)	Postal Directories (designation/ firm and year of directory)	Merchants' House Matriculation Book (designation and year of registration)	Burgess and Guild Brethren of Glasgow (designation and year of registration)	Advertise-ments of shipping in Glasgow Courier 1829	100 Glasgow men (description of business and Chapter number)	Records of the Glasgow WIA, Dennistoun, Buchanan & Co., and James Finlay & Co.
William Milroy	Milroy, Turnbull & Co., manufacturers (1829)		merchant, of Milroy, Turner & Co., manufacturers (1828)			
William Mirrlees	saddler (1829)	merchant (1834)	hammerman (1802) or merchant (1844)			
Patrick Mitchell	calico printer (1829)	calico printer (1825)	merchant (1823)			
Henry Monteith (Carstairs 1843)	Henry Monteith & Co., bandana & yarn warehouse, dye works (1829)	possibly home trader (1790)	merchant (1786)		H. Monteith & Co. (Turkey-red, print works at Barrow-field) (Chap. 88)	
Duncan Morrison (95 Hutcheson)	Duncan Morrison & Co., manufacturers (1829)	merchant (1833)	weaver (1812)			
Hugh Morrison	manufacturer (1829)	merchant (1819)	merchant (1813)			
William Morrison	merchant (1829)	merchant (1832)	merchant (1828)	William Morison (EI, SA, US)		
John Muir	Muir, Brown & Co., manufacturers (1829)				Muir, Brown & Co. (Chap. 45)	
Thomas Muir (Madeira 1844)						
James Oswald (MP 1843)	Alex. Oswald & Sons (1829) James Oswald & Co., spinners, mill at Barrowfield (1833)	home trader (1813)	merchant (1808)			

(*Continued*)

Appendix III. (*Continued*)

Name and other information (title, address, etc.)	Postal Directories (designation/ firm and year of directory)	Merchants' House Matriculation Book (designation and year of registration)	Burgess and Guild Brethren of Glasgow (designation and year of registration)	Advertise-ments of shipping in Glasgow Courier 1829	100 Glasgow men (description of business and Chapter number)	Records of the Glasgow WIA, Dennistoun, Buchanan & Co., and James Finlay & Co.
James Paterson		home trader (1790) or home trader (1817)				
William Patrick Paton	commission merchant and agent (1829)	foreign trader (1830)	merchant (1830)			
Mathew Perston, Junior	M. & J. Perston, manufacturers (1829)	foreign trader (1830)	merchant, manufacturer (1823)			
John Reid	gingham & pullicate agent (1829)	X	merchant & agent (1817)			
James Reid		merchant (1834)				
John Robertson		manufacturer (1831)				
Laurence Robertson	Royal Bank (1829)	banker (1829)	merchant, Royal Bank (1828)			
Rowand Ronald						
Michael Rowand	cashier, Ship Bank (1829)	banker (1817)	merchant (1808)		Ship Bank (Chap. 26)	
Thomas Samuel	merchant (1829)	home trader (1817)	merchant (1815)			
George Scheviz	merchant, at Campbell, River & Co. (1829)	foreign trader (1817)	partner of Campbell, Rivers & Co., merchants (1816)		Campbell, River & Co. (Shipping house) (Chap. 41)	
John Scott (L.L.D. 1844, London 1843)						
William Shand (49 Miller st.)	W. & A. Shand, manufacturers (1829)		merchant (1808)	W. & A. Shand (EI)		
William Shedden (11 Ingram st.)	William Shedden & Co., manufacturers (1829)	home trader (1821)	merchant (1808)			

Appendix III. (*Continued*)

Name and other information (title, address, etc.)	Postal Directories (designation/ firm and year of directory)	Merchants' House Matriculation Book (designation and year of registration)	Burgess and Guild Brethren of Glasgow (designation and year of registration)	Advertise-ments of shipping in Glasgow Courier 1829	100 Glasgow men (description of business and Chapter number)	Records of the Glasgow WIA, Dennistoun, Buchanan & Co., and James Finlay & Co.
John Smith, Youngest (Clutherland 1843)		X				
William Snell (20 Ingram st.)	sen. of William Snell & Co., manufacturers (1829)		merchant (1813) or weaver (1809)			
Robert Speir	R. & T. Speirs, manufacturers (1829)	merchant (1832)	merchant, at R. & T. Speirs (1822)			
A. G. Speirs	Culcreuch Cotton Co. (1829)					
George Stevenson	Stevenson & Sons, cotton spinners (1829)	merchant (1833)				
George Stirling	William Stirling & Sons, merchants (1829)	home trader (1827)	merchant, partner of Wm. Stirling & Sons, calico printers (1815)		William Stirling & Sons (printing & dyeing trade) (Chap. 88)	
John Stiven	Stiven, Blair & Co., manufacturers (1829)	possibly home trader (1790)	merchant, of Stiven, Blair & Co. (1829)			
James Struthers	Thom & Struthers, yarn warehouse (1829)	foreign trader (1829)	merchant (1808)			
Charles Tennant	C. Tennent & Co., manufacturers of bleaching powder & drysalters (1829)	home trader (1817)	merchant (1807)			

(*Continued*)

Appendix III. (*Continued*)

Name and other information (title, address, etc.)	Postal Directories (designation/ firm and year of directory)	Merchants' House Matriculation Book (designation and year of registration)	Burgess and Guild Brethren of Glasgow (designation and year of registration)	Advertise-ments of shipping in Glasgow Courier 1829	100 Glasgow men (description of business and Chapter number)	Records of the Glasgow WIA, Dennistoun, Buchanan & Co., and James Finlay & Co.
Andrew Tennant	merchant (1829)	home trader (1815)	merchant (1807)	Andrew Tennent (EI)		
John Tennant	C. Tennent & Co., manufacturers of bleaching powder & drysalters (1829)	home trader (1817)	merchant (1817)			
Charles James Tennant	C. Tennent & Co., manufacturers of bleaching powder & drysalters (1829)	home trader (1829)	Merchant, of Charles Tennant & Co. (1829)			
Alexander Tennent	James Oswald & Co. (1833)	merchant (1832)	merchant, cotton broker (1828)			
Robert Thom	spirit-dealer (1829) or possibly, Thom & Struthers, Rothay yarn warehouse (1829)	wine merchant (1837)	merchant (1815)			
William Thomson		X				
Robert Thomson, Senior	Robert Thomson & Sons, Adelphi cotton works (1829)	(R. Thomson, Jun.) home trader (1806)	merchant (1795) or merchant (1799) or merchant (1786)			
Robert Thomson, Junior	Robert Thomson & Sons, Adelphi cotton works (1829)	(R. Thomson, tertius) home Trader (1817)	merchant, cotton spinner (1829)			
Charles Todd (79 Queen st.)	merchant (1829)	home trader (1825)	merchant (1827)			
Daniel Walkinshaw	Walkinshaw, Adam & Co., merchants (1829)	home trader (1825)	merchant, partner of Walkinshaw, Barlas & Co., merchants (1817)	Walkinshaw, Adam & Co., merchants (EI)		

Appendix III. (*Continued*)

Name and other information (title, address, etc.)	Postal Directories (designation/ firm and year of directory)	Merchants' House Matriculation Book (designation and year of registration)	Burgess and Guild Brethren of Glasgow (designation and year of registration)	Advertise-ments of shipping in Glasgow Courier 1829	100 Glasgow men (description of business and Chapter number)	Records of the Glasgow WIA, Dennistoun, Buchanan & Co., and James Finlay & Co.
Andrew Whyte (W U & Co.)	White, Urquhart & Co., manufacturers (1829)	(Andrew Whyte), home trader (1817)	weaver (1808) or merchant (1802)			
Andrew Wingate	Wingate, Son & Co., silk & shawl warehouse (1829) or Black & Wingate, manufacturers (1829)	home trader (1804)	merchant (1800)			
John Wright, Junior	Walker & Co., Lanark Cotton yarn warehouse (1829)	merchant (1835)	merchant (1828)			
James Wright		foreign trader (1823)	merchant, of Findlay, Connal & Co., merchants (1823)		Managed the cotton department of Findlay, Connal & Co. (having several branches including the cotton department and yarn and calico manu-facturing) (see Chap. 22)	

Notes: In the 'Merchant House Matriculation Book' and 'Burgess and Guild Brethren of Glasgow' columns, X indicates that there are too many of the same names recorded in the books to identify individuals. In the column for shipping advertisements in *The Glasgow Courier*, WI represents the West India trade, EI the East India trade, NA the North America trade, SA the South America trade, US the US trade, and EU the European trade.

Source: Glasgow East India Association List of Members from 1829 (MS 891001/16); Subscription Book from 1829 to 1833 (MS 891001/17); Postage Book from 1829–1845 (MS 891001/18); *Glasgow Postal Directories*, 1829 and 1833; Merchants' House of Glasgow Matriculation Books; Anderson, *The Burgess and Guild Brethren, The Glasgow Courier*, 1829; J. MacLehose, *One Hundred Glasgow Men*; Abstracts of the Minute Books of the Glasgow West India Association (The name of James Bogle appeared on 7 March 1823; Arthur Connell on 17 December 1823 and 14 June 1827; James Ewing, between 7 March 1823 and 14 June 1827; William Mathieson between 11 December 1832 and 23 January 1833; George Scheviz, on 24 January 1824); Minute Book of Dennistoun, Buchanan & Co. Glasgow 1806–42 (MS Murray 605, Glasgow University Special Collection Department), 14 February 1825; C. Brogan, *James Finlay & Company Limited: Manufacturers and East India Merchants, 1750–1950*, 1951, pp. 10–2.

Appendix IV. List of the Magistrates & Town Council of Glasgow, 1828–33.

Offices	1828–1829	1829–1830	1830–1831	1831–1832	1832–1833
Provost	*Alexander Garden*	*Alexander Garden*	*Robert Dalglish*	*Robert Dalglish*	*James Ewing*
Merchants rank baillie	William Gray	Hugh Robertson	*Matthew Fleming*	*John Smith, ygst.*	James Martin
	Robert Paterson	*John Buchanan*	*John Smith, ygst.*	*John May*	*Hugh Cogan*
Youngest merchants baillie	Charles Stirling, Jun. (refused/declined the position)	*Matthew Fleming*	David Ferguson	James Martin	John Somervil
Crafts rank baillie	Archibald McLean, Jun.	James Graham	Robert Ferrie	George Burn	William McLe
Youngest trades baillie	James Graham	Robert Ferrie	George Burn	William McLean	William Wilso
Eldest baillie of the town of Port-Glasgow and Newark	William Hamilton	David Gilkison	David Gilkison	James Barclay, eldest	Archibald Falconer, eld
Councillors from the merchants	*John Buchanan*	David Ferguson	*John Buchanan*		*John Buchanan*
	Robert Dalglish	*Robert Dalglish*	*Robert Dalglish*		*Robert Dalglis*
	Donald Cuthberson	Donald Cuthberson	Donald Cuthberson		Donald Cuthberson
	William Graham	William Gray	William Gray		James Campb
	William Hamilton	Robert Paterson	*Hugh Corgan*		David Ferguso
	Robert Hinshaw	Robert Hinshaw	James Martin		*Matthew Fleming*
	Alexander McGrigor	Alexander McGrigor	Alexander McGrigor		*William Gilmour*
	John May	*John May*	*John May*		John Leadbett
	John Muir	*John Muir*	*John Muir*		*John Muir*
	George Scheviz	*George Scheviz*	*George Scheviz*		Henry Paul
	John Smith, ygst.	*John Smith, ygst.*	*John Robertson*		*Jon Smith, ygst*
	Hugh Robertson	Stewart Smith	Stewart Smith		Stewart Smith
Councillors from the traders	John Alston	Archibald McLellan, Jr.	John Alston		John Alston
	George Burn	George Burn	James Graham		Joseph Brown
	William Craig	William Craig	William Craig		Archibald McLellan
	Walter Ferguson	Walter Ferguson	Walter Ferguson		Alexander Mitchell
	Robert Ferrie	James Paterson*[1]	James Paterson*[1]		James Paterso
	William Frew	William Frew	William Frew		John Niel
	John Fulton	*William Snell*	*William Snell*		*William Snell*
	William McLean	William McLean	William McLean		John Small
	William McTyer	William McTyer	Henry Taylor, Jr.		Henry Taylor, J
	William Rodger	William Rodger	William Rodger		William Rodge
	Alexander Wood	Alexander Wood	Alexander Wood		Alexander Wo
Dean of Guild	Stewart Smith	Stewart Smith	*James Ewing*	*James Ewing*	*James Hutchis*

Appendix IV. (*Continued*)

Offices	1828–1829	1829–1830	1830–1831	1831–1832	1832–1833
Deacon Convener	William McLean	John Alston	John Alston	Archibald McLellan	Archibald McLellan
Treasurer	Peter Mirrlees	William Hamilton	Archibald McLean	Laurence Craigie, Jun.	Robert Ferrie

Note: *[1] James Paterson on the list may be a member of the association. Names in italic type indicate that they were the members of the Glasgow EIA.

Source: R. Renwick (ed.) *Extracts from the Records of the Burgh of Glasgow with Charters and Other Documents, Vol. XI, A.D. 1823–1833*, 1916, pp. 300–1, 345–6, 397, 401–2, 442–4, 498; *Glasgow Herald*, 18th, October, 1828, 16th, October, 1829, 22nd, October, 1830, and 15th October, 1832

Appendix V. List of the members of the Liverpool Committee in 1829 and their designations, the regions with which their firms traded, and Liverpool merchants' associations to which they belonged.

Name	Gore's Directory	Liverpool Mercury 1829	Liverpool's Associations (from Gore's Directory)
J(ohn) T(homas) Alston	merchant	Alston, Finlay & Co. (EI, SA, US)	EICA (1832)
Edward Baines, Jun.			
T(homas) B(rockhurst) Barclay	merchant		ACC (1825, 1835)
Robert Benson	merchant (Cropper, Benson & Co.)	Cropper, Benson (EI, US)	ACC (1818) EIA (1818, 1825)
John Bolton	merchant	Bolton, Ogden & Co. (US)	
Henry Booth	corn merchant		
John Bourne	Esq. (J. Bourne & Co. coal proprietors & iron merchant)		
Thomas Brocklebank	merchant	T. & J. Brocklebank (E, EI, SA)	EIA (1825)
James Cropper	merchant	Cropper, Benson & Co. (BA, E, EI, US)	
W. Wallace Currie	merchant & fire office agent		
William Earle, Jun.	merchant	T. & W. Earle & Co. (E, US, WI)	
Hardman Earle, Jun.	broker (Salisbury, Turner & Earle.)		
Willis Earle, Jun.	merchant		
John Ewart	broker (Ewart, Myers & Co.)	Ewart, Myers & Co. (US, WI)	EIA (1818, 1827)
John Garnett	merchant		EIA (1818) MLA (1825, 1829, 1832)
John Gladstone	Esq.	J. Gladstone, Grant & Wilson (EI) Gladstone, Grant & Co. (WI)	BA (1818) EIA (1818) SOA (1818)
George Grant	merchant	J. Gladstone, Grant & Wilson (EI) Gladstone, Grant & Co. (WI)	PBA (1818) SOA (1818) WIA (1834, 1835)
Ormerod Heyworth	merchant (Ormond Heyworth & Co.)	O. Heyworth & Co. (SA, E)	PBA (1818)
Adam Hodgson	merchant		
Samuel Hope	banker (Samuel Hope & Co.)		
Joseph Hornby	merchant (Joseph, Thomas & William Hornby & Co.)	J., T. & W. Hornby & Co. (E, EI)	
Charles Horsfall		C. Horsfall, Son & Co. (AF, EI, SA, WI)	SOA (1825, 1829, 1832) WIA (1834)

Appendix V. (*Continued*)

Name	Gore's Directory	Liverpool Mercury 1829	Liverpool's Associations (from Gore's Directory)
Thomas Leathom	merchant		ACC (1818, 1829) EIA (1825) MLA (1825, 1829, 1832, 1834, 1835)
Joseph Leigh	rope maker/Esq. (Russian Consul) (J. Leigh & Co)	Leigh & Co. (E)	
Thomas Littledale	Esq. (Thomas & Harold Littledale & Co.)	T. & H. Littledale (WI)	
Alexander Maxwell		W., A. & G. Maxwell (E, SA, US)	
A. Melly	merchant (Melly, Prevost & Co.)	Melly, Prevost & Co, (E, US)	
William Myers	broker	Ewart, Myers & Co. (US, WI) W. Myers (US)	
William Potter	merchant (Taylor & P.)	Taylor, Potter & Co.(EI, WI)	EIA (1825) EICA (1837)
Richard Radcliffe	attorney		ACC (1825, 1829) MLA (1825)
William Rathbone	gentleman	Rathbone, Brothers & Co. (AF, EI, US)	
Nicholas Robinson	Esq.	N. Robinson (E)	
Edward Roscoe	iron merchant (Mather, Roscoe & Co.)		
William Rotherham	cutler/merchant (W. Rotherham & Co.)	W. Rotheram (E)	
Edward Rushton	gentleman		
John Smith			
Charles Tayleur	merchant (Charles Tayleur, Son & Co.)	C. Tayleur, Son & Co. (SA, US)	
Thomas Thornely	(Thomas & John Daniel Thornely, merchants)	T. & J. D. Thornely (US)	ACC (1837)
William Ward	merchant		
Daniel Willink	Esq. merchant & consul for the Netherlands	D. Willink (E, EI, US, WI)	ACC (1818) EIA (1825) EICA (1829) LBSAMA (1825)
Daniel Willis	Daniel & Thomas Willis	D. & T. Willis (E, EI)	
Joseph B(rooks) Yates		J. B. Yates & Co. (WI)	SOA (1827, 1834, 1835)
John A(shton) Yates	broker		ACC (1818, 1825)

Note: AF=Africa, BA=British America and Newfoundland, E=Mediterranean, Holland, France, Spain, Portugal, Azores, Germany, Prussia, and Russia, EI=East India, SA=South America and Brazil, US=United States, WI=West India and Bahamas.

ACC=American Chamber of Commerce, BA=Baltic Association, EIA =East India Association (late EICA=East India and China Association), LBSAMA=Liverpool, Brazil, South American and Mexican Association, MLA=Mediterranean and Levant Association, PBA =Portugal and Brazil Association, SOA=Ship Owners Association, WIA=West India Association.

Source: *Gore's Liverpool Street Directory*, 1818, 1825, 1827, 1829, 1832, 1834, 1835, and 1837; "Imports" in *The Liverpool Mercury* 1829 (EI: From 2 January until 25 December, and others from 2 January until 26 June).

BIBLIOGRAPHY

Primary Sources

Manuscripts

Baring Archive
209803

British Library
Add. MSS. 38410 Liverpool Papers
Add. MSS. 38758, 38765 Huskisson Papers
Loan 57, Bathurst Papers, Vol. 5

Flintshire Record Office
Glynne-Gladstone MSS 288, 330

Glasgow City Archives
T-MH-17, Merchants' House of Glasgow Matriculation Books

Glasgow Mitchell Library
Records of the Glasgow East India Association
Glasgow East India Association Committee Minute Book
MS 891001/1, 1812–1813
MS 891001/2, 1829–1834
Correspondence Incoming
MS 891001/3, 1812–1813
MS 891001/4, 1829–1830
MS 891001/5, 1831–1832
MS 891001/6, 1833–1834
Correspondence Outgoing
MS 891001/12, 1812–1814
MS 891001/13, 1829–1830
List of Members from 1829
MS 891001/16
Subscription Book from 1829 to 1833
MS 891001/17
Postage Book from 1829 to 1845
MS/891001/18
Records of the Glasgow West India Association
MS 891002, Abstract of the Minute Book of the Glasgow West India Association
Vols. 1, 3

Glasgow City Archives
CO1/1/13, Lanark County Council, Commissioners of Supply Minutes 30th April, 1825 to 30th April, 1835, No 13
CO2/1/5, Renfrew County Council Commissioners of Supply Minutes 1819–1830

Glasgow University Archives
Records of James Finlay & Co. Ltd.
UGD91/1/4/1/3/1, Balance Book, 1798–1800
UGD91/1/5/5, Dec. 1818–Dec. 1854, Book of overseas consignments of stock-monetary value and account

Glasgow University Library Special Collection Department
GB 0247 MS Murray 605, Minute Book of Dennistoun, Buchanan & Co. Glasgow 1806–42

Liverpool Record Office
352 MIN/COUI 2/8, Liverpool Town Books

Manchester Archives and Local Studies
Minutebook of the Chamber of Commerce of Manchester
M8/2/1, 1821–1827
M8/2/2, 1827–1833
M8/2/3, 1833–1839

Parliamentary Papers

State of commercial credit. Report from the Select Committee, 1810–11 (52) Vol. II. *Supplement to the Appendix to the Fourth Report from the Select Committee on the Affairs of the East India Company*, 1812 (151) (182).
Minutes of Evidence before the Committee of the Whole House of Commons relating to Orders in Council, 1812.
Minutes of Evidence Taken before the Committee of the Whole House, and the Select Committee on the Affairs of the East India Company, 1812–1813 (122) Vol. VII.
Report [Relative to the Trade with the East Indies and China] from the Select Committee Appointed to Inquire into the Means of Extending and Securing the Foreign Trade of the Country, and to Report to the House, 1821 (476), Vol. VII.
Second Report from the Select Committee Appointed to Consider of the Means of Improving and Maintaining the Foreign Trade of the Country, 1821 (535).
Third Report from the Select Committee Appointed to Consider of the Means of Improving and Maintaining the Foreign Trade of the Country, 1821 (746).
First Report from the Select Committee on the Affairs of the East India Company and the Trade between Great Britain, the East Indies and China, 1830 (644).
Reports from Committees: 1831–2. East India Company's Affairs. II. – Finance and Accounts – Trade. Vol. III, 1832 (735-II).
Minute of Evidence Taken before the Select Committee on the Affairs of the East India Company; and also an Appendix and Index, II. – Finance and Accounts – Trade, 1832.
Minutes of Evidence before the Select Committee of the House of Commons on Manufactures, Commerce and Shipping, 1833 (690), Vol. VI.
Memorials Addressed to Her Majesty's Government, by British Merchants Interested in Trade with China, 1840.
Return of Contracts with any Company for Making Railways Public Roads, Canals, Works for Irrigation, or Other Public Works in India, 1859, Session 1 (259), Vol. XIX.

Journal of the House of Commons

Sess. 1830

The Parliamentary Debates

Vols. IX, XII, XXI, XXII, XXIII, XXIV, XXVI

Hansard's Parliamentary Debates

New Series Vols. IX, XXII

Papers Respecting the Negociation for a Renewal of the East-India Company's Exclusive Trade

Nos. I, II, III, IV, VII

Newspapers

Glasgow Courier, 1829, 1830
Glasgow Herald, 1811, 1812, 1813, 1828, 1829, 1830, 1832
Liverpool Courier 1812, 1813, 1830
Liverpool Mercury 1812, 1827, 1828, 1829, 1830, 1831, 1832, 1833
Manchester Guardian, 1829, 1830
Wheeler's Manchester Chronicles, 1829, 1830

Magazines

The Gentleman's Magazine and Historical Chronicle, 1787, Vol. 61, Part 1.

Postal Directories

Glasgow Postal Directories, 1812, 1813, 1815, 1829, 1833
Gore's Directories, 1807, 1810, 1818, 1825, 1827, 1829, 1832, 1834, 1835, 1837
The Pigot & Son's General Directory, Manchester, Salford, &c., 1829

Printed Contemporary and Near Contemporary Sources

An Impartial Reporter (1813) *The Preliminary Debates at the East India House on Tuesday, the 5th January, 1813, on the Negotiation with His Majesty's Ministers Relative to a Renewal of the Charter* (London: Black, Parry, and Co.).

Anon. (1832) *Speech of Sir Daniel K. Sanford at a Meeting of Electors and Inhabitants of Glasgow, in the Traders' Hall, Wednesday, September.*

Anon. (c. 1832) *Letter to James Ewing, Esq. L.L.D. of Dunoon Castle* (Glasgow).

Anon. (c. 1829) *Report of the Proceedings at a General Meeting of the Inhabitants of Calcutta, on the 15th of December, 1829* (London).

Anon. (1812) *Letters on the East India Monopoly, Originally Published in the Glasgow Chronicle, with Addition and Correction, Second Edition* (Glasgow: D. Prentice & Co).

Baines, T (1852) *History of the Commerce and Town of Liverpool, and the Rise of Manufacturing Industry in the Adjoining Countries* (London: Longman, Brown Green and Longmans).

Brought, A (1786) *Consideration on the Necessity of Lowering the Exorbitant Freight of Ships Employed in the Service of the East-India Company* (London: printed for G.G.J. and J. Robinson).

Bruce, J (1811) *Reports on the Negociation, between the Honorable East-India Company and the Public Respecting the Renewal of the Company's Exclusive Privileges of Trade for Twenty Years from March, 1794* (London: Black, Parry, and Kingsbury).

Buckingham, JS (unknown) *Subscribers to a Public Fund for Effecting a Voyage round the Globe, by the Route of India, China, Japan, and the Pacific Isles.*

Idem (1830) *History of the Public Proceeding on the Question of the East India Monopoly, during the Past Year* (London: Hurst, Chance, and Co.).

Crawfurd, J (1830) *China Monopoly Examined* (London: James Ridgway).

Idem (1829) *A View of the Present State and Future Prospects of the Free Trade & Colonization of India* (London: James Ridgway).

Idem (1828) *Journal of Embassy from the Governor-General of India to the Court of Siam and Cochin China Exhibiting a View of the Actual State of Those Kingdoms* (London: Henry Colburn).

Idem (1820) *History of Indian Archipelago: Containing an Account of the Manners, Arts, Languages, Religions, Institutions, and Commerce of its Inhabitants* (Edinburgh: A. Constable).

Cropper, J (1823) *Relief for West Indian Distress Shewing the Inefficiency of Protecting Duties on East-India Sugar* (London: Ellerton and Henderson).

The East India Company (1812) *Correspondence and Proceedings in the Negotiation for a Renewal of the East India Company's Charter* (London: Black Perry and Co.).
The Liverpool East India Association (1829) *Report of the Public Meeting at Liverpool on Wednesday, January 28, 1829, for the Purpose of Taking into Consideration the Best Means of Removing the Restrictions Imposed upon Commerce by the Present Charter of the East India Company.*
Idem (1828) *Report of the Committee of the Liverpool East India Association, on the Subject of the Trade with India: Presented to the Association at a General Meeting, 21st March, 1828.*
Idem (1822) *Report of a Committee of the Liverpool East India Association, Appointed to Take into Consideration the Restrictions on the East India Trade.*
The London East India Association (1841) *The Fifth Report of the Committee of the East India Association* (London).
Idem (1838) *Report of the Committee of the East India Association* (London).
MacLehose, J. (1886) *Memoirs and Portraits of One Hundred Glasgow Men* (Glasgow: James MacLehose).
Maitland, J [Lord Lauderdale] (1809) *An Inquiry into the Practical Merits of the System for the Government of India under the Superintendence of the Board of Controul* (Edinburgh: Archibald Constable).
The Rambling Reporter (1868) *Reprint of Jones's Directory; or, Useful Pocket Companion for the Year 1787. With an Introduction, and Notes of Old Glasgow Celebrities* (Glasgow: Robert Graham).
Stewart, G (1881) *Curiosities of Glasgow Citizenship* (Glasgow: James Maclehose).
Thomas, A (1879) *The Old Country Houses of the Old Glasgow Gentry* (Glasgow: James Maclehose).

Secondary Sources

Unpublished Works

Bargen, RB (1974) "An Historical Analysis of the Critical Parliamentary Debates on the Renewal of the Charter of the British East India Company in 1793 and 1813", unpublished PhD thesis, University of Nebraska, Lincoln.
Bourne, JM (1977) "The Civil and Military Patronage of the East India Company", unpublished PhD thesis, Leicester University.
Devine, TM (1971) "Glasgow Merchants in Colonial Trade, 1770–1815", unpublished PhD thesis, University of Strathclyde.
Eyles, D (1955) "The Abolition of the East India Company's Monopoly 1833", unpublished PhD thesis, University of Edinburgh.
Nenadic, SS (1986) "The Structure, Value and Influence of the Scottish Urban Middle Class: Glasgow, 1800 to 1870", unpublished PhD thesis, University of Glasgow.

Books

Anderson, JR (1935) *The Burgesses & the Guild Brethren of Glasgow 1751–1846* (Edinburgh: Scottish Record Society).
Barbar, WJ (1975) *British Economic Thought and India 1600–1858* (Oxford: Clarendon Press).
Bowen, HV (2006) *The Business of Empire: The East India Company and Imperial Britain, 1756–1833* (Cambridge: Cambridge University Press).

Brogan, C (1951) *James Finlay & Company Limited: Manufacturers and East India Merchants, 1750–1950* (Glasgow: Jackson & Company).
Butt, J (1967) *The Industrial Archaeology of Scotland* (Newton Abbot: David & Charles).
Cain, PJ and Hopkins, AG (2001) *British Imperialism: 1688–2000* (London and New York: Longman).
Idem (1993) *British Imperialism: Innovation and Expansion 1688–1914* (London and New York: Longman).
Catling, H (1970) *The Spinning Mule*. (Newton Abbot: David & Charles).
Chapman, SD (1992) *Merchant Enterprise in Britain: From the Industrial Revolution to World War I* (Cambridge: Cambridge University Press).
Idem (1987) *The Cotton Industry and the Industrial Revolution* (Basingstoke and London: MacMillan Education).
Chaudhuri, KN (ed.) (1971) *The Economic Development of India under the East India Company 1814–58: A Selection of Contemporary Writings* (London: Cambridge University Press).
Checkland, SG (1971) *The Gladstones: A Family Biography 1764–1851* (Cambridge: Cambridge University Press).
Collins, N (1994) *Politics and Elections in Nineteenth-Century Liverpool* (Aldershot: Scolar Press).
Darvall, FO (1969) Popular Disturbances and Public Order in Regency England (London: Oxford University Press).
Davis, R (1979) *The Industrial Revolution and British Overseas Trade* (Leicester: Leicester University Press).
Idem (1962) *The Rise of the English Shipping Industry in the Seventeenth and Eighteenth Centuries* (Newton Abbot: David & Charles).
Devine, TM (2003) *The Scottish Empire* (London: Allan Lane).
Idem (1975) *The Tobacco Lords: A Study of the Tobacco Merchants of Glasgow and Their Trading Activities* (Edinburgh: Donald).
Donnachie, I (2000) *Robert Owen: Owen of New Lanark and New Harmony* (East Linton: Tuckwell Press).
Dumett, RE (ed.) (1999) *Gentlemanly Capitalism and British Imperialism* (London and New York: Longman).
Dutt, R (1956) *The Economic History of India under Early British Rule, from the Rise of the British Power in 1757 to the Accession of Queen Victoria in 1837* (London: Routledge & K. Paul).
Ellis, G (2003) *The Napoleonic Empire* (second edition) (New York: Palgrave Macmillan).
Ellison, T (1968, originally published in 1886) *The Cotton Trade of Great Britain* (London: Frank Cass & Co.).
Farnie, DA (1979) *The English Cotton Industry and the World Market 1815–1896* (Oxford: Oxford University Press).
Fry, M (2001) *The Scottish Empire* (East Lothian: Tuckwell Press; Edinburgh; Birlinn).
Fieldhouse, DK (1973) *Economics and Empire 1830–1914*. (London: Weidenfield and Nicolson).
Furber, H (1948) *John Company at Work: A Study of European Expansion in India in the Late Eighteenth Century* (Cambridge, MA: Harvard University Press).
Greenberg, M (1961) *British Trade and the Opening of China 1800–42* (Cambridge: Cambridge University Press).
Gibson, JF (1953) *Brocklebanks, 1770–1950* (Liverpool: Henry Young & Sons Ltd.).
Hamilton, H (1966) *The Industrial Revolution in Scotland* (London: Frank Cass & Co. Ltd.).
Hamilton, H (1963) *Economic History of Scotland in the Eighteenth Century* (Oxford: Oxford University Press).
Heckscher, EF (1922) *The Continental System: An Economic Interpretation* (English Edition) (Oxford: Clarendon Press).

Hide, W (1973) *George Canning* (London: Collins).

Hyde, FE (1971) *Liverpool and the Mersey: An Economic History of Port 1700–1970* (Newton Abbot: David & Charles).

Imada, S (2000) *Pakusu Buritanika to shokuminchi Indo* [*Pax Britannica and the Colonial India*] (Kyoto: Kyoto daigaku gakujutsu shuppann kai).

Keay, J (1993) *The Honourable Company: A History of the English East India Company* (London: Harper Collins).

Lawson, P (1993) *The East India Company: A History* (London: Longman).

Le Pichon, A (ed.) *China Trade and Empire: Jardine, Matheson & Co. and the Origins of British Rule in Hong Kong 1827–1843* (Oxford: Oxford University Press).

Lenin, VI (1982) *Imperialism, the Highest Stage of Capitalism* (Moscow: Progress).

Lythe, SGE and Butt, J (1975) *An Economic History of Scotland 1100–1939* (Glasgow & London: Blackie).

Lloyd-Jones, R and Lewis, MJ (1988) *Manchester and the Age of the Factory* (London: Croom Helm).

Marshall, PJ (1974) *East India Fortunes: The British in Bengal in the Eighteenth Century* (Oxford: Clarendon Press).

Idem (1968) *Problems of Empire; Britain and India 1757–1813* (London: George Allen and Unwin Ltd.).

Mathias, P (1969) *The First Industrial Nation: An Economic History of Britain 1700–1914* (London: Methuen & Co. Ltd.).

Matsumoto, M (1996) *Igirisu no Indo touchi* [*India under the Control of Britain*] (Kyoto: A-un sya).

Mitchell, BR (1988) *British Historical Statistics* (Cambridge: Cambridge University Press).

O'Brien, DP (1970) *J. R. McCulloch; A Study in Classic Economics* (London: George Allen & Unwin).

Orbell, J (1985) *Baring Brothers & Co., Limited. A History to 1939* (London: Baring Brothers & Co., Limited.).

Philips, CH (1940) *The East India Company, 1784–1834* (Manchester: Manchester University Press).

Read, D (1958) *Peterloo: The 'Massacre and its Background* (Manchester: Manchester University Press).

Redford, A (1934) *Manchester Merchants and Foreign Trade 1794–1858* (Manchester: Manchester University Press).

Renwick, R (ed.) (1916) *Extracts from the Records of the Burgh of Glasgow with Charters and Other Documents, Vol. XI, A.D. 1823–1833*, (Glasgow: Corporation of Glasgow).

Robins, N (2006) *The Corporation That Changed the World: How the East India Company Shaped the Modern Multinational* (Oxford: Peter Lang).

Scottish Record Office (c. 1987) *Court of Session Productions c. 1760–1840* (Surrey: List and Index Society).

Smith, A and Cannan, M (ed.) (1904) *An Inquiry into the Nature and Causes of the Wealth of Nations*, Vol. II, (London: Methuen & Co.).

Tripathi, A (1979) *Trade and Finance in the Bengal Presidency 1793–1833* (Calcutta: Oxford University Press).

Webster, A (2009) *The Twilight of the East India Company: The Evolution of Anglo-Asian Commerce and Politics 1790–1860* (Woodbridge: The Boydell Press).

Idem (2007) *The Richest East India Merchants: The Life and Business of John Palmer of Calcutta 1760–1836* (Woodbridge: The Boydell Press).

Idem (1998) *Gentlemen Capitalists: British Imperialism in South East Asia 1770–1890* (London and New York: Tauris Academic Studies).

William, E (1994) *Capitalism & Slavery* (Chapel Hill and London: The University of North Carolina Press).

Williams, JB (1972) *British Commercial Policy and Trade Expansion 1750–1850* (Oxford: The Clarendon Press).

Whyte, I (2006) *Scotland and the Abolition of Black Slavery, 1756–1838* (Edinburgh: Edinburgh University Press).
Yokoi, Y (2004) *Ajia no umi no daiei teikoku* [*The British Empire in the Asian Sea*] (Tokyo: Kodansha).

Secondary Articles

Anderson, BL (1977) "The Lancashire Bill System and its Liverpool Practitioners: The Case of a Slave Merchant", in Chaloner, WH and Ratcliffe, BM (eds.) *Trade and Transport: Essay in Economic History in Honour of T.S. William* (Manchester: Manchester University Press), pp. 59–97.
Bowen, HV (2002) "Sinews of Trade and Empire: The Supply of Commodity Exports to the East India Company during the Late Eighteenth Century", in *The Economic History Review*, New Series, Vol. LV, No. 3, pp. 466–86.
Idem (2002) "No Longer Mere Traders: Continuities and Changes in the Metropolitan Development of the East India Company, 1600–1834", in Bowen, HV, Lincoln, M and Rigby, N (eds.) *The Worlds of the East India Company* (Woodbridge, Suffolk: Boydell Press), pp. 19–32.
Idem (1989) "Investment and Empire in the Late Eighteenth Century: East India Stockholding, 1756–1791", in *The Economic History Review*, New Series, Vol. XLII, No. 2, pp. 186–206.
Cain, PJ and Hopkins, AG (1987) "Gentlemanly Capitalism and British Expansion Overseas II, New Imperialism, 1850–1945", in *The Economic History Review*, New Series, Vol. XL, No. 1, pp. 1–26.
Idem (1986) "Gentlemanly Capitalism and British Expansion Overseas I. The Old Colonial System, 1688", in *The Economic History Review*, New Series, Vol. XXXIX, No. 4, pp. 501–25.
Campbell, RH (1995) "The Making of the Industrial City", in Devine, TM and Jackson, G (eds.) *Glasgow, Vol. I, Beginning to 1830* (Manchester: Manchester University Press), Chapter 5.
Carlos, AM (1992) "Principal-Agent Problems in Early Trading Companies: A Tale of Two Firms", in *The American Economic Review*, Vol. 82, No. 2, pp. 140–5.
Charlton, K (1972) "Liverpool and the East India Trade", in *Northern History*, Vol. VII, pp. 55–72.
Idem (1971) "James Cropper and Liverpool's Contribution to the Anti-Slavery Movement", in *Transaction of the Historic Society of Lancashire and Cheshire*, 1971, Vol. 123, pp. 57–80.
Idem (1971) "The Present State of Ireland in the Eighteen-Twenties: James Cropper's Plan", in *Irish Historical Studies*, Vol. XVII, No. 67, pp. 320–39.
Chaudhuri, KN (1983) "Foreign Trade and Balance of Payments (1757–1947)", in Kumar, D (ed.) *The Cambridge Economic History of India, Vol. 2: c.1757–c.1970* (Cambridge: Cambridge University Press), Chapter X.
Idem (1966) "India's Foreign Trade and the Cessation of the East India Company's Trading Activities", in *The Economic History Review*, New Series, Vol. XIX, No. 2, 1966, p. 345–63.
Checkland, SG (1958) "American versus West Indian Traders", in *The Journal of Economic History*, Vol. XVII, No. 2, pp. 141–60.
Idem (1957) "Two Scottish West Indian Liquidation after 1793", in *Scottish Journal of Political Economy*, Vol. 4, pp. 127–43.
Idem (1954) "John Gladstone as Trader and Planter", in *The Economic History Review*, New series, Vol. VII, No. 2, pp. 216–29.
Idem (1952) "Economic Attitudes in Liverpool 1793–1807", in *The Economic History Review*, New Series, Vol. V, No. 1, pp. 58–75.
Devine, TM (1995) "The Golden Age of Tobacco", in Devine, TM and Jackson, G (eds.) *Glasgow, Vol. I, Beginning to 1830*, Chapter 4.
Idem (1978) "An Eighteenth-Century Business Elite: Glasgow-West India merchants, c. 1750–1815", in *Scottish Historical Review*, Vol. 57, pp. 41–67.

Fores, M (1981) "The Myth of a British Industrial Revolution", in *History*, Vol. LXVI, Issue 217, pp. 181–98.

Furber, H (1938) "The Beginnings of American Trade with India 1784–1812", in Rocher, R (ed.) *Private Fortunes and Company Profits in the India Trade in the 18th Century* (Aldershot: Variorum), Chapter II.

Gherity, JA "Adam Smith and the Glasgow Merchants", in *History of Political Economy*, Vol. 24, No. 2, 1992, pp. 357–68.

Henderson, WO (1985) "The American Chamber of Commerce for the Port of Liverpool, 1801–1908", in *Transactions of the Historic Society of Lancashire and Cheshire*, Vol. 85, pp. 1–61.

Hyde, FE and Parkinson, BB (1951) "The Port of Liverpool and the Crisis of 1793", in *Economica*, New Series, Vol. 18, No. 72, pp. 363–78.

Killick, J (1974) "Bolton, Ogden & Co.; A Case Study in Anglo-American Trade, 1790–1850", in *Business History Review*, Vol. 48, No. 4, pp. 501–19.

Lawton, R (1953) "The Genesis of Population", in Smith, W, et al. (eds.) *A Scientific Survey of Merseyside* (Liverpool: The University Press of Liverpool).

Lee, CH (1981) "Regional Growth and Structural Change in Victorian Britain", in *The Economic History Review*, New Series, Vol. XXXIV, No. 3, pp. 438–552.

Longstreth, F (1979) "The City, Industry and the State", in Crouch, C (ed.) *State and Economy in Contemporary Capitalism* (London: Croom Helm), pp. 157–90.

Marshall, PJ (1993) "Private British Trade in the Indian Ocean before 1800", in Marshall, PJ, *Trade and Conquest* (Aldershot, Hampshire; Brookfield, VT: Variorum), Chapter XIII.

Maver, I (1994) "Politics and Power in the Scottish City: Glasgow Town Council in the Nineteenth Century", in Devine, TM (ed.) *Scottish Elites* (Edinburgh: John Donald), Chapter 5.

Moss, DJ (1976) "Birmingham and the Campaigns against the Orders in Council and East India Company Charter 1812–1813", in *Canadian Journal of History*, Vol. XI, Issue 1, pp. 173–88.

Nairn, T (1977) "The Twilight of the British State", in *New Left Review*, Jan.–April, pp. 3–61.

Nenadic, S (1990) "Political Reform and the 'Ordering' of Middle-Class Protest", in Devine, TM (ed.) *Conflict and Stability in Scottish Society 1780–1850* (Edinburgh: Donald), Chapter 4.

Parker, JG (1985) "Scottish Enterprise in India, 1750–1914", in Cage, RA (ed.) *The Scots Abroad: Labour, Capital, Enterprise, 1750–1914* (London: Croom Helm), Chapter 7.

Peers, DM (1990) "Between Mars and Mammon: The East India Company and Efforts to Reform its Army, 1796–1832", in *The Historical Journal*, Vol. 33, no. 2, pp. 385–401.

Rubinstein, WD (1977) "Wealth, Elites and the Class Structure of Modern Britain", in *Past and Present*, No. LXXVI, pp. 91–112.

Idem (1977) "The Victorian Middle Classes: Wealth, Occupation and Geography", in *The Economic History Review*, New Series, Vol. XXX, No. 4, pp. 602–23.

Sheridan, RB (1958) "The Commercial and Financial Organization of the British Slave Trade, 1750–1807", in *The Economic History Review*, New Series, Vol. XI, No. 2, pp. 249–63.

Smith, R "Manchester as a Centre for Manufacturing and Merchanting Cotton Goods, 1820 to 1830", in *University of Birmingham Historical Journal*, Vol. IV, 1953–4, pp. 47–65.

Tolley, BH (1969) "The Liverpool Campaign against the Order in Council and the War of 1812", in Harris, JR (ed.) *Liverpool and Merseyside: Essays in the Economic and Social History of the Port and Its Hinterland* (London: Cass), Chapter 5.

Ward, JR (1994) "The Industrial Revolution and British Imperialism, 1750–1850", in *The Economic History Review*, New Series, Vol. XLVII, No. 1, pp. 44–65.

Webster, A (2006) "The Strategies and Limits of Gentlemanly Capitalism: The London East India Agency Houses, Provincial Commercial Interests, and the Evolution of British Economic Policy in South and South East Asia 1800–1850", in *The Economic History Review*, New Series, Vol. LIX, No. 4, pp. 743–64.

Idem (2005) "An Early Global Business in a Colonial Context: The Strategies, Management, and Failure of John Palmer and Company of Calcutta, 1780–1830", in *Enterprise & Society*, Vol. 6, Issue 1, pp. 98–133.

Idem (1990) "The Political Economy of Trade Liberalization: The East India Company Charter Act of 1813", in *The Economic History Review*, New Series, Vol. XLIII, No. 3, pp. 404–19.

Idem (1987) "British Exports Interests in Bengal and Imperial Expansion into South-East Asia, 1780–1824: The Origin of the Strait Settlements", in Ingram, B and Simmons, C (eds.) *Development Studies and Colonial Policy* (London: Cass), pp. 138–74.

Williams. DM (1969) "Liverpool Merchants and the Cotton Trade 1820–1850", in Harris, JR (ed.) *Liverpool and Merseyside*, pp. 182–211.

Conference Papers

Webster, A (2006) "Liverpool and the Eastern Trade 1800–1850: A Paper for the CLAMS Conference on Liverpool and Empire".

Online Sources

Chew, ECT "Dr. John Crawfurd (1783–1868): The Scotsman who made Singapore British" [http://www.scholars.nus.edu.sg/landow/post/singapore/history/chew/chew11.html, accessed 10, May 2005].

Crosby, AG (2004) "Baines, Edward (1774–1848)", in *Oxford Dictionary of National Biography* (Oxford University Press) [http//www.oxforddnb.com/view/article/1089, accessed 29 May 2006].

Whitaker, MD, "Raw Materials and the Division of Labor: Textile and Consumption in Urbanization from Manchester to Mohenjo-Daro, General Theory and Empirical Specification II"
[www.ssc.wisc.edu/~mwhitake/files/rmadol_ARTICLE2_2-23-02.doc, accessed 17 October 2006].

Wills & Testaments, ScotlandsPeople, SC36/48/8 Alexander Oswald dated 18/03/1814 [http://www.scotlandspeople.gov.uk/, accessed 10 April 2007].

INDEX

www.ingramcontent.com/pod-product-compliance
Lightning Source LLC
LaVergne TN
LVHW010657300926
849161LV00005B/1149